LINGUISTICS AND PHILOSOPHY

Linguistics and Philosophy

An Essay on the
Philosophical Constants of Language

ETIENNE GILSON

Translated by John Lyon

University of Notre Dame Press
Notre Dame, Indiana 46556

Originally published in 1969 as
*Linguistique et Philosophie: Essai sur les
constantes philosophiques du langage*
by Librairie Philosophique J. Vrin

Library of Congress Cataloging-in-Publication Data

Gilson, Etienne, 1884–1978.
    Linguistics and philosophy.

    Translation of: Linguistique et philosophie.
    Bibliography: p.
    Includes index.
    1. Languages — Philosophy.   2. Semantics (Philosophy)
I. Title.
P106.G4513   1987   401   87-40348
ISBN 0-268-01284-9

Every thought sets in action a throw of the dice.
—Stéphane Mallarmé

Contents

Translator's Foreword

The greatest joy involved in preparing this translation, outside of that of dealing with a mind as acute and as subtle as that of M. Gilson, is that reserved for last, namely, the opportunity I have here of thanking those to whom I owe so very much in connection with this work.

In the first place I must mention Russell and Annette Kirk, to whom this volume is dedicated. Indeed, without them this translation would not have been possible. They not only assisted me in securing a grant from the Wilbur Foundation (to which I owe separate acknowledgment and thanks, here formally but sincerely given) but personally shepherded me as one of their erstwhile wayward flock during a period in which my soul was contorted as a result of trying to adjust incommensurable entities to each other, a period in my life characterized by "continental discontinuities." Their deep concern and almost daily expression of it is most appreciated and will not be forgotten.

I have found my friend and former colleague, Dr. Bernard Doering, of the Department of Modern and Classical Languages at the University of Notre Dame, ever ready to assist me when I needed him. Much more knowledgeable of the French language than I, he has had the patience requisite to tolerate the folly of my sophomoric and quite amateur translatory efforts. For the hours of his time which I have forced him to displace into journeyman's work in the language of which he is a master, I am both deeply grateful and sincerely apologetic. His continued friendship is one of the pillars of my being.

I should thank at this point Mrs. Joyce Parrish, formerly my secretary in Whitney Young College at Kentucky State University, who took my initial typescript and keyed it onto a word processor. She dealt with the chore stoically over the several months required to produce the handsome copy she returned to me. Again, I am in debt to the patient, methodical, and consistent work of John Ehmann at the University of Notre Dame Press for seeing this volume through to publication.

To Father Stanley L. Jaki, O.S.B., I owe the suggestion that this work be translated. His influence and inspiration are deeply felt and appreciated.

Either nature or convention has predisposed me to matutinal habits, and age has sharply shaped the curve of my energy disposal, so that I have nothing significant to say, and think only in platitudes, after about three o'clock in the afternoon. This translation has consequently been accomplished only in part thanks to the generosity of numerous restaurateurs who have allowed me to occupy sometimes expensive space for hours in the mornings while consuming nothing more than innumerable cups of tea and latterly, as pressures have increased, coffee. The beverages were always hot, if not of exquisite quality, and the company was generally pleasant. (I am convinced that intellectual work should be done in the presence of others of one's species who are, preferably, eating and conversing, or otherwise pleasantly disposed; such work suffers greatly, I fear, when composed in monastic isolation.) Only the "Muzak" offended, that wallpaper for the ear, and it not always.

In addition, necessity has made me peripatetic in these last years, as the location of those institutions I wish to thank here will suggest. To the following providers of modest comestibles and libations, then, my thanks and respect: "The Rustic Inn," Castle Danger, Minnesota; "Grandma Lloyd's," in Stockton, Illinois; "Seymour's," in Mount Pleasant, Michigan; "Simon's" in South Bend, Indiana; the two local restaurants in Mecosta, Michigan; "Wendy's" on Rte. #127 in Frankfort, Kentucky; "The Anderson House," in Wabasha, Minnesota; "Randall's," in Winona, Minnesota; "The Edgewood Inn," in Howard's Grove, Wisconsin; Stoeckigt's Family Restaurant, in Cleveland, Wisconsin.

I have often wanted to dedicate a work explicitly to my children, although in a sense all my productions have been due to them. Quite really, this volume has depended for its completion on their constant support and understanding over the past few years. Perhaps "the next one" will be explicitly theirs. Let me at least pause here to recognize their loyalty, courage, and self-possession, and to thank them publicly for their maturity and balance.

The ghosts of so many others crowd about my typewriter now demanding recognition. To this perforce nameless throng all I can do is apologize, and hope that, given enough more years, I may show myself not to be utterly unresponsive to that which they justly deserve.

John Lyon
Lakeland College
Sheboygan, Wisconsin
April 10, 1987

Translator's Introduction

The reader of these pages should be immediately forewarned that the translator is neither a linguist nor a linguisticist, and that only by a most generous stretching of the imagination could he be considered a philosopher. Gilson, by profession a philosopher, makes no pretension to specific linguistic competence, calling himself "a simple layman in such matters." I, then, must confess to being a layman twice removed from the professional competence directly relevant to the matter at hand.

With all an amateur's awkwardness, then, let me try to specify most briefly how I have chosen to translate two pairs of words and one triplet which are of central importance in this work, and to mention some of the confusion that surrounds their meaning. The French terms are: 1) *signe/symbole;* 2) *signifié/signifiant, -ante;* 3) *langage/langue/parole.*

The necessity of saying something about the French use of *signe* and *symbole,* and comparing that use to English practice, arises in the first chapter of the present work, particularly in connection with Gilson's analysis of the human ability to symbolize and the relation of this ability to endowing signs with meaning, to "signifying," to creating signification. This analysis culminates at about page 40 of this chapter, in particular in connection with a passage from Ferdinand de Saussure's *Cours de linguistique générale* cited by Gilson in note 20.

Despite the close English cognates of these words, translating them is far from a simple task. So far as the first pair (*signe/symbole*) is concerned, both the French and the English languages seem to be striving, albeit somewhat inchoately, to allocate meaning to one or the other on the basis of whether the thing re-presented and the (verbal) representation are associated by natural or conventional ties. If I understand the brief disquisitions on the Indo-European roots of "sign" and "symbol" in the *American Heritage Dictionary* (1979: see *sekw-* and *gwel-*), this striving has been going on for some time in our family of languages. One suspects, however, that it is a chimerical attempt in languages as derivative and conglomerate as French and English.

xi

So far as the present work is concerned, the struggle to distinguish or amalgamate meanings for the two words centers around some linguists' desire to create a universal semiology, a semiology with no reference to a semantology, in order that language might be treated with all the rigor traditionally associated — at least in the mind of a layman — with the physical sciences. Gilson thinks this an impossible, indeed a self-contradictory, task. For him the imposition of names is an arbitrary process, "arbitrary" meaning here voluntary or free. For de Saussure (and apparently even more so for many linguists who have come after him), naming is also an arbitrary process, but here "arbitrary" means, for example, "a thing that is tolerated [by a community] and not a rule to which all freely consent" [Ferdinand de Saussure, *A Course in General Linguistics*, p. 71].[1] For de Saussure symbols and systems of symbols "have a reasonable basis," or have "a natural relationship with the thing signified," which language does not have. For him the word "symbol" ought not then designate linguistic signs (73, 68).

Gilson, citing Lalande's *Dictionnaire*, finds "symbol" defined as "that which characterizes something else by virtue of an analogical correspondence" (p. 22 below). He then proceeds to argue about the matter in the following fashion: "[Generally] . . . there is no analogy between words and the things they signify. One can find an analogy between the image of a dog and the notion of fidelity, or between that of an anchor and steadfastness of faith, but the words 'dog' and 'faith' are not the symbols of anything; they are only sounds without analogy to the ideas, which are moreover abstract, which they signify. It is necessary to choose between maintaining that signs are arbitrary or assigning them a symbolic content based, then, on reality" (p. 22 below).

Gilson sees the purpose of the distinction that de Saussure makes between sign and symbol to be the exclusion of "meaning," "intellect," or "mind" from the would-be science of linguistics. Some linguists, he further notes, have even devised the belief, "or it is at least spoken of as if believed, that it is the sign itself which created the meaning, and the sig-

---

1. I have not had access to the 1968 edition of Ferdinand de Saussure's *Cours de linguistique générale* (Paris, Payot) which Gilson regularly cites. I have, however, checked the 1969 edition by the same publisher, with which Gilson's citations are compatible. I have used another edition for my work, however, the critical edition prepared by Tullio de Mauro (Paris: Payot, 1980). The page numbers of de Saussure's text in this edition are identical with those in the 1969 edition and hence accurately reflect Gilson's citations. I have also used the English translation of the *Cours* prepared by Wade Baskin (New York: McGraw-Hill, 1966). Unless otherwise specified, all English citations are from this edition. Throughout the text and the footnotes, matter provided by the translator has been inserted within brackets.

nifier the signified" (p. 23 below). This belief is a philosophical opinion at the least, Gilson notes, and is not a proposition verifiable within a science of language.

I should say immediately that my main concerns are with Gilson and intelligibility, and not with de Saussure and modern linguistics. I am attempting to translate Gilson, not de Saussure, to deal with living language, not the cadaverous thing deconstructionists cut up. Gilson endorses the linguists' attempt to create a science of language (a universal semiology) so long as this is a pragmatic tactic, a properly decorous obeisance before the shrine of positive science for those who worship therein. He denies, however, the correspondence of such an artificially forced precipitate with living language. The transmutation of this tactic into a universal strategy has as its consequence the destruction of the proper object of a potential science of language. This transmutation, we might add, is attempted through a sort of reverse alchemy, as it were, turning the gold of language into the lead of linguistics by means of substituting "linguistic value" for "meaning." As Gilson himself puts it: "Real language is not that which the linguist studies" (p. 78 below).

My policy has been to put the French word in question in brackets after the English word I have chosen as its equivalent, given the context and what I understand to be the meaning conveyed.

Fortune seems to have contrived things so that an equally lengthy discursus on *signifié/signifiant, -ante* can be avoided. One does, of course, find the direct English equivalents of these terms in use, "the signified" and "the signifier." *Robert* defines *signifié* as "the contents of the sign. V. Meaning [that which a sign signifies]," and *signifiant, -ante* as the "material manifestation of the sign. . . ." However, perhaps the best clue to a common understanding of these terms is given in a footnote added by the translator of the *Cours:* "From May to July of 1911, De Saussure used interchangeably the old terminology (idea and sign) and the new (signified and signifier)."[2] One might wish to substitute "meaning" or "sense" or, more generally, "concept" for "idea" at times; and one must admit that both "idea" and "meaning" foreshorten or tend to foreshorten the triadic analysis of speech which Gilson espouses (see especially ch. IV, particularly in those sections in which Gilson deals with Plotinus and Aquinas and in notes 6, 25, 26, 27). As Mortimer Adler puts the issue (see n. 25), the three terms in question are "the verbal sign, the things that we use language to talk about, and our understanding or knowledge of these things." The point here is that, unlike Locke's usage, the concept is treated as that *by* which we know, never as that *which* we know.

---

2. Ibid., p. 75 (Baskin trans.).

Our real difficulties in discriminating meanings arise, however, in disentangling and translating the senses of *langage, langue,* and *parole.*

I have ordinarily translated Gilson's *langage* as "language" and his *langue* as "speech" or "tongue." Where this is not the case, I have inserted the French word in question in brackets in the text next to my choice of word for the English translation. When dealing with de Saussure, however, I have followed the practice of his translator, Wade Baskin, a practice presumably conformable to that of modern linguistics. Consequently, I have in these instances rendered *langue* as "language" and *langage* as "speech" unless otherwise noted by the insertion in brackets of the French term in question. "Tongue" being in general an archaism with us when used to refer to anything other than the bodily organ, I have tried to avoid its use. This has entailed translating Gilson's *langue* as "language" upon rare occasions, but I have, of course, noted this by the insertion of the controverted word in French in brackets.

Much of the basis for confusion in this area appears to stem from de Saussure's desire to separate out what he calls the "executive side" of "speech" [*langage*] — those idiosyncratic, "hazardous," momentary, accessory, accidental, individual acts of speaking — from something he will insist is a datum quite concrete, social, systematic, essential, "self-contained," something that is consequently a proper subject for scientific analysis. This de Saussure will call *langue,* and the Baskin translation renders this as "language." This datum "has first place in the study of speech" [*langage*]. The executive side of the phenomenon de Saussure calls *parole,* which is rendered as "speaking" in the standard translation. The broadest and most general phenomenon he calls *langage;* this, of course, is not to be rendered as its nearest English equivalent, "language." It comes across the linguistic barrier as "speech." In a nutshell: *"Langue et parole forment le langage"* [*Robert,* citing de Saussure].

For de Saussure, then, the sole object of linguistics is "language" [*langue*]. This "language" [*langue*], however, is not to be confused with human "speech" [*langage*], for it is only a part of the latter. "Speech" [*langage*], is the whole; "language" [*langue*] is the part. One suspects that general English usage would have it the other way around, and so have I translated the words elsewhere in this work than when translating de Saussure.

Again, I have tried to proceed in my translation as I sensed the text in question and contemporary English usage have demanded. In defense of my practice as outlined above, consider but one problem. Would there really be any alternative to translating the key word in the French subtitle of Gilson's work (*Essai sur les constantes philosophiques du langage*) as "language"? "An Essay on the Philosophical Constants of Speech" would hardly do.

In a manner, though, de Saussure himself allows us an easy way out of the translatory morass centering around *langage* and *langue*. Quite early in the *Cours*, and apropos his definitions of "language," "speech," and "speaking," he interjects: "Note that I have defined things rather than words; these definitions are not endangered by certain ambiguous words that do not have identical meanings in different languages. . . . No word corresponds exactly to any of the notions specified above; that is why all definitions of words are made in vain; starting from words in defining things is a bad procedure" (Baskin, tr., 14).

Plausible; perhaps all too plausible. But in moving *toward* words, then, are we to start from "things" or from "notions"? Is a "notion" a "thing" for de Saussure? Are all "things" "notions"? De Saussure's strident insistence on the realism of his approach here puts one uncomfortably in mind of Marx's naive assertion in the "Preface" to the *Economic and Philosophic Manuscripts of 1844* that his work results from an entirely empirical analysis of political economy. In the presence of such apparent naiveté perhaps one ought immediately to sense the enveloping presence of ideology. An "imperial" ideology it may be, of course — a sort of positivistic metaphysics.

Ultimately one must agree with Gilson on the central matter here: "one finds language [*langue*] as such in grammars and treatises on general linguistics, which concern words and sentences composed of signs and significations, abstraction having been made of knowing whether things signified correspond to them in reality . . . real language is not that which the linguist studies" (p. 78 below). A universal semiology may be possible, but arriving at it would entail a classically autophagic process of the denial of meaning. It is indeed hard to conceive of or imagine a sign that would not be a sign of something, that is, have meaning, or, more simply, be a word.

John Lyon
Department of English
Lakeland College

Preface

The title of this essay precisely specifies its object. It is completely oriented toward philosophy and metaphysics. Consequently, it is not in the least a book of linguistics. It makes no claim whatsoever to instruct linguists. On the contrary, the author feels himself to be entirely in their debt, having received from them extraordinarily rich material for philosophic reflection. A simple *layman* in such matters, he has not been tempted to formulate the least linguistic opinion. Even less has he set up the slightest linguistic critique against the opinion of any linguist. Insofar as linguists and linguistics are in question, it is simply that the author has undertaken to philosophize on the subject.

My book has taken shape and been provoked into being by the liberty which numerous linguists grant themselves of philosophizing as linguists and presenting their philosophy as if it were a matter of their science. This same attitude is not unknown to physicists or biologists either. It does not bother them if the philosophy thus bandied about under the name of science often consists in a denial of the validity of philosophical positions accepted by those whose *metier* is philosophy. A scientist [*savant*] who, with good right, would become indignant upon seeing a philosopher with a casual acquaintance with science uttering supposedly scientific opinions, will not himself thereupon refrain from philosophizing. Holding reasonably that it is necessary to have learned a science in order to be authorized to speak about it, he does not for an instant doubt that it is a matter of indifference who may be authorized to speak of philosophy, provided only that he knows some other discipline.

For the philosopher nature is what the physicist and the biologist tell him it is. Language is for him what the linguist tells him it is. In these two cases he comes across two kinds of scientists [*savants*]. All of them agree to hold all philosophical speculation in the background, and as scientists, they are reasonable to refuse to go beyond the realm of reasoned observation and experience. But all of them do not observe the same attitude toward reality. Some of them, for whom the fear of philosophizing is the beginning of science, methodically ignore or deny on principle the aspects of language use which provide reflection for the philosopher. Whether or not this attitude is of use to linguistics is for linguists to decide among themselves. Others — a short time ago Edward Sapir, today Emile Benveniste and Noam Chomsky for example — are equally solicitous to prevent their science from losing its way in the indistinct landscape of philosophy, and in particular metaphysics. These, however, have great concern in their descriptions to maintain the mysterious aspects of language for him who observes it merely as a scientist [savant]. These are precisely the aspects which retain the attention of the philosopher, for whom the philosophical constants of language are but a particular case of metaphysical constants. The philosopher whose reflection profits from their work hesitates between two alternatives. He may simply not admit his debt to them, or he may publicly recognize it. If he does the latter, he runs the risk of compromising them in the judgment of those of their colleagues who stand to profit from reproaching them for what they will hold, wrongly, to be a mixing of genres. But after all, why should this disturb one? Philosophical reflection on language cannot lead to much, but short of holding all philosophers as senseless, there must be something in the reality of language such as it is that invites one to philosophize.

Among linguists to whom I feel particularly indebted I want to mention first of all the name of Joseph Vendryès. It was impossible to know him without liking him, and no one contributed more than he to maintaining intact the salutary sense of the complexity of linguistic facts. Incidentally, I take the occasion to recall to those who classify him among the representatives of the outmoded school of historical linguistics that, having written his great work on languge as an introduction to an encyclopedic collection devoted to the history of humanity, he had every reason to emphasize that which makes of language a properly historical reality. J. Vendryès loved language for its own sake, for its creative as well as its rational characteristics. I remain grateful to him for having shown me by example that even a linguist can share some at least of the wonder of the philosopher.

I owe even more to M. Emile Benveniste. To begin with, he proved to me by example that a purely scientific observation of language shows more things than our philosophy could ever have imagined. I thank him for having generously authorized me to reproduce important parts of his essays, particularly that truly admirable one which he devoted to "linguistic time." Those pages are so perfect, in my estimation, that it is impossible either to summarize them or to express them in different terms without ruining them.

I regret not having been able to profit more from the works of Noam

Chomsky, with whom, it seems to me, a philosopher ought to be able to communicate. It is only through extracts published in the *Forum* that I have come to know something of his book (*Language and Mind*: Harcourt, Brace and World, 1968) [unavailable to Gilson when he wrote the present work].

Knowing philosophers, these illustrious linguists will not be surprised to see me get involved in discussions in which I can only play the role of the amateur. Philosophers are thus by nature: teach them something, and they undertake directly to explain to you what you came to teach them. But we have known ever since Molière that the Master of Philosophy is a comic figure. I am certain that the linguists will indeed be willing to excuse me.

Experience has taught me that no linear composition is possible in a book on language. Each part is an exercise of thought preparing one for a final conclusion. This conclusion, which in large measure is the expression of submissiveness to evidence, has been present furthermore from the beginning. One strives in this matter to speak of obscure things with a reasonable clarity, if it only be to outline with some precision the exterior contours of their obscurity. The epigraph borrowed from Mallarmé renders homage to the poet which the philosopher is happy to give, for where it is a question of language, the philosopher (and likewise the linguist) is only the commentator; the poet is the author.

This "thought" of Mallarmé's, like a new roll of the dice, casts words each time beyond the scope of reckoning. It does so nevertheless without becoming discouraged, because this will-to-hazard is its very essence. Here, perhaps, in this "thought" is what I laboriously tried to describe in its incessantly renewed action. Even at present, after much reflection, I find myself still with the same incredulous astonishment in the presence of language. Chateaubriand wrote: "One had the impression of hearing that nameless bird which consoles the traveler in the vale of Kashmir." What sense do these two magical lines make? In what does their meaning reside? In the words or in the totality of the phrase? Whatever the case may be, what conceivable connection could there be between the word and the phrase? All the philosophical constants of language are tied up in this mystery, which remains impenetrable to me but which it has appeared important to admit.

The names of Mallarmé and Chateaubriand opportunely remind us of the basic fact that, especially for whoever writes a book, the spoken word is only with difficulty distinguished from the written. No attempt then will be made to disjoin them, except in the two chapters where the question will be posed explicitly. That will be our last cast of the dice.

1

The Myth of the
Decomposition of Thought

The title of the celebrated memoir of Maine de Biran, *On the Decomposition of Thought*, gives evidence of the survival at that late date of an ambition that Condillac and, in his wake, many an Italian or French ideologue deluded themselves with already having accomplished. The history of ideology in France and Italy describes moreover a situation not without analogy with that of linguistics today. One ideology could always be replaced by a new one, and all were almost equally legitimate, as their authors themselves have come to realize. Furthermore, if thought is truly decomposable, it is assuredly necessary to decompose it in order to know it better. Nothing could be more Cartesian, and much of the Cartesian spirit remains in Condillac's enterprise,[1] but he thought that the labor of decomposing thought had already been done for us and brought to a successful issue by language.

Heir to the school of the great philosophical grammarians Arnauld and Lancelot, Condillac set forth as a rule at the beginning of his own *Grammaire:* "I regard grammar as the first part of the art of thought. In order to discover the principles of language it is necessary to observe how we think. It is necessary to look for these principles in the very analysis of thought. Now, the analysis of thought is completely accomplished in discourse. This is so with more or less precision according as languages [*langues*] are more or less perfect, and relative to whether or not those who speak them have a more or less precise mind. This is what makes me think of languages [*langues*] as so many methods of analysis." Thereafter two parts of the work are described:

In the first, which I entitle "On the Analysis of Discourse," we shall look for the signs which languages [*langues*] furnish us for the analysis of thought. This will be a general grammar which will reveal to

1

us the elements of language and the common rules of all languages [*langues*]. In the second part, entitled "On the Elements of Discourse," we shall observe the elements with which the first part has provided us and we shall discern the rules that our language [*langue*] prescribes to us for maintaining the greatest clarity and precision in the analysis of our thoughts.

Condillac's style illustrates perfectly his ideal of language. One cannot call into question his bias for analytic simplicity without renouncing equally his clarity, but the latter is secured only at the price of capabilities which he is perhaps wise not to take into consideration.

Condillac's enterprise takes its place in a long tradition whose fundamental propositions are not in doubt. It is, going back beyond their successors at Port Royal, that of the philosophical grammarians of the Middle Ages, particularly the founders of the *grammatica speculativa*. For them there was only one single common grammar in all languages [*langues*], since all are the expression of the human spirit, one and the same at all times and in all places. Variations in vocabulary, by nature accidental, could therefore be neglected by grammar, which ought to consist uniquely in an inventory of the fundamental operations of a thought expressing itself.

One senses from the beginning of his work, however, a hesitation in the manner in which Condillac expresses himself. He announces at first that in order to discover the principles of language, one must observe how we think. It appears then that he proposes to move from thought to language; but he immediately adds that the analysis of thought is entirely accomplished in discourse, to such an extent that languages [*langues*] appear to him to be analytical methods for the analysis of thought, which now reverses the first scheme and moves from language to thought. This is the first indication of an ambiguity for which one ought not perhaps blame Condillac, for the ambiguity is less in his mind than in its object. Each science attains philosophical status when, going back to its principles, it achieves steadiness of purpose [*elle se fait sagesse*]. This ambiguity is the very one which would later be the torment of Ferdinand de Saussure when, in meditating on the object of general linguistics which he worked to build up, he ran into that evidence, at once invincible and disconcerting, "that *language*, under whatever point of view it is studied, *is always a twofold object*, composed of two parts, each of which is worthless without the other."[2] The duality of thought and the discourse which expresses it is perhaps only the first of these dualities — yet the most fundamental — for discourse is always discourse of thought, and this thought always tends to express itself in discourse. It is therefore natural that Condillac hesitates between approaching the analysis of language [*langue*] through that of thought or proceeding the other way around; yet this is always why, whether the linguist wishes it or not, grammar is philosophy and all philosophy implies a certain view of language. It is entirely legitimate for the grammarian and the linguist to refrain from all philosophical speculation devolving from the ends of philosophy. But that the very matter upon which they reflect should be charged with philosophical substance is not a matter within their control, and the philosopher does not have the privilege not to be interested in this.

Condillac's enterprise has the merit of considering grammar as comprising part of the art of thought rather than speech [de parler]. One rests assured, therefore, that his analysis of language will be in fact an analysis of thought. But this analysis presumes as a condition of its initiation that thought is analyzable, and that therefore it is composed of parts. Such analysis, further, presumes that thought breaks down under analysis into parts which are the parts of speech [discours]. It maintains, finally, that this analysis will contribute a general grammar that will be, so to speak, a grammar of human language.[3]

There is nothing impossible in these suppositions, but they all depend upon the first one, which presents a difficulty. Condillac means by "analyze" the same thing as "break down" [decomposer], and "analysis is nothing else but successively and orderly observing" (I, 1). But it first would be necessary to know if there is succession in thought. One could in fact admit either that there is in thought a succession of which analysis only recognizes and imitates the moments or that these moments are introduced by the very act of analysis into a thought which is itself instantaneous. Under the second hypothesis it would not be permissible to speak of the analysis of thought, in that sense designating an operation which consists in distinguishing in a whole the elements of which it is composed. In fact, if thought is simultaneous, what results from analysis thus understood is no longer thought. Now, in reading Condillac, whom we use here only as a particularly lucid witness to a common attitude, one cannot help but understand him as meaning the operation in the first sense. Thus, just as a mechanic takes apart a machine and puts the pieces of which it is composed side by side, so the philosophical grammarian "uncovers the principles of language" in the very analysis of thought. The parts or principles are, then, already there. It is not a question of putting them there, but rather of finding them there.

Read a bit more closely, Condillac shows himself to be a more subtle observer, however. In the chapter of the Grammaire which he devotes to the "language of action" (I, 1), whether it be natural or artificial, he notes that in the language of natural action "each thought is expressed instantaneously and not sequentially." For example: fixing my eyes upon an object, I make a sign that I would like to eat it. Many phrases are required to say so, but a gesture suffices to signify my intentions. Condillac puts it this way with his customary eloquence: "Action is quite complicated, for it indicates the object which affects (the subject) and at the same time it gives utterance to both the judgment that the subject makes and the sentiments that it feels. *There is no sequence within [dans] its ideas.* They present themselves all at once in the subject's action, so they are present all at once in his mind. One can understand it in the twinkling of an eye, while in order to explain it a long discourse is necessary."

Successfully pursuing the course of his ideas, Condillac next observes that "the language of simultaneous ideas is the only natural one." Is it necessary to conclude from this that the natural condition of ideas is to be simultaneous, therefore given instantaneously, all at once? Condillac seems to want to convince us of this by what he immediately adds: "We develop such a great familiarity for language consequent upon its articulation *that we believe that ideas proceed one after the other in the mind* because we utter words one after the other. Yet the matter is not as we conceive it. *And as each thought is necessarily intricate [composée],* it follows that the language of simultaneous ideas is the only natural language. That language of successive ideas, on the contrary, is an art from its very beginnings, and it is a great art when it is carried to its perfection."

It seems that Condillac is not concerned with responding to our question or that we have not managed to be interested in his. We would like to know if there is distinction and succession in thought anterior to language; he simply states that all thought is naturally complex and can be expressed by gestures rapidly but confusedly, or by language distinctly but slowly. No one has better sensed than he the "lifeless" characteristic of spoken language in comparison with gesture, this language of action which, to the extent that it remains natural, "always offers a multitude of ideas all at once." "With our languages [langues], on the contrary, we shuffle laboriously from idea to idea and appear to be embarrassed to say all that we think." It is true that the language of action daily becomes less natural. Also concerned with clarity, it breaks itself down into elements and, in its turn, becomes analytic, as can be seen in the method of the Abbe de l'Epée in his *Institution des sourds-muets par la voie des signes methodiques* (1776). This language will become more and more analytical because the more "men analyse, the more they feel the need of analyzing." It is, then, above all the opposition between the rapidity of natural language, the instantaneous expression of a complex but completely present thought, and the embarrassed awkwardness of all analytical language, whether of gesture or of the spoken word [parole], which holds the attention of Condillac.

It is curious to watch this subtle mind, both aware of the complete presence of thought to itself and pressed to desert this unproductive soil as soon as possible in order to transport us with him to the painstakingly cultivated terrain of analysis, where all is clear and distinct. He never tires of returning to this theme: "Languages [*langues*] are proportionate to ideas. . . ." As with ideas, so with words. "Consciousness precedes words, since we only fashion words to express ideas we already have." Because these ideas respond to the same needs and betoken the same objects, they are the same for all men. "Thus the system of ideas is basically the same for savage and for civilized people. It differs only because it is more or less elaborated [*étendu*]." Finally, returning once more to the connection between the progress of languages [*langues*] and that of analysis, which distends them as it were and spreads them out over time: "Languages [*langues*] perfect themselves only to the extent that they become analytical. Instead of offering instantaneously *confused masses*, they present ideas one after the other. . . ." (I, 2).

The difficulties with which Condillac struggles are instructive rather than something for which he ought to be reproached. Like all of us, he becomes less and less explicit to the extent that he approaches the heart of the question. That which he wishes to inculcate in his reader is, first, that languages [*langues*] *are not only*, not even principally, means of communicating thought. Important as it may be, this function only comes in second place, for in order to communicate thought it is necessary that it be communicable, and it is so only under the form of distinct ideas which are themselves inconceivable except under the guise of words. Languages [*langues*] are before all else then "analytical methods," that is to say, implements which man creates for himself in order to constitute distinct thought by analyzing confused thought, which naturally comes first. "The first object of language is therefore to analyze thought." Condillac remarks as follows: "As a matter of fact, we can only point out to others seriatim the ideas which coexist in our minds to the extent that we know how to display them to ourselves one after the other, that is to say that we only know how to speak to others to the extent that we know how to speak to ourselves" (II, 6).

This view affects the totality of Condillac's doctrine, insofar as it is set forth in the celebrated *Traité des sensations*. However, one sees developing in this treatise that new, and in a sense unforeseen, idea, that the analysis of thought, which proceeds with that of language, is begun and, as it were, set on its way by nature. This natural power to break things down [*décomposer*] belongs to the realm of sensation, for the diversity of the data pertaining to sight, hearing, touch, etc., puts us in the presence of distinct data. To the extent then that it provides irreducible information about reality, "each sense decomposes" (I, 5). If nature did not first begin to decompose things, "we should not be able to do so ourselves. But no sooner has she begun than she stops. Satisfied with having given us direction, she departs, and it is up to us to take the next step."

In order to move forward it is necessary that natural analysis become an art. Since nature decomposes thought to the extent that she engenders in us naturally distinct ideas, the art of decomposing thought will consist in recovering the order of the natural generation of our ideas. This is the entire secret of the *Traité des sensations*, but the *Traité* shares this secret with the *Grammaire*, because ideas are named to the extent that they are generated. Through the spontaneous play of nature men are led first to analyze without knowing it, automatically, by the simple fact that they sense. They must speak if they are to continue to analyze and be conscious of it. So it is with language. Condillac introduced into his doctrine an active element opposed to the general passivity of thought. It is indeed this which allows for the reconciliation of the two apparently antithetical aspects of his doctrine. One has access to language only through thought, for without thought man would have nothing to say. But one has access to distinct thought (except in the case of the natural distinction of primary sensations) only through language, for it is language which allows us to unravel the skein of thoughts simultaneously presented in the mind. "If all the ideas which make up a thought are simultaneously in the mind, they are successive in discourse. It is then languages [*langues*] which supply us with the means of analyzing our thoughts" (I, 3). One comes back thus to the same question: How does it come about that thought is still not analyzed, although it is analyzable?

The example of arithmetic counts for much in the conviction, soon formulated by Condillac, that signs are necessary "in order to develop ideas of all kinds." In his *Art de penser* (I, 6) he recalls that Locke "speaks of some Americans who did not have any idea of the number one thousand, because in fact they only had devised nouns which allowed them to count to twenty." In the way Condillac conceives it, the idea of number is composed of three elements: "The idea of unity, that of the operation by which the mind has added unity to itself several times, and finally the remembrance of having devised signs in the order of the exposition that he has just proposed" (I, 6). One hesitates when he rashly adds: "But why should not that which is true in arithmetic be true in the other sciences?" It is quite true that we could never reflect upon metaphysics and morals had we not devised signs for the purpose of fixing our ideas, to the extent that we have composed any new ones; but this fact does not obviously justify the question which Condillac immediately puts to himself: "Ought not words stand in that relation to the ideas of all the sciences which numbers hold in relation to the ideas of arithmetic?" Condillac sees in the ignorance of this truth one of the causes of the confusion which reigns in works of metaphysics and morals. One sees why he thought so. There is a unit whose combination with itself according to certain rules allows for the production of all other ideas. This is sensation. Why could not metaphysics and morals be kinds of arithmetics of sensations and their images?

To this question we ourselves would reply that it is because thought is not truly composed of units. Condillac's response is different, and gives cause for reflection on other grounds. It is, he says, that "the mind is so limited that it is not able to recall a great number of ideas for the purpose of reflecting on them all at once" (I, 6). This is why, when it is necessary to consider many ideas together, the mind combines many ideas under one symbol [signe] and thinks of them all together as if they were but one. The response is clear, as is always the case with Condillac, but disconcerting by its very simplicity; for, in short, if consciousness is so limited that it can only envisage a small number of ideas, under what form of the mind is it able to contain all of them? It is obvious that language allows for the enumeration, counting, and composition of ideas in a thousand ways. But can the metaphysician create them as one creates numbers, at will? Are the ideas of metaphysics and morals really the sums of units? Can *The Republic* or the *Nicomachean Ethics* be broken down into elementary images and into sensations?

One willingly follows the track of this agile mind, so charmed by its own clarity that it does not see anymore the obscure background it stands out against. It wants to persuade us that thought can be analyzed right down to its first elements, and it demonstrates this by establishing that the language in which thought expresses itself is already, in fact, an analysis of thought, as if language, which is material, were comparable to thought, which is not. Throughout his *Art de penser* he works unceasingly to prove that if we did not have words at our disposal, we would be incapable of forming complex ideas, although the problem would be rather to know how we could create symbols [signes] representing complex, abstract notions without first having in our minds the notions which these signs are supposed to signify. "When we have brought together ideas which we see nowhere put together, what is it that could arrange them in categories if we were not to connect them to words which are like bonds which prevent them from escaping?" (I, 6). This is an excellent question, but it presumes another one: According to what model do we assemble those ideas which we see nowhere put together? Condillac calls them "complex ideas which we form without models." But since his empiricism rejects all innate knowledge, and since we find them neither outside nor inside ourselves, will it be necessary to admit that the mind itself arranges them before language is there for the purpose of symbolizing them? If this is the case, language is not an analysis of thought. Language does not explain thought. Thought explains language.

Condillac works to show that verbal signs are necessary to the exercise of thought. "If you believe that names are useless to you, tear them out of your memory and then try to reflect upon civil and moral laws, virtues and vices, and, finally, on all human actions. You will recognize your error." We are in no way tempted to act in this fashion. We only ask whether Condillac himself has not committed another error whose presence he ends up suspecting through reflection. "Signs [*signes*] and reflection," he says at last, "are causes which lend each other mutual assistance and which concur reciprocally in their progress." But if reflection is only a certain methodical use of symbols [*signes*], the latter can only combine with themselves. "How much reflection has been necessary in order to form languages [*langues*], and of what assistance are languages [*langues*] to reflection?" (I, 6). If reflection forms languages [*langues*] (which have first been presented as natural and spontaneous analyses of thought), it is not possible that these same languages [*langues*] should be a natural analysis of thought. The latter ought to be different from what it becomes in the state of linguistic decomposition. Thought expressing ought to be other than thought expressed. Moreover, there are moments when Condillac does not deny this: "Gestures, sounds, numbers, letters: it is with these instruments *so foreign to our ideas* that we put them to work in order to raise ourselves to the most sublime knowledge" (I, 6). Then what can we learn about thought from an analysis of the materials which thought puts to work if they are foreign to it?

Basically Condillac is sustained in his enterprise by a simple and optimistic vision which he would not defend to the end if one were to press him to justify it, but which inspires all his views. This vision is that ideas are as enumerable as things are and that, whether it be a question of objects of sensation or of objects of thought obtained by reflection, there is always a possible sign for each idea and one idea for each sign. If that were the case in fact, then it would be possible to be in a kind of Eden inhabited by perfectly rational beings. Man, according to Condillac's heart, "would only devise signs to the extent that he experienced new sensations and made new reflections. . . . He would combine these first ideas . . . ; he would fix each collection of ideas by particular words; and when he wished to compare two complex notions, he could easily analyze them. . . . Thus *never devising words except after having ideas*, his notions would be always specific, and his language [*langue*] would not be subject to the obscurities and equivocations that ours is" (II, 5). Such is not our present condition; but we ask ourselves what ideas anterior to words are and what they can be for a thought which does not yet have words to name them.

This vision of an order of signs and an order of ideas whose elements would correspond each to each did not die with Condillac. Far from it! Condillac had invented the droll method which allows anyone to proceed to a simultaneous decomposition of thought and language. This method treats mind as a thing composed of parts; and since in fact mind is not a thing and is not composed of parts, each person could begin the operation anew with the certainty of succeeding, but also with the certainty that the operation could be resumed after him by anyone else with the same degree of success. The numerous family of ideologues—Destutt de Tracy, Garat, Cabanis, Laromiguière in France; Soave, Gioia, Delfico, and many others in Italy—are the witnesses of a school which profited by the mind's limitlessness in order unrestrainedly to attack it through all kinds of limitations. Because thought is not made up of parts, it is always possible to devise a new manner of breaking it down. The greatest of the ideologues, Maine de Biran, who came finally to throw off the yoke of ideology, did not escape its influence. The Institut de France, moreover, found it necessary to submit ideology to consideration as the subject of a gathering: *Decomposing the Faculty of Thought and Showing the Elementary Faculties Which Are to Be Seen There.* In whatever fashion one responded to the question, it was necessary to admit that thought is composed and decomposable. One might hesitate in determining the elementary faculties of which it is composed, but not over the fact that it might have some. On this point witness the *Mémoire sur la décomposition de la pensée* which Maine de Biran wrote for this occasion. I would only dare affirm that Biran marked the coming of age of the movement descended from Condillac. The *Intelligence* of Taine was perhaps a tardy prolongation, if not of de Tracy, at least of Cabanis. From the "Preface" of his work to its very end Taine expressly quotes from Condillac, from his "analysis" and from his "language [*langue*] of calculation." Henri Bergson did battle with this rear guard of ideology without moreover winning a decisive victory. The old hydra has subsequently grown new heads. Doubtless there always will be amateurs to propose anew decompositions of thought. Imagination does its calculating there in default of reason.

Things have nevertheless changed quite a bit since Condillac's death, and he would not readily recognize the scene were he to come to life in our own intellectual milieu. Assuredly he was a *philosophe* in the French style of the eighteenth century. A great admirer of Locke, he was incapable of following his method (even as much as a Frenchman could). He was also as systematic as Descartes had been, an enemy of Scholastic empiricism as he had been,[4] and like him a private man. His great circumspection moreover suited his situation as "Monsieur l'Abbé," private tutor to the inheritor of a princely house and, in that capacity, one of the "household retainers" of whom Bossuet and Fénelon were the best known French examples. A priest, naturally, as this sort of function required at that time (it is even said that he celebrated Mass at least once), he had taken his theology at the Sorbonne, as that is learned in times of *aggiornamento*, and he remembered it upon occasion. That is obvious in the precaution he takes, at the beginning of his *Art de penser*, of recalling that he is going to describe the soul such as it is at the present time, after original sin. Before such sin the soul had ideas anterior to the usage it made of the senses, "but things have changed since its disobedience." Now it is the soul such as it has become — Locke's soul, the only soul of which we have experience — that Condillac sets out to describe, for considered in itself and absolutely, "the soul being distinct and different from the body, the latter can only be the occasional cause of what it seems to produce in the soul." The history of European philosophy offers few more illustrative episodes. It is impossible to determine to what extent the Abbé Condillac wishes us to believe what he says, but taken literally, man would be living at present under the regime of a peripateticism of accidental origin, waiting upon the restoration of Malebranchian occasionalism whose effects sin has provisionally suspended.[5]

What has transpired between Condillac's time and ours? A bit of the same that has transpired between Newton and Einstein, where the disappearance of God has, although delayed, entailed the disappearance of absolute movement. In the present case it is the soul which has disappeared. Condillac still believed in it, and it is what allowed him to hold to the common origin of speech [*parole*] and thought. To the extent that he affirmed the existence of a soul, one could at least assume that it is there that ideas reside prior to language. There dwell the thoughts which proceed to become words by virtue of a mysterious incarnation. It is there that thought takes place, in me and for me. But the separate agent intellect taught by Avicenna and Averroes has been dead since the end of the sixteenth century. God the Light of Minds, still quite alive in the eighteenth century, died with ontologism toward the middle of the nineteenth century. The concept of the soul has been brought into disrepute by modern positivist psychology to such an extent that when today a person looks for an explanation of the status of thought outside of language, one does not find anymore anything either inside or outside himself to respond to the question.

The word "science" exercises the same fascination on minds at present as the word *scientia* did upon the masters of scholasticism. Everything, then, must take on the form of science in order to become matter which can be taught. This was the case with theology. The *Summa Theo-*

logiae of St. Thomas Aquinas had no other object than to offer to the schools a systematic exposé of it *per modum scientiae*, that is to say, as a series of consequences deduced from principles. But grammar, at the bottom of the ladder, displayed the same ambition as theology at the top. The *grammatica speculativa*, the *sprachlogik*, tended to replace in all the schools the empirical teaching of classic authors founded on the traditional grammars of Priscian and Donatus.[6] After having been for so long an instrument in the formation of literary taste and esthetic culture, grammar next became scholarship trying to explain the structure of language by means of the operations of the mind. In a similar respect we ourselves are today entangled in an eminently scholastic age, wherein philology and linguistics put the ancient [i.e., classical] *grammatica* through an analogous transformation. But today the transformation is followed under novel conditions which render it more difficult. The principal difficulty consists precisely in the disappearance of any God: God the light of Minds, the Divine Light, the Soul of the World, even the Agent Intellect charged with rendering possible the operations of language in fecundating thought. One does not even know anymore if it is "scientific" to suppose an immaterial reality at the origin of speech [*parole*]. Many doubt it, and Marxist materialism denies it. The linguist cannot expect that agreement should be arrived at in these paralinguistic questions. He moves on then; yet the very nature of his object does not allow him to forget such questions. Everything would be simple if language did not mean anything, but this is not the case, and so in order to avoid difficulties which are perhaps not "formalizable," as current usage has it, the linguist does his best to deal with signs while leaving out of the question their signification.

All the difficulties are gathered together in the notion, so simple in appearance, of "word" [*mot*]. When, principally in order to put food on the table, but also moved by the irresistible attraction which words exercised on his poetic imagination, Mallarmé wrote his treatise *Les mots anglais*, he announced his intention of studying language [*langue*] "according to the book." Whoever has the least experience of studying a foreign language [*langue*], whatever it may be, knows that it is impossible to proceed in this fashion. The book is indispensable for the purpose of learning the grammar of the tongue. This is quite important, but one could know English grammar thoroughly (supposing that English has a grammar) and possess an extended familiarity with its vocabulary, not only without being able to understand a single spoken phrase of English but even without having the least idea of what it means. For a tongue [*langue*] is before all else speech [*parole*], language [*langage*], and even song. English is an indeterminate number of tongues [*langues*] spoken differently depending on whether it is the English of Great Britain or the Anglo-American of the

United States. In Great Britain, again, it is a matter of the English of England, Ireland, Wales, or Scotland. In England, too, there is variation between the "King's English" and Cockney English. The subdivision could go on practically to infinity, as it could with Anglo-American speech. It is above all the spoken language [*langue parlé*] which is the true language [*langue*], that which, in any language [*langue*] in the world, women do not speak like men do, and the difficulty begins with the word. "Phonetic pronunciations" themselves do not do away with the difficulty, because when they are not simply ridiculous, they are of use only to the reader to whom the actual sounds of the language [*langue*] are familiar. One understands what sort of English "u" or "a" is at issue providing that one already knows what the diverse ways of pronouncing them are.

Here one runs into the first of the contingencies which encumber the study of languages [*langues*], that of the written word in relation to the spoken word. Mallarmé declares that his book is "a written work whose teaching is limited to the specific characteristics of writing, let us say, *spelling* and *meaning*." Pronunciation is another matter. So be it. Let us take a book then. I open it; what do I see there? "*Words*, first of all, recognizable themselves by means of the *letters* which compose them. They connect with each other, and we have sentences." How many words are there in the English language [*langue*]? About forty or fifty thousand. However that may be, the grammarian-poet does not doubt for a moment that English is made up of words and that he will know how to perceive, recognize, and classify them. All philology contains two things, Rules and Vocables. The volume which the poet offers contains words.[7]

Let us not quibble over it. Everyone understands what Mallarmé wants to say. But neither are we unaware that it is practically impossible to come to know a word isolated from any phrase, because, taken by itself, every word is susceptible of many different senses. The creative analogy, at work everywhere in language, at the heart of each tongue [*langue*] and even in the usage which the speaker makes of each word, brings it about that it is impossible to assign to any of these words a precise and universally applicable meaning. *Horse* does not necessarily signify a quadruped in the expression "battle horse," and the most important thing is that one does not even know, in terms of that expression taken alone, if it is a question of an actual or a purely metaphorical animal. It is indeed true that sentences are made up of words which determine their meaning, but it is almost as true to say that it is the sentence which determines the meaning of the words of which it is composed. Each word owes its meaning to the ensemble of its relations with the other words with which, in all given phrases, it forms an intelligible articulation. Even its direct, fundamental, and immediate meaning is retained better if one understands this meaning in connection with some other word. For these reasons one can say that languages [*langues*] are composed of a literally innumerable quantity of words, since each word in a language [*langue*] bears many meanings and is consequently in reality many words. Pushing the analysis to its limit, one could even say that language is not composed of words but of what the poet called quite appropriately "understandable mouthfuls." Every "mouthful" is uttered all together, and as legitimate as it might be to try to analyze it, the elements which one distinguishes in it do not possess really distinct existence. That makes for an obscure situation, but language itself is, finally, obscure.

This existence of the word as a distinct unit can be observed more clearly still if one considers the frequent case of homophones. The sound "o" signifies indifferently the words *au, eau, haut, aulx*. It could even signify an "O" (the letter O). All of these words are different since their respective meanings are different. It is indeed here that writing enters into play as a constituent element of language,[8] creating thus the scourge of spelling which saddens the life of some adults and of all students. At least one part of the function of orthography is to distinguish, by their different spellings, the different words which speech expresses by the utterance of identical sounds. It is evident that the written letter depends upon the spoken word. There are no spoken letters. Spoken words are not composed of letters but of sounds.[9]

One cannot hope to advance to the source of language by starting from the written word, for that only signifies spoken language, which itself signifies the meaning. The history of writing, or of the diverse ways of representing language by conventional signs, of which alphabetic writing is only a part, makes immediately obvious that contingency of which we spoke, that of the dependence of writing upon speaking, this time adding to that the contingency of writing upon writing. The point is of great practical bearing, for certain ideogrammatical languages [*langues*] betray a tendency to alphabetization. In any case, the problem inevitably arises within the most developed written languages [*langues*]. The existence of homophones makes it obvious that more ideas exist than there are sounds to express them, since the same sounds can signify entirely different ideas, and these same sounds can be signified by different letters. Writing comes, then, to the aid of speech [*parole*] in order to create as many written words as there exist meanings for the same sound: *saint, sein, seing, ceint, sain*.

At the origin of this fact there is a contingency more deep-seated still than that of all written signs, traced in black on white or otherwise by an instrument whatsoever upon any surface whatsoever, in connection with any sound whatsoever. When the homophone is a homograph, no artifice of writing can be of any help. A *coin* [French] is an angle formed by two lines or two planes; it is a tool for splitting wood [a wedge]; it is a piece of steel grooved for the purpose of striking medals or money [a die]; it is a piece of wood or iron designed to fill in the space between two parts of an object or building and to tighten them up [a quoin]. But it could be many other things also: a patch of woods, a small piece of land, a chimney corner, a corner of the eye, of the mouth, an out-of-the-way place, etc. One perceives at the same time from these examples the scarcity of spellings for expressing different ideas and different meanings. A fact of capital importance presents itself immediately to our reflection: the paucity (if we must take back again from English an ancient French word which we have today lost)[10] of signs at our disposal compared to the indefinite number of meanings which we ask them to signify. We insist that this is not a question of numerical inequality, but rather of incommensurability between the order of the signifiers and that of the things signified. There is literally no proportion between the two orders.

The grammarian who wishes to be nothing else can define the word in various ways. For example: a sound or an ensemble of sounds corresponding to an idea. It is the smallest verbal unit taken separately. A syllable has meaning only if it signifies a monosyllabic word. If it does not make sense outside of a polysyllabic word of which it is a part, it is then only a simple syllable, not a word. That was Aristotle's doctrine in the treatise "On Interpretation," chapter 2. Under that simple form the notion is easily managed: *monosyllabe* is a single word composed of four syllables, *mo, no, syl, lab*, any one of which is but a monosyllable [in French].

Nothing could be more simple in appearance, but linguists are not of this mind. "All efforts to give to the term *word* a properly scientific status come up against the fact that in addition to some cases which we can decide without hesitation, there are other cases in which none of the utilizable criteria allow us to determine the issue simply."[11] The philosopher does not have the competence to begin or conclude inquiries of this sort, but one can at least observe that if it is impossible to find a satisfactory definition of the vocable "word," it is probable that a science of language is not possible, or that the idea that has developed of such a science does not agree with the reality which it has been charged with explaining. "The notion of word," the same linguist continues, "completed by that of enclitic, allows us to give a good account of the structure of articulation in inflected languages [*langues*] such as Greek or Latin. In other languages [*langues*] it allows us to group certain facts together in a useful fashion, but its extension to the aggregate of all articulations often complicates the exposition of the grammar more than it simplifies it."[12]

It is perhaps the case that the most simple grammatical fact does not at all lend itself to an exhaustive explanation. What is proposed for the purpose of simplifying grammatical exposition? It is suggested today that we replace "the *word* in linguistic practice by the much more supple concept of *syntagma.*" Under this term will be designated "any cluster of a number of irreducible signs" [*de plusiers signes minima*]. In order to be a part of a syntagma, or cluster of signs [*mots*] forming a unit, a minimal sign ought to be connected to the other signs of the same group by "relations more intimate than those which connect it to the rest of the articulation." For example, let us say the phrase "an enormous rock overhung the railway" breaks down naturally into three syntagmas: *an enormous rock, overhung, the railway.*[13] It appears to the ordinary user of grammar that the new terminology does not change anything that concerns the word, for it can be said of each syntagma, whether it is a *minimum* (*overhung*) or is composed of several *minima* (the railway [in French: *la voie ferrée*]), that it is a word or a group of words. "Word" remains what it always has been, the smallest part of speech which can make sense.

No difficulty would remain in the mind of the analyst if he did not ask himself what a "minimal sign" is. When in response to that question we reply, "the word," the linguist easily demonstrates to the grammarian that the word itself is a syntagma. This is evident in the case of "overhung," which signifies "properly projecting beyond the vertical." This meaning is not simple, particularly since it includes in itself that of the word "vertical," which is already compound. Quite unlike the German language, which disposes infinite resources in this regard, the French does not much like compounds. It contains a large number of them, but we see here why it mistrusts itself on this score, for it is not certain that the word chosen says what one wants it to say. It is rare that a railway would be constructed below rocks which overhang it. Doubtlessly one wishes to say only that the railway passes at the foot of a rock whose height towers above it, but one already sees two things there: that the meaning of the polysyllabic syntagma can only be defined by a sentence and that this meaning cannot completely be determined starting out from an isolated word. Here once more our decision about the meaning of the word requires taking into consideration the meaning of the entire sentence. When we say that the word is the smallest part of speech, we are not saying that its meaning is one and indivisible, as the word itself is. On the contrary, the meaning of the simplest word expands from the moment that we try to define it. Even if the word is divisible, its meaning is not, for in adding the meaning of *over* to that of *hang* one does not obtain that of *overhang,* which, moreover, does not properly apply to the case in question. Once again, we do not find here "parts of thought" which could correspond to "parts of speech."

Thus there is still carried on today the many-centuries-old enterprise of the decomposition of thought, although it is done in a new spirit and according to novel methods (which remain nevertheless the same old methods). It is carried on always with a predilection for the means of analyzing language, formerly grammar, now linguistics, and completely filled with its resolution to make itself a science. Contemporary decomposition even does this successfully, for it is not its fault if philosophers present questions to it which are not in its domain, questions to which it cannot, then, respond. It is completely true that language expresses thought, in this sense, that through it the initiative of one thought appeals to another thought in the legitimate and normally justified hope that the words spoken and the words heard will be spoken and heard univocally enough so that the message is effectively communicated. The communicability of thought is a great and incontestable fact, and it is only possible through language. But everything suggests that thought by its very nature remains essentially other than its means of communication. J. Vendryès believed this was the case when he thus summed up one of the major conclusions of his vast experience: "The discord between grammar and logic consists in this, that grammatical categories and logical categories quite rarely overlap. Almost never do the numbers of the two coincide." And toward the end of his book, as if he were more and more convinced of the truth of his conclusion, Vendryès added: "there is no connection that has been established between the categories of the mind and the number or the complexity of the categories of grammar."[14]

The philosopher who notes these conclusions, insofar as the matter concerns him, can deduce from them only that there is a fundamental and primary heterogeneity between speech [parole] and thought. Between the one and the other there seems to be interposed a kind of creative liberty which is called mind. But one is then in the midst of metaphysics, in a domain which linguistics and grammar incessantly skirt. Perhaps they even inadvertently venture into it, but they never dwell there with complete ease.

It is all the more interesting for the philosopher to see such a linguist, as rigorous in the idea that he develops of his own science as he is scrupulous in the handling of his methods, allow himself to be so seduced by metaphysical reality that he consistently feels it, even if he refuses to engage in it.

The question is not one of knowing whether one ought to refuse to face the issue, but rather whether one could confront it in the event one should want to. It is impossible to confront it because here the observer is part of the observed. One cannot move away from language in order to consider it from outside, because it is impossible to represent it without using it. Such is the destiny of man, the metaphysical animal, or at least the animal engaged in metaphysics, with which his physical being is in intimate, incessant, inevitable relation, even though he himself may not know exactly what the nature of this relation is.

Nothing shows this better than recently multiplied efforts by linguists designed to carry to term the many-centuries-old undertaking of a decomposition of thought brought about by a decomposition of language [*langue*].

There simply are no limits to the possibilities of this decomposition, and linguists deploy a remarkable virtuosity in it. It goes without saying that in this endeavor one continually moves from the design of the language [*plan du langage*] to that of speech [*langue*]. It is inevitable, since one cannot even conceive of a language which is not the language of a certain tongue [*langue*]. A private language would still fit this case. Furthermore, it is impossible to escape from the fatal objection already noted by de Saussure, who finds it necessary to pose "on the horizon of science and of philosophy the notion of *sign* as a two-sided unit."[15] This necessity is more especially embarrassing as the two sides of this notion, equally necessary, are, however, not homogeneous, since as the same linguist says, "language has this as an eminent distinction, that it always is established upon two planes, that of the signifier and that of the thing signified."[16] As communication is impossible without language, it therefore follows that every signifier and everything signified is, in its turn, at one and the same time signifier and signified. The result of this is that the "tensions and transformations" entailed by this fundamental "dysharmony" make it difficult, if not impossible, to constitute a properly objective science of an object so naturally ambiguous.

Looking at the efforts of contemporary linguistics trying to move beyond this ambiguity is most instructive. Departing from the initial distinction between signifier and the thing signified, one first notices that every linguistic sign consists precisely in their union. As a matter of fact, there is no sign where there is nothing signified, but one notes also that "in current language" it is rather to the signifier that the name of sign will be reserved. This is the initial "dysharmony," if one wishes so to think of it, for one hardly sees how the signified could itself be a sign. The sign post is not the route which it points out.

This is not the last asymmetry with which the sign may be burdened. One distinguishes signs into units of primary articulation, which are, in short, what but recently were called words, and units of secondary articulation, which are those units into which, in their turn, words are decomposed. Thus, in *I have a headache* one counts five units of primary articulation (*I, have, a, head, ache*). The units of secondary articulation are those which make up the vocal, or "phonetic," form of each unit of primary articulation. In short, these are the letters (or their phonetic equivalents) of which the words are composed. Thus *head* is composed of three units of secondary articulation, which are the letters *h, e, d.* There is nothing objectionable in this analysis. It is just necessary to add that it decomposes language into heterogeneous elements, of which some, the units of primary articulation, truly belong to it, while the others only belong to it through the first and in an indirect fashion. Put otherwise, these two orders of units are not of the same nature. Because "head" is a word, it constitutes an ultimate linguistic element which cannot be broken down into smaller elements. As the linguist whose analysis we follow here puts it so well, this unit of primary articulation "could not be analyzed into successive smaller units endowed with meaning: the whole *head* means 'head', and it is impossible to attribute to 'h', 'e', and 'd' any distinct meanings whose sum would be equivalent to *head.*" On the contrary, the letters or sounds which form the secondary articulation of language do not have their own meaning. The words which set them forth only contain these sounds or letters: *h* is *h, e* is *e.* In fact, since they have no intelligible meaning of their own, these signs do not have any "signified" and thus are not signs. They are but the elements with which one can make signifiers endowed with signifieds. Taken in themselves, they are no more elements of language than would be the babbling or indistinct vocal noises such as those of infants in the cradle, who do not yet "speak." The units of primary articulation are of language; those of secondary articulation, taken in themselves, are not units of language. They are physical facts divested of signification.

This is not all. In order better to distinguish two sorts of units, it is proposed to call the units of primary articulation *monemes,* each of them a minimal sign, one which is not analyzable into other signs. The units of secondary articulation of which the first are composed are to be called *phonemes.* We simply observe that the preceding comment holds here also for this new distinction. The "monemes" are of the nature of language, the "phonemes" are not, except that they make up the monemes without participating in their nature or possessing any of their properties. This is why, furthermore, "monemes" were recently called "semantemes," because they are endowed with signification. Today it is desired that the "phonemes" also have a signification. And they do, but the signification of a phoneme is of another nature than that of the moneme. It is not properly a signification but a "consignification." In itself "working" signifies something; but the "ing" of "working," if one separates this ending from its root [*radical*], signifies nothing.[16a] "Ing" is an element of secondary articulation which is a part of an element of primary articulation and has signification only in this connection. It is only in an equivocal sense that one can hold a phoneme to be an element of language, for, signifying nothing by itself, it is not a sign.

If, however, one wishes to follow this analysis to the end to which it inevitably leads, one must next divide language into two elementary groups so frankly heterogenous that one will assign different names to them. One will call *lexemes* all monemes endowed with their own, or, in any case, distinct, signification; and one will reserve the name *morphemes* for the elements of language which, although not alien to signification, do not however signify by themselves. One then ends by conceiving of all language [*langue*] as composed of two sorts of elements contained in two distinct sorts of books, dictionaries and grammars. One will call *lexemes* "those of the monemes which find a place in a dictionary and not in a grammar," and one will reserve "*morpheme* to designate those which, like *-ing* (in *working*), appear in grammars." Thus the fundamental heterogeneity of signifier and signified in the sign, after being installed, at the interior of the sign itself, between the elements of the moneme which are lexemes and those which are only morphemes, ends by solidifying under the form of two distinct books, the one destined to gather the first class of monemes, the other to gather the second.[17]

It seems difficult to push further into the decomposition of thought through that of language, since we reach the point where it is language itself which is found to be decomposed. Whatever one thinks of the result, the effort itself captures attention and, moreover, piques the curiosity. One senses in the whole series of these analyses a sort of obstinate will to provide the science of language with an object which it could deal with "scientifically," with all the rigor and the full objectivity that a physicist brings to the study of physical facts, or that we nonscientists imagine that study achieves everywhere and always. An obstacle, always the same, that thwarts the striving of the linguist toward the ideal of perfect scientific rigor is the fact that words have meaning. Of the two aspects of the sign there is one which does not allow itself readily to yield to the laws, rules, accounting, and measurements dear to every linguist enamored of scientific rigor. This aspect is naturally not the signifier but the signified.

Thus one comes to comprehend the possibility of that consequence, at once monstrous and inevitable, which is the ambition conceived by certain linguists, namely, of constituting a science of language which would begin by "eliminating the meaning" of it. Nothing is more curious than the attitude of certain moderate or reasonable linguists who, without going this far, do not disguise the sorrow that the difficulty of the enterprise activates in them. Too difficult to execute, such a science does not appear to them either absurd or impossible. To deal with words scientifically, without allowing their meaning to intervene, "would give more rigor to linguistics by eliminating a domain wherein experience shows that it is not easy to arrange facts." With a little ingenuity, however, one could "go rather far in this regard" and distinguish, solely by the inspection of forms, those which correspond to lexemes or to phonemes. "One could thus attain to a complete analysis of language [*langue*] which would allow one to establish a grammar, and even a vocabulary which would only lack the definitions of our dictionaries." One cannot but sense a secret pleasure to see this method crowned by the triumph of a complete dictionary in which the words would lack nothing except their meanings.

One understands the nuance of regret which informs the remark of a certain scholar that, in fact, "no linguist ought to analyze and describe a language [*langue*] of which he understood nothing. According to all appearances such an enterprise, if it were to amount to anything, would demand a consumption of time and energy which has caused those very ones to back off who see in this method the only theoretically acceptable one."[18]

To devise a linguistics which should succeed in treating language abstracted from its meaning is to demand a science founded on the preliminary suppression of its object. One must choose between the traditional principle, simply taken up again by de Saussure and many another modern linguist, of the essential duality of language, and the notion, more recent than that but false, of a linguistic dealing with a system of signs divested of meaning, or at least treated as if they were so as a matter of fact. The idea of such is absurd because vocal forms divested of meaning are not signs. They do not, then, constitute a language, and a linguistics without a language is impossible. That these vocal forms nevertheless may have a meaning from which one merely abstracts, because one does not know it, has, moreover, as a consequence that we condemn ourselves not to know the connection of these forms with the meaning which explains them in part, since their reason for existing, or proper function, is to signify that meaning. The enterprise whose difficulty is regretted is in fact quite other than "difficult." It is contradictory and impossible. Its absence is only the absence of a chimera. There is nothing to be regretted here.

There is no mystery about this. On the contrary, it bears the mark of a sort of inevitability. It is only the paradoxical but logical issue of the desire to eliminate from the object of linguistics the element of thought which prevents it from becoming a natural science entirely subject to the laws of mechanics. Everything immaterial, unpredictable, and free in the formation and functioning of language [*langue*] ought consequently be denied or devaluated and, at the very least, subordinated to the material and properly physical element of language.

This tendency reveals itself in many ways. It inspires the harmless but symptomatic remark of linguists who begin by prudently declaring their resolution of avoiding all philosophical discussion and, above all, of not coming to any decision about the philosophical questions which the study of language might suggest. In the first rank of these questions there naturally occurs that of the connection of language to thought. "Right away," firmly declares one of them whose thought is moreover perfectly well-balanced, "the linguist, for his part, considers that no thought exists without language, and that, consequently, the understanding of the world is determined by the expression that it receives."[19]

The linguist who makes this declaration has the right to make it, but not by virtue of being a linguist. To affirm that thought cannot exist without language is to set forth a proposition that most hold to be true, but which is not a linguistic proposition. It is to set forth a philosophical proposition exactly in the same sense as it would be to set forth the contrary. Our linguist doubtless considers that to maintain the possibility of thought without language would be to assume a philosophical responsibility, and he is right; but the negation of a philosophical and metaphysical thought is itself a philosophical and metaphysical proposition. This is what Peguy called "a negative affirmation," of exactly the same nature as that to which it is opposed. We concede, at least provisionally, that there is no thought without language, but could there be language without thought? Even the linguists who aspire to the perfect linguistic of a language which, for them, would be devoid of meaning admit that it would at least be necessary for that subject of their study from which they abstract the meaning to be truly a language [langue] in order for them to abstract from it. And, nevertheless, of the thought which conceives this meaning they know nothing precisely insofar as they are linguists.

An analogous problem presents itself with regard to what language signifies. The same eminent linguist does not hesitate to affirm that "language reproduces the world." He even invites us to take this doubly extraordinary affirmation literally. He himself truly has no intentions however of imposing on us the more theological than philosophical idea that the world was produced. It cannot be then a question for us of reproducing it. Language, moreover, does not produce anything other than sounds endowed with meaning. If I say "horse," I produce the word "horse," but no horse. It is only of the Divine Word that Scripture teaches: *dixit et facta sunt* [He spoke, and it was accomplished], but this unique case would not enhance any linguistics. If one replies that the idea of reproduction is only a simple metaphor here, it will be in place to ask what the meaning of it is. Some ideograms represent, if one will, the objects which they signify, but at best they represent the image of it. They do not reproduce anything real of it.

This is still more true, if possible, of the spoken or written words of which languages [langues] are composed. They are decorated with the name of "linguistic symbols" [symboles linguistiques], but the manifest abuse that is made today of the idea of symbol is explained quite well by the desire to conjure away the difficulty of the problem. By definition the symbol "is mediating" [*mediatisant*], for it is a material sign endowed with signification. But de Saussure already put his hearers on their guard against the imprecision of the word, and rightly so. "A symbol," says Lalande's *Dictionnaire*, "is that which characterizes something else by virtue of an analogical correspondence." Now, as a general rule there is no analogy between words and the things that they signify. One can find an analogy between the image of a dog and the notion of fidelity, or between that of an anchor and steadfastness of faith, but the words "dog" and "faith" are not the symbols of anything; they are only sounds without analogy to the ideas, which are moreover abstract, which they signify. It is necessary to choose between maintaining that signs are arbitrary or assigning them a symbolic content based, then, on reality.[20]

Supposing that one insists on calling the linguistic sign a symbol, one will ask, From whence comes its power of symbolizing? The most serious linguists ask themselves: "What is the source of the mysterious power which resides in language [*langue*]? Why are the individual and society, together and with the same necessity, *founded* in language? Because language [*langue*] represents the highest form of a faculty which is inherent in the human condition, the faculty of *symbolizing*."[21]

Let us admit this "symbolizing faculty" and that it "allows in fact the formation of the concept as distinct from the concrete object which is only an exemplar of it."[22] The response annoyingly recalls the classical explication of the properties of opium by a *virtus dormitiva* [dormitive power] of which the effect would be *sensus nostros assoupire* [put our senses to sleep]. We shall not rail at this response, however, for perhaps we have nothing more precise to say on our side. Only we do not claim that the *virtus significativa* that is alleged could be a scientific explanation. The Cartesian critique of substantial forms has perhaps taught us only this, but it did teach us this, and one is a bit surprised that it should be those who hold to a scientific linguistics who invite us today to understand this "faculty of symbolizing," even understood in a quite broad sense, as "the faculty of *representing* the real by a 'sign' and of understanding the 'sign' as representing the real, thus establishing a connection of 'signification' between something and something else."[23] Here is matter for astonishment, for, precisely, even if this faculty exists, it is reduced to creating signs which do not "represent" anything, attaining its perfection in the language of mathematics where any sign whatever, numerical or algebraic, can signify indifferently quantities of whatever sort.

So many efforts to decompose thought by a progressive decomposition of language into words, into monemes, then into phonemes, finally into letters, crowned by an avowed hope of producing a science of language preliminarily freed of all signification, betoken finally the desire of constituting a science of language comparable in objectivity and certitude to the most indisputably "scientific" parts of the sciences of nature. This desire betrays many signs which suggest the intention of relegating to the background the intellect and the role, however decisive, that it plays as cause of the spoken word. If it is not the sole cause of it, the intellect certainly contributes to producing it, since it is to the intellect (or to what we designate by this name) that is owed the meaning of signs.

In order to disembarrass itself completely of this intruder, meaning, the belief has been devised, or it is at least spoken of as if believed, that it is the sign itself which created the meaning, and the signifier, the signified. One of the most hackneyed objections against metaphysics is that the metaphysician takes grammatical categories of language for the expressions of reality. Because in our tongue [langue] sentences are composed of a subject, verb, and predicates, we spontaneously infer that there are in nature substances working causal actions which are undergone by other substances. The adjectives modifying substantives immediately become for us the accidents of as many substances, and so on. Our language [langue] begins then at once in this fashion to model our world, and since it models our thought at the same time, we think a world which our language [langue] has first modeled.[24]

It is possible that this could be true, but it is a philosophical position foreign to linguistics. It is an appendage to that other opinion, equally accepted among linguists, that there is no thought without language. If a linguist says to me that it is our language [langue] which first models the world that we think, I know that he is not speaking to me as a linguist but as a philosopher who, moreover, would excuse himself from giving me any philosophical justification for his opinion. Not only do I not know if the argument in the previous paragraph is true, but I do not even know why it seems to him to be true. He who formulates this argument assumes, however, an enormous philosophical responsibility, for it would be a question of knowing if thought has not first been modeled by that world which it is said that thought models. And if thought has modeled language (which is at least not impossible), could it not be the world which, through language, had modeled thought?

This is what perhaps prompted the first philosophy of Ludwig Wittgenstein. In his Tractatus Logico-Philosophicus he unself-consciously maintained that the structure of language reproduced that of reality.[25] It is hard to know with any accuracy if one ought to attribute to Wittgenstein the philosophical notions which appear to us to be presupposed or implied by his own words. Others who are practitioners of the sciences of nature, however, do not leave us any doubt about what they actually think. The biologist Walter M. Elsasser wrote: "Ordinary conceptual language has clearly been invented for biological ends, and fundamental concepts are modeled on biological classes."[26] In short, we say trees, cows, cockroaches, because there exist in fact, as distinct classes, trees, cows, cockroaches. One must not then reproach philosophers at one and the same time with wanting to impose on nature the categories of grammar while also conceiving of language as a simple reflection of reality. The universe could have modeled language [langue], and language [langue] the universe, but not at one and the same time and in the same manner. The Saussurian principle will then be conceded, that "linguistics has for its unique and true object language [langue] envisaged in itself and for itself." But one cannot presume on it to exorcise from that science the phantom of metaphysics, for it is possible that language could be metaphysical in itself and by full right.

The first remark of W.M. Elsasser leads to another: "When the complexity [of science] reaches a certain degree, common, everyday language can clarify the mind better than a thicket of mathematical formulas." By pushing a bit further in the same direction one comes to ask oneself whether it is not the case that when the object to be defined is immensely complicated, one is led at times to ways of posing the problem invented and used as a certainty over the centuries by philosophers whose positions are commonly held as irrevocably superceded. "If the relations become too complex," the same biologist notes, "it can come about that the conceptual expression becomes the most appropriate manner to formulate certain aspects of the theory."[27] One readily sees of what conceptualization he is thinking when he proposes elsewhere to replace the scientific concept of *classes* by that of *universals*.[28] It is only a question there of an imagined substitution and of a suggestion of which one expects no practical consequences, but it suggests that the interminable Scholastic controversy between nominalists and realists had meaning and that reflection upon language might not be able to escape from the necessity of this controversy. It is annoying for the linguist that language should have a meaning, but it is of its essence that it have one.

2

Word and Meaning

Ferdinand de Saussure introduced into linguistics the word "value." Perhaps this innovation was suggested to him by Humboldt,[1] but de Saussure assured the diffusion of it by making what was with others only a casual expression a technical term endowed with a precise meaning.

Chapter IV of the *Cours de linguistique générale* is entitled "*La valeur linguistique*," but the preceding chapter has already established this idea as belonging to the science of language. Comparing the latter to economics, in which political economy and economic history are to be distinguished, Saussure says that the same internal necessity that obliges economics to make this distinction makes it necessary "to divide linguistics into two parts each having its own principle." And he gives the reason for this: "It is that there, as in political economy, one is faced with the idea of *value*; in the two sciences it is a question of *a system of equivalences between two things of different orders:* in the one, work and salary; in the other, a signified and signifier."[2]

This idea is bound up in the thought of de Saussure with the distinction between the two manners of situating facts, according to *the axis of simultaneities* and *the axis of successivities*. We shall return to this later, but for the moment we mean by this the axis of values considered in themselves and the axis of these same values considered as functions of time. "It is on the linguist," writes de Saussure, "that this distinction imposes itself most imperiously, for language [*langue*] is a system of pure values which nothing determines outside of the momentary state of its terms." What does he mean by "pure values" or "values pure"? Insofar as his text allows one to conjecture on it, linguistic values are pure because they are rootless, without any foundation in reality. It is not so in economics, where the values are tied to reality. For example, "the value of an estate is in proportion to what it brings in." The connection of an economic value with the realities which it "is worth" assures it a natural, real foundation. Linguistic values are completely different. They are "pure" because they have no foundation in reality. They are totally arbitrary, which means to say "that in linguistics natural 'givens' do not have any place."[3]

Sentences which contain the words *always* or *never, all* or *none,* are rarely completely true. In the present case this same linguist will readily demonstrate that in linguistics it is difficult to form a proposition in which the natural "givens" do not truly find any place. But this is not the question here. The usage which de Saussure makes of the word "value" is the source of the difficulty. It is not its customary usage; yet modern dictionaries are so properly made that one finds Saussure cited in them as testimony to this new usage, and one can then all the less protest against the legitimacy of the linguist establishing the purely arbitrary character of language. If, then, it is his pleasure to call "value" what is habitually called "meaning," no one has in fact the least right to oppose it.

In cases of this sort, however, a change of terminology is not unconnected to a change in the meaning of the proposition concerned. Here Saussure wants to underline the fact that the meaning of the word varies with its context. Certainly. That has always been known. There is no schoolboy who is unaware of the problem: search out in the dictionary among the possible meanings of a word that which fits the rest of the sentence. A professor of French in a school in Toronto (Canada) told me how perplexed he was at reading in a paper of one of his students, as a translation of a corresponding English sentence, "My father is not a well" [*Mon père n'est pas puits*]. It took him some time to figure out that the English sentence to be translated was simply: "My father is not well." In fact, *well* is a perfect homophone and a perfect homograph. One can only figure out the meaning of the word from that of the sentence. The intellect spontaneously eliminates the sentence in which the word in question would not make any sense.

But everyone knows that the meaning of a word depends on its context, and to be mistaken as above in not a "misvalue" [*contre-valeur*]; it is simply what is called a misinterpretation [*contresens*]. The value here is the modification of meaning undergone by the word by reason of its context, and what the word signifies is real; but since the meaning of a word depends almost always on its context, the idea of value does not add anything to that of meaning. It becomes interesting then to search out why Saussure and the linguists who follow him want to add this particular sense to all those which are already attributed to the word "value." And the only reason I can imagine is the desire to eliminate the word "meaning."

We have already said that this elimination is impossible, as long, at least, as one intends to speak of language. Saussure justifies the application to language of the idea of value because what is at stake is a system of equivalences, but this is to define a word by the repetition of the same word. There is equivalence when there is equality of value. Now our problem is to know if the sign has a value, if the signified has a value, and if these two values are equal.

Here is a sum of silver, or gold, or paper. It has exchange value either because it possesses some intrinsically real properties which make it desirable in itself, or else for its power of procuring other goods, each of which is desirable in itself. Even symbolic money, such as all fiduciary money is, only has exchange value by virtue of the gold it represents, or, in the absence of a gold standard, the purchasable objects, products of work which are exchangeable for those of other work, of which it is a symbol. Assuredly, since speech is free, nothing prevents our holding as goods the intelligible word which we know, and the meaning of that word. There is no decisive reason, then, for refusing the name of value either to speech [*langue*] or even to language [*langage*], but one lays oneself open by so doing to creating a fundamental equivocation about the nature of what one designates by this name. No exchange is possible without language, even though it be the language of bearing and gesticulation. But in real exchange he who gives in exchange loses the property of what he gives and acquires the property of what his partner gives him. Directly or otherwise, the property, as we say, "changes hands." It is not so with the signs involved in the operation of speech [*langage*]. He who speaks loses neither the particular property of the words that he pronounces nor their meaning. We say that those who speak "exchange remarks," but this is a metaphor which tells us that their remarks answer one another. One does not want to say that one of the interlocutors parts with the remarks he has and thus makes himself the possessor of those of the other, or that the other might part with anything whatever to the profit of the first. Each remains the indisputable proprietor of his word and thought. It is not even a case for applying the idea of equivalence, for words do not cost anything and are not worth anything.

It is not sufficient to consult a dictionary, however well-constructed, in order to know whether the new usage of the word "value" is legitimate. Since de Saussure made use of it in this sense, all that the lexicon can do is to note it down. You consult it in order to understand Saussure; it responds to you with Saussure.[4] You have not advanced any then. Saussure himself, and others after him, search for other analogies, in arithmetic, for example; but in arithmetic relations of quantity are at issue. One can consequently say that 100 is worth 100 units because in fact, for him who counts, the number 100 "contains" unity 100 times. But the word that one pronounces does not contain its meaning by any means. One hundred is not worth one hundred times one; it is that. In solfeggio a half note is worth two quarter notes, and a full note is worth two half notes, because the duration of one of these notes contains twice the duration of the other. But the meaning of a word is not quantitatively measurable. It no more lasts in time than it extends in space. A word then does not have "value" in the sense that a note has. The analogy is worthless.

Perhaps it is the sense of this which led Saussure to compare language to a game of chess in which words would be the pieces.[5] Perhaps Ludwig Wittgenstein also found there an inducement for setting forth and developing his second philosophy, that of language games.[6] But there are only quite superficial resemblances between a word endowed with its meaning and a chess piece of any sort whatsoever. In the first place, Saussure appears to have forgotten along the way his own definition of the idea of value as equivalence between things of a different order. There is no equivalence between chess pieces and anything else whatever. Each piece is exactly what it is, nothing else, whatever movement one might give to it. And if it is licit to compare two successive states of a language [*langue*] to two successive states of a chess board, there exists no resemblance whatever between the diachronic aspects of a language [*langue*], whose game, if that is the name you want to give its history, plays itself out, and the game of chess, all the successive movements of which are reflective, calculated, premeditated. Saussure himself admits this fundamental difference between the two cases: the chess player "*has the intention* of bringing about the move . . . ; in order that the chess game might resemble language [*langue*] at all points of play, it would be necessary to suppose an unconscious and unintelligent player."[7] It becomes difficult then to assimilate language to a game whose player would be deprived of intelligence, for language is almost universally accorded to be the privilege of man, the intelligent animal.

In whatever manner one intends it, the notion of value is not applicable to language. The intelligible has a value; it is even endowed with the highest of all value after being. Truth is a good in itself; it is the good of the intellect. Everything that is has a value in proportion to its being. The meaning of a word and the word itself have, then, their value, but their being is not composed of their values. They are not exchangeable equivalents for anything whatever.

The question is basically metaphysical, since the debate bears on transcendentals. It is a question of knowing if the meaning of language, which is of the intelligible order and is the object of the intellect, can conceive of itself as if it were a good and an object of the will. In its proper sense the value of an object is a characteristic measurable to the extent that this object can be exchanged. Nothing is measurable in the signifier, nothing in the signified, nothing in their relation. The meaning is not a desirable and possessible good; it is given as coessential to the intellect.

It is doubtlessly superfluous to recall that nothing in the preceding paragraphs ought to be understood as a linguistic proposition. We are only concerned here with the philosophy implied in certain linguistics which are not themselves linguistic but philosophical. De Saussure did no more than state a fact in saying, we recall, that "the linguistic phenomenon constantly presents two faces."[8] It is necessary to add, however, that these two faces, although corresponding, are heterogeneous, and that given the one in the other, the nature of their correspondence, and even its possibility, escapes us. Since the physical face is the only one which could be measured and scientifically described, every linguistics which wants to be a science tends to reduce the transphysical or nonphysical face to the physical. This, moreover, does not prevent any serious inconvenience as long as one does not deny the existence of the face that one has decided to ignore. At that moment philosophy cannot excuse itself from intervening in order to recall the rights, not of philosophy, but of reality.

The point of juncture of these two elements of language whose manifest duality was always recognized is the word [mot]. We must then return to it in order to examine it more closely.

I have looked for the definition of "word" in the *Dictionnaire technique et critique de la philosophie* of André Lalande (1967). Its place would normally be found between *morule* and *moteur* [the French term is "*mot*"], but it is not to be found there. The same is the case for *name* [*nom*], which ought to go between *nolonté* and *nombre*, but it is not to be met with there either. The Societé Francaise de Philosophie, under whose responsibility Lalande's *Dictionnaire* is edited, has doubtless considered, as has Lalande himself, that these vocables are related to grammar and not to philosophy.

More philosophical in this respect than the philosophical dictionary, the *Littré* on the contrary defines "word" as "a monosyllabic or polysyllabic sound composed of several articulations, which has a meaning." *In cauda venerum;* but *Littré* cannot do anything about it.

After having given a similar but more technically elaborate definition, the *Dictionnaire alphabétique et analogique* of Paul Robert (IV, 668) mentions two other definitions authorized by linguists. One is from James Darmesteter (*La vie des mots*, p. 36): "In every spoken language [*langue*], the word is a sound or a group of articulated sounds to which those who speak the language [*langue*] attach an intellectual meaning. It is a *sonorous* sign which calls back by means of a regular association of ideas either the image of a material object or the idea of an abstract notion. . . . The word is the servant of the idea. . . ." The other definition, taken from André Brunot's *Pensée et langue*, p. 22, has its origin frankly in a thought which is quite remarkable for a grammarian who wanted to be considered, as we say, modern: "Every idea, simple or complex, expresses itself by sounds, groups of sounds, and noises, which form words, the signs of ideas: *inkstand, to live, tomorrow.*"

All these definitions recognize and even give evidence of the essential duality that de Saussure called attention to in his turn. The problem is one other than that of nominalism and realism, which bore upon the object of the concept, not on the word. But the problem presents itself already on the level of nominalism, for even if one grants that the concept is only a *flatus vocis* [mere breath], it remains to know how a breath of voice could have a meaning. When a modern nominalist tranquilly declares that the concept is nothing other than the name, but "the name, significant and understood," he presents the ambiguity of the idea of "word," for insofar as it is nonsignificant it is simply a noise, just as is, moreover, to us every word in a foreign language [*langue*] of which we do not know the meaning. That which is "word" for one is "noise" for the other, like the clicking of the operator who telegraphs in Morse code is a sound for those who know this alphabet and a noise for those who do not know it. The meaning that is attributed to it does not partake in any way in the nature of the noise, and inversely. It is in the hearer, not in the sound, that the metamorphosis of meaning from noise, of sign from sound, is made. With the word a person has already left the purely physical. The grammarians and linguists fly over the metaphysical realm without always noticing it.

The sound and the sense [*sens*] whose union constitutes the word are not, however, distinct things. First of all, the sense is not a "thing"; the sound alone is such. Besides, even taken as a sign, the sound, or noise, does not always signify a "thing." The vocal sign signifies first of all a verbal image which itself is capable of signifying either other verbal signs or other "things." The heterogeneity of the two elements of the word of which we speak makes obvious here that the same word can have several meanings. This is the case with "word" itself, for which Littré distinguishes twenty-six different usages. In turn Robert's dictionary devotes more than four columns to "word" [*mot*], beginning by noting that it comes from the low Latin, *muttum:* grumbling, grunting (English, to mutter, muttering).[9] The play of analogical slidings of sound and sense, that of the multiple alliances possible between one word and another, result in the indefinite diversification of meaning. The sound, as such, can remain the same nevertheless. A single signifier, one same physical reality, can have twenty-six different meanings at one and the same time due to the meanings or nuances of meanings that it signifies, while remaining itself only one single thing at a time, the sound that it is.

This heterogeneity of sounds and senses appears in homonyms, identical sounds signifying not only different usages of the same word but different words which signify different objects. They are the same word phonetically (homophones), but they differ in meaning. We have already noticed the case of voiced homonyms, or homophonic words, which can only be distinguished by reading because of their different spellings: *sein* (part of the thorax where the mammary glands are located [breast]); *seing* (signature of an act) [archaic: sign manual]; *saint* (consecrated, venerated); *sain* (in good health); *ceint* (surrounded, as with a girdle, a surrounding wall, etc. . . . .). These homophones are not homographs, but some are, as "the dog, a celestial constellation, and the dog, a barking animal." One can, if one wants to be precise about it, write the name of the constellation with a capital letter: "The Dog," a minimal difference in writing for an immense difference of meaning.

Lists of such words, moreover, give no idea of the multiplicity of secondary, derivative, or analogical meanings of each of the words involved. In propositions of this sort nothing is ever absolutely true. Sapir assures us that no language [*langue*] is (exactly) translatable into another, and this is strictly true. However, to speak with the same precision, no language [*langue*] is perfectly translatable into itself. This is so in that there is no word for which one could supply a perfect equivalent by means of other words. All those who have worked on a dictionary know this well. In this regard, to translate one language [*langue*] into another or to define in the same language [*langue*] is to come up against analogical difficulties, except that to translate is more often easier than to define.

All words do not appear similarly in this respect, depending upon whether they are of primary or secondary imposition. The Ancients understood by that phrase the act of attributing a meaning to a word. In fact, this is the same thing as signifying, since each time that a word is used, even though it is already in usage, it can be given a particular signification. Speaking loosely moreover, words have a meaning middlingly defined, and it turns out that words of primary imposition (those which designate beings, material objects whether living or not) are easier to define than the names of secondary imposition, which signify names of primary imposition whose objects exist only in thought. In "horse feed" [*manger du cheval*] the word *horse* designates an animal; it is a noun of primary imposition. In "horse is a noun" [*cheval est un substantif*] the same word is a noun of secondary imposition. In any language [*langue*] whatever it is possible to say what a noun of primary imposition signifies and to translate this noun into another language [*langue*]. In this sense, whether one says *hippos* or *caballus* or *equus* or *cheval* or *horse* or *Pferd* or *lochad*, etc., he who understands the word can make himself a mental picture of an animal of the same species. If one tells two men of different languages [*langues*] to indicate, in a group of animals, those which correspond to the French *cheval*, they will indicate the same kind.

It is the same with words signifying acts or movements perceptible to the senses and representable in memory by sufficiently precise generic images: to march, to run, to take, to stop, to sit down, to get up, etc. Provided that one knows the being, the object, or the operation which corresponds to one of these vocables in a certain language [*langue*], the translation into another language [*langue*] of the names which signify them is always possible. There is no reason why machines should not take over this operation.

It is not that, even in these clearly defined cases, the operation is simple. It is simple if it is only a question of translating each word by another word. But if one undertakes to define the meaning of one of these names of primary imposition in the very language [*langue*] to which it belongs, the difficulty immediately appears. One puts one's finger on it in trying to write a sentence in which the definition replaces the defined. If this sentence began with "the horse," one might write then, for example: "hoofed, soliped mammal of the family equidae," etc. This would hardly allow him who had never seen one to recognize a horse. Perhaps then another definition will be offered (I cite a dictionary): "A large, prominently maned mammal, bigger than the ass, domesticated by man as a draft animal and for transportation. The word is especially applied to the male of the species (contrasted with the mare), and the adult male (contrasted with the colt.)" One is a bit more informed, but unless one knows what an ass is one has hardly progressed. It goes without saying that if one refers back to the word "ass" in the same dictionary, one finds it defined as a domestic animal "smaller than the horse," an imperfect description more especially as it is easy to find horses smaller than certain asses. It is useless to specify that the ass is an animal with long ears, for one must have seen a horse in order to know that the ears of the ass are ordinarily longer than those of the horse.

In order to know the meaning of "horse" one must have seen one, and it suffices to have associated the name of the animal with the animal in question, or its image,[10] in order that signification should take place. No definition or description of any animal whatsoever is sufficient to give an idea of it. One must have a sketch, a photograph, in a word, some sort of an illustration such as those which adorn encyclopedias. Moreover, it suffices to open one of those illustrated dictionaries in order to establish the fact that the illustrations are connected entirely with names of primary imposition. One sees there images of plants, animals, utensils, towns, monuments, celebrated personages represented by sometimes totally imaginary effigies, musicians, and musical instruments. One even will find there symbolic images representing faith, hope, or charity; but they will always be material, concrete, tangible, or visible objects, even if they are only diagrams, drawings, or maps. An individual representative of a species is fit matter for illustration. One can represent a dog, not the species "dog" or the genus "animal." The sentiments are capable of being symbolized: We have innumerable Eroses and Cupids to symbolize love, but such symbols [emblèmes] only have the value of characters in hieroglyphic writing. One can choose to sculpt a dog or to write "fidelity."

Abstract words can only be defined with difficulty. Their meanings cannot be shown by exhibiting specimens of the class which they signify. They can only be explained by other words of analogous meaning, in connection with which an apparent problem can be posed. The meaning of the word "love" is defined thus by a dictionary: "An affective and positive disposition in regard to that which is felt or recognized as good, diversified according to the object which inspires it." One would not dream of criticizing this noble effort, but such a definition, or any other of the same sort, does not give to "love" an idea more distinct than "domesticated mammal: *carnivores, canidae*" gives one an idea of dog. Furthermore, one has doubtless seen dogs, but no one has ever seen Love, except under the form of Cupid.

To translate abstract words is easier than defining them, above all in the heart of the same linguistic family. For example, *magnanimité* is already found in Greek under the form *mégalopsukhia*, then in other languages [langues] under corresponding forms: *magnanimitas, magnanimity, Grossherzigkeit, viélikodouchié*, etc. But these words have been copied from one another, and their correspondences are far from being rigorous. In the case in point one sees that as early as the Greek model from which the other forms are derived by imitation, a wavering of meaning imposes on the translator the obligation of making a choice.

In fact, *mégalopsukhia* is a metaphor. Having no spatially measurable dimensions, the soul cannot be held to be either great or small. For such semantic correspondences to be possible it is necessary that apparent analogies should be accepted and carried over from one language [langue] to another through the initiative of some writers. But since there exists in reality no objective model of the signified, it is natural that some variations of detail should be produced in the process of translation. There is even some play within the same language [langue]. Magnanimity signifies at one time nobility of soul, at another its generosity, most often perhaps both at once. However, "generosity" and "nobility" are words each charged with several possible meanings. In order to choose among them the translator will inevitably refer to the authoritative commentary which Aristotle himself gives of *mégalopsukhia* in his *Nicomachean Ethics* (IV, 7, 9) [IV, 1–3]. He will however find himself by this same stroke at grips with three chapters of moral philosophy, each technical word of which raises in its turn analogous difficulties. When he shall have come to the end, the reader will find out that *mégalopsukhia* and magnanimity do not signify the same thing.[11] One can hesitate between the two words "generosity" and "pride" in order to render the meaning of the Greek word. Consequently, one will search among words related to *magnanimité* in French in order to determine which to choose. There are quite a few of them, and one's perplexity is great. After *magnanimité* itself (as an obsolete usage, Robert assures us; but is it so?), a choice is offered between nobility [*noblesse*], benevolence [*bonté*], clemency [*clémence*], "heart" [*coeur*], generosity [*générosité*].[11a] "Pride, moreover, is not offered us as an option here, though it neverthe-less would render more faithfully the Aristotelian meaning of *mégalop-sukhia*. Many another word would lend itself to analogous considerations, for all linguistic families teem with "false friends." That day when trans-lating machines shall know how to choose between the plurality of dif-ferent ideas that a single word signifies within but one language [*langue*] they will give evidence of a power of divination for which the intellect will envy them. For it is divination that one needs to find between lan-guages [*langues*] equivalents which at best will only be approximations.

It is good to accustom oneself by reflections of this sort to conceive of the relation between language and thought as radically contingent be-fore trying to conceive of the connection between word and meaning with some precision.

The first analogy that presents itself is the connection of the soul and the body which it animates. This analogy has been proposed for cen-turies, and we shall return to it before long in order to consider its co-gency. But de Saussure forbids us to rally to that analogy anymore. He has rejected it for an obscure reason, but the acceptance which it enjoys among some linguists forbids us to neglect it. After having recalled once more that the linguistic entity only exists through the association of the sigifier and the signified, and that "from the moment that one retains only one of these elements, it vanishes," he adds: "This double-faced unity has often been compared with the unity of the human person, composed of body and soul. The comparison has little merit. One might think more appropriately of a chemical compound, water for example. It is a com-bination of hydrogen and oxygen. Taken separately, each of these elements has none of the properties of water."[12]

In reading these lines one must keep in mind that we only have of the *Cours de linguistique générale* of Saussure a reconstruction owed to the care of auditors who have claimed "complete responsibility" for it. The passage in question does not reproduce his whole thought on a quite dif-ficult problem. Perhaps it even fails to recognize the meaning of it, for it is hard to believe that he would have been able to compare a chemical compound, whose components are perfectly homogenous, with a linguistic compound of which he has not ceased to say that it is made up of an irreducible duality. Hydrogen and oxygen are gases whose combination gives water, which is not a gas. The sign and the signifying [*le signe et le signifiant*] belong to two different orders, one physical and the other apparently non-physical; and far from combining into a new *tertium quid* which would not be either the word or the meaning but something else, they remain perfectly distinct for the observer who, hearing a language [*langue*] spoken which he does not understand, knows that the sounds that he hears are words even though he does not comprehend their meaning. One would with difficulty find a comparison less well adapted to the situation than that proposed in de Saussure's text. Just as one can synthesize water, so can one analyze it. One secures then one volume of oxygen and two of hydrogen. But one can only analyze the word by making use of other words. Language is only a compound of itself and can only be decomposed into itself. One can no more divide it than one can a living body, the life of which is no more separably observable than the meaning is taken apart from the word. A biological comparison, imperfect as it also doubtlessly is, would be much more satisfactory than the chemical comparison approved by the text of the *Cours*. It is astonishing that it should ever have been proposed.

Must we then return to the presently discredited conception which saw in word and meaning a particular case of "hylomorphic" composition, that is to say, of matter and form? This is at least a perfect example of what such a composition might be according to the principles presented by Aristotle and exploited endlessly by the Scholastics of the Middle Ages. In the same way that the body is the matter of which the soul is the form (vegetable, animal, or human makes little difference), the word would be the matter of which the meaning is the form. To know whether this form can exist apart from its matter is a metaphysical problem which we shall not escape dealing with, but it does not present itself at the level of immediate observation to which we are subjecting language. In fact, meaning and word are always given together, since the absence of the one or the other does away with all intelligible speech [*parole*].

Language was a quite normal case of a law that was universal for the Scholastics, so that its possibility was never in question in their eyes. It had held the attention of St. Augustine precisely because, under the influence of Plato, he had conceived of man as a soul inserted in a body. This *anima utens corpore*, like a pilot in his ship, evidently did not form a substantial unit with the body which it directed or of which it made use. Nor was it evident that memory, the treasury of concepts and images, could embody itself in sounds and by its alliance with them form words.

One finds many a remark about language in the works of Aristotle and the Scholastics, and we shall return to them, but the possibility of language presented no difficulty for them. Everything being composed of matter and form, why should language be the sole exception? It is equally natural that the possibility of language should become a distinct philosophical problem from the moment that Descartes determined upon the suppression of the "substantial forms," that is to say, the forms which, in the hylomorphic system, constituted by their union with matter a distinct substance. If there were no more "substantial forms," one evidently could no longer conceive of the word as a substance of which the sound would be the matter and the meaning the form. Thereby the philosophical possibility of language was found to be put in question.

It is not certain that Descartes himself saw this. Every Cartesian metaphysical adventure is dominated by his project of conceiving of matter as pure extension in space such that it allows the constitution of a mechanical type of science wherein everything would be explained by extension and movement. No more substantial forms in physicochemical bodies or in living bodies; no more souls then in plants, animals, or men, all these breaking down into two elements at one and the same time really distinct although really united: body, that is, pure extension; and soul, pure spirit.[13] Descartes, having created the paradoxical situation and escaped it without damage, left to his successors the problem of straightening things out. How can one explain the union and reciprocal interaction of two elements really distinct (that is to say, of which one does not possess any character in common with the other) and nevertheless really united, as one sees this in the case of man, composed of body and soul? One could say, in the language of his time, that "Monsieur Descartes had left the game at that point." What can be called the entire Cartesian school was employed in resolving this problem, insoluble by definition, of "the communication of substances." Malebranche, Spinoza, Gueulinckx, Leibniz, and a number of others of lesser stature each applied themselves to furnish a different solution.[14] Among the latter, one at least perceived that if the soul and the body were really distinct in the sense that Descartes understood that word, language became extremely difficult to conceive, for it came consequently to consist in words formed by a body, the sound, and by a sort of soul, the meaning, divested of all relationship, of all natural connection, and of all unity.

That "petty Cartesian," Gérard de Cordemoy, set forth his views on the problem in an essay whose importance did not escape Noam Chomsky. Thanks perhaps to the influence of what this eminent linguist said of it, this essay has come to be reedited.[15]

The essay is entirely dominated by the Cartesian problematic. It is always a question, first and last, of *distinguishing* soul from body, that is to say, of showing that nothing which is part of the nature of the one is part of the nature of the other. These Cartesians at least have the merit of being perfectly clear: "I have set forth in the six preceding discourses[16] the means of knowing oneself, and I have shown that it only consists in discerning in oneself the operations of the soul and those of the body. I now set forth the means of knowing others, and this means is Speech [*la Parole*]. I explain, insofar as I can, what it is; and always following my first design, I exactly discern in this discourse all in it that is of the soul and all that it borrows from the body."[17] To discern, discernment; it is not a question of anything else. If a union of some sort is necessary in order to explain the word, one will bring oneself to recognize this only when it shall become impossible to evade it.

The Cartesian position on the question once understood, one enjoys seeing the reasoning develop to its term, which is at one and the same time necessary and, even metaphysically, perfectly arbitrary. In fact, to speak is "to give signs of one's thought." On the other hand, a quite remarkable character of these signs "is that they do not have any conformity with thoughts but are joined to them by making them so [*par institution*]." For Cordemoy this observation is a matter of lively satisfaction, for the total absence of resemblance between signs and their significations proves to him that things as dissimilar as body and soul can, however, be united. On that, pushing reasoning to its limit, he finds in the connection of word and meaning the explanation of the relation between soul and body. The philosophy of language here serves as a model for metaphysics, from which, ordinarily, it ought to borrow principles. Since signs are tied to things signified 'by making it so,' it is thus that bodies are tied to souls, by making it so. And since the author of this "making it so" could not be man, he can only be God. There, anyway, is "the best means of conceiving of what the union of body and soul truly consists. For, finally, if one imagines that men can, by "making it so," join certain movements to certain thoughts, it ought not be difficult to imagine that the Author of Nature, in forming a man, should unite as well some thoughts from his soul to some movements of his body, that these movements could only be excited in the body immediately upon thoughts being excited in the soul, and that, reciprocally, as soon as the soul wishes that the body should be moved in a certain fashion, it is so moved at that time."[18]

In this fashion, just as Malebranche invented the occasionalist system in order to surmount the Cartesian paradox, and Spinoza imagined the parallelism of thought and extension, and Leibniz conceived his pre-established harmony in view of the same end, the modest Cordemoy contented himself with seeing in the union of the soul and the body a matter of divine institution as free as the human institution of the connection of words and meanings, which is the very essence of language, can be. The word here becomes the paradigm for man. In return, since man is only a talking machine instituted by God, one must establish [*constater*] that the notion of such a machine has nothing impossible about it. Simply, one must be God and be able to create souls in order to fabricate such a machine.

That one should have to have recourse to a metaphysic and even to a theology that is occasionalist in order to give an explanation of a fact so simple, or at least so evident, as language ought not be a recommendation with linguists.[19] Yet one readily speaks today of "Cartesian linguistics" — as if the philosophy of Descartes had not had the immediate result of making language itself, if not impossible, then at least paradoxically improbable and almost self-contradictory. It is highly improbable that those who today remember Cordemoy agree with his thought entirely and conceive that certain movements of the body should be the occasion for the soul to form certain thoughts, or that certain whims [*volontés*] of man should be for his body the occasion of executing certain movements, as the pronunciation of certain words are for us the occasion of conceiving certain meanings. All that remains, then, to "Cartesian" linguistics is positions of the most common sort: language consists in signs endowed with meaning; there is no connection between these signs and their signification; it is necessary then that their association should be "conventional"; and as regards how physical signs may be related to intelligible ideas in thought, nothing is known.

It is doubtful that the efforts to constitute a synchronous linguistic order distinct from a diachronous one clarify the idea of language. I imagine that a linguistic historian of languages [*langues*] such as J. Vendryès would hesitate greatly to commit himself thoroughly in this direction. Every fact of language [*langue*] is at the point of intersection of synchronous and diachronous axes. So it is with all beings endowed with life. The transverse cut through a tree allows one to read its age; the age of a living body is inscribed in the condition in which the anatomist finds it. One cannot work in a dictionary — a synchronous work on the present state of a language [*langue*] — without writing after certain still living words the indication "dated" [*vieilli*]. Moreover, it is frequent that in the course of an academic discussion of this sort individual protests arise: such a word, dated for one, is not so for another; nevertheless, as we say, words "date." And their "dates" are perceived by those who make use of words. Certain words are presently judged to be new, whether in themselves or in the acceptance that is given them.[20] The diachronous is part of the synchronous; the synchronous has always been a moment of the diachronous. This is not to deny the legitimacy or the utility of that distinction. If it serves the researches of the linguist, it is justified. The philosopher only questions himself about his subject in order to assure himself of its speculative bearing insofar as it might clarify the nature of language, and he doubts that its reach is of serious consequence.

From the philosophical point of view, which we take here, the balance sheet of the so-called Cartesian linguists is not much more favorable. The direct observation of language reveals first of all the radical heterogeneity of the signifier and the signified [sign and meaning: *du signifiant et du signifié*]. With some reservations about details without real bearing, all those who have spoken of language right up to our time have admitted the fact. The sole consequence of Cartesianism in this domain appears to have been to transform this factual condition into a theoretically justified one [*situation de droit*]. Far from having concluded, with Saussure, that the connection of meaning to the word is not analogous to that of the soul to the body (which would be moreover to explain one enigma by another), the Cartesians have made that connection the model of the union of soul and body (or inversely), leaving their successors at grips with the exact same difficulty, henceforth rendered insurmountable because philosophically warranted.

The heterogeneity of word and meaning can further be observed at a higher level in the repeated frustration of attempts made to create a universal language [*langue*]. Enterprises of this sort could succeed only on condition that one could make up ahead of time a complete lexicon of ideas, paralleled by a system of signs each of which would designate always and univocally one of these ideas and one alone.

Consulted on the question by Mersenne, Descartes responded in a letter of November 20, 1629, that he found many difficulties in the project. In fact, he saw only two things to be learned in all languages [*langues*], to know "the signification of words, and grammar." He foresaw no difficulties in fabricating a simple grammar, one without irregularities and thus quite easy to understand. He foresaw, on the contrary, that the creation of a common vocabulary would come up against serious obstacles.

How would one choose the basic words of such a vocabulary? How make them up? Descartes, who came to simplify algebraic notations, could foresee the infinite complexity of the new problem. First of all, one would have to give oneself over to an exhaustive analysis of all simple ideas which enter into the human mind, to define them, enumerate them, arrange them, and write them by means of suitable signs. It is obvious that Descartes did not doubt as evident that there exist in thought "simple ideas," what he elsewhere calls "simple characters [*natures simples*]," those which finally it is only a question of having to count. For if such exist, one in fact ought to be able to count them, make a lexicon of them, and invent a script in which to signify them. If it existed, such a language [*langue*] "could be taught in a very short time, and that methodically, that is to say, establishing in order all the thoughts which can enter into the human mind in the same way as such an order is naturally established among numbers. And just as one can learn in a day to name all the numbers right to infinity, and to write them in an unknown language [*langue*], which numbers are actually an infinity of different words, so one could do the same thing with all the other words necessary to express all the other things which come into the minds of men."

A more exact description of the mode of exposition and the method of demonstration that Descartes later on came to put to work in his *Meditations* could not be desired. At times we ask ourselves how he was able to convince himself that his metaphysics was mathematically demonstrated. It is because his mathematics and his metaphysics were dominated by an unconscious linguistic. He spontaneously believed that there were simple ideas each of which can be represented by a sign and that the connection between these ideas is of the same nature as that which is seen between numbers, that is to say, a connection of order. One must know which ideas came before, which after, after which all that remains is to compute them. Unfortunately, concepts, philosophical or otherwise, are not of the nature of numbers. There are no simple ideas which one could number and combine with each other so as to form compound ideas always decomposable again into their simple elements without any surprise being feared. The thin intelligibility of the language of the *Meditations* is thereby explained. Descartes tried to transform into simple and univocal signs words whose meanings are as complex as thought, extension, movement, liberty, even God. He believed that "that which thinks" was a simple nature safe from all equivocation, whereas Gasendi, Hobbes, and others had to draw his attention at once to the obscurities which such a notion entailed. But Descartes went further. When his reflection led him to unite two ideas which he had up to that point worked to distinguish, he believed it possible *to write* them together, as if it sufficed to put down the binomial "union of soul and body" in order to restore, by this simple artifice of writing, an idea which he himself had at first rendered inconceivable. From this date (1629) he knew that, in any case, "the invention of that language [*langue*] depends on true philosophy, for it is impossible otherwise to enumerate all the thoughts of men and put them in order, let alone to distinguish them in such a fashion that they should be clear and simple," which was, to his mind, "the greatest secret that one might have in order to acquire sound science."

There are not any ideas so clear and simple that one could work with them as the mathematician works with numbers. We admire the ingenuity of this powerful mind, which believes that one could devise a universal language [*langue*] "quite easy to understand, to pronounce, and to write," one that would even exclude all possibility of error from men's minds, if only "someone had truly set forth what the simple ideas are which are in the imagination of men." He himself is quite conscious that this is nothing but a dream realizable only in the world of novels. But the blame there is man's, he thinks, and does not lie in the nature of things. Whatever may be the cause of it, the fact is that, "completely against the grain, the words that we have, have almost only confused significations, which the human mind being accustomed to for a long time past, is the reason that it understands hardly anything perfectly." Cartesian philosophy was an attempt to establish that list of "simple ideas," clear and especially distinct, upon which order could be imposed with an obviousness such that one would not have any more trouble to discover it.

But the nature of thought is such that the notion of unity cannot be applied to the idea. Philosophers persist in believing that it is a matter of negligence, of ill-will, or of bad habit that words have almost only confused significations. In fact, except in mathematics, where signs do not signify concepts, those that make up language never offer any meanings that hinder one from saying that any one among them signifies another thing at the same time. A more serious problem is that one can always cause a sign to signify something else provided one wants to. And that is not a defect of speech [*la parole*]; it is its very essence. It is a free creative act, which would not know how to impose limits to its own creative liberty. Everyone talks about observing how children learn to speak. One could just as well say: how we hinder each child from creating his own language, for left to itself, each human being, each group, each social body sets up for itself a vocabulary of its own which it always tends to use in full liberty. What is a *porrier*? In my childhood it was a working man of the port of Vermenton (Yonne). At that time many logs coming from Morvan floated down the River Cure. Logs do not come anymore, and *porriers* are not now spoken of there. But people of my age still know the word, an ephemeral creation like all verbal significations of ephemeral objects. One dies, another is born, and *homo loquens* never ceases to devise them.

This devising is not totally determined or totally arbitrary. When there was a port for logs at Vermenton, it was indeed necessary to name those who gained their livelihood in working there. We were not inclined to create the word other than by analogy. He who works with cuisine is a *cuisinier*, he who works at the gate [*porte*] is a porter, he who works at a por(t) is quite precisely a *porrier*. But precisely because the number of sounds is limited while the number of meanings is infinite (their creation being free), language avoids an excessive verbal proliferation and makes one word serve for many different significations. The arbitrariness of the relation between signifier and signified reaches its summit in such a case, since, as we have noted, one single word can be several words at the same time. For this to be possible it suffices that some sort of a thread connect the various objects signified. J. Vendryès cited as an example the word *fille* [girl, daughter]. If one says, "I present my *fille* to you," one signifies a parental relation. If one says, "Madame X has had a child; it is a *fille*," one signifies the sex. If one says, "Beware of Mademoiselle X . . . she is a *fille*," one signifies a person of doubtful morals. Some people would rather say a *garce* [trollop], but that is only the feminine of *gars* [boy], as *fille* is that of *garçon* [young man, etc.]. One cannot put one's foot in these quicksands without sinking in. If the word is the unity of the sign and the meaning, the word *fille* is, at least, three different words.

Perhaps, then, in order to conceive of the union of the word and the meaning, one must harken back to that of the soul and the body. The meaning is not a soul, or a being, or a thing, but the relations are comparable in nature, and the perception of every analogy is in itself an intellectual gratification. To speak of the "life of language" is a metaphor; it is also justified, however, by the same analogy, for if the meaning is to the word what life (whatever may be its nature) is to the body, it is natural that language should have a life of its own and that words should be born, mature, flourish, mutually fecundate each other, grow old and die as all living things do. This is why every artificial language [*langue*], be its inspiration mathematical or logical, is a language [*langue*] born dead. The same linguist remarks of them: one can create artificial languages [*langues*] which are logically satisfying,

> but these languages [*langues*] must not become living; they would immediately deteriorate. There would be set up between the forms differences of value; certain forms would dominate others, the law of analogy would come into play, and disorder would succeed to the initial good order. . . . Ideal, logical language [*langue*] is only a dream. It puts one in mind of a gardener who should think that, as a result of having planted identical seeds in a regular pattern, and having given them all the same care, his garden ought always to have plants of the same height, arranged in the same way, with equal numbers of flowers and fruits. Too many varying causes modify the biological conditions, and some causes are beyond human control. The same is true in linguistics, where analogy is often the enemy of logic, though it responds to the need for uniformity and uses reasoning to satisfy this need.[21]

Nothing could be said more appositely, except perhaps this: if the proliferation of growth in gardens confounds our search for causes which escape human control, the proliferation in language is due, on the contrary, to the practically unlimited and incessantly creative invention of human phonic power. The history of Esperanto is a case in point. Created about 1887 by Zamenhof, this quite ingenious and, at least for Europeans, quite easy language was about twenty years old when I amused myself in learning it. I had hardly begun to use it when I learned that the mathematical logician Couturat had invented an improved version, which he called *Ido* (the son [*le fils*]).[22] I was assured that the son was of more value than the father, but I abandoned them both immediately. Vendryès was right: when Esperanto began to live, it was already consigned to death.

3

Language as a Human Achievement

Leaving linguistics to its desire to make itself into a science of language, of nothing but language, and of all language, let us return to a few very ancient ideas which have been reiterated since the beginning of philosophical inquiry simply because they were obvious and because those who came to this sort of inquiry first were also those who saw them and spoke them first. For this very reason we shall often have to deal with Aristotle. His name alone is sufficient to irritate those who cannot forgive him for having come before them and for having seen and declared simple, profound truths, truths obvious with an almost artless obviousness, truths which one can do no more today than rediscover, for lack of the ability "to move easily beyond" them.

Before the Philosopher only Plato belongs to this order of inquiry, but the "Cratylus" lacks that simple and direct objectivity which allowed Aristotle to say things the way he saw them. There never was any "Aristotelian philosophy," any "Aristotelian system." Reality replaced any system for him. Plato tackled the problem of the origin of language, his mind already occupied by a metaphysic (the dialectic of ideas) and by the concerns of a candidate for the role of legislator. The "Cratylus" gives witness above all to the presence of the author of the *Republic* and the *Laws*. Setting out from the evidence that symbols [*signes*] are not imposed by nature, he could see no one other than the legislator to impose them, but he also thought that the wise legislator would know how to give to each object the name which fits its nature, in such fashion that, according to Plato, symbols [*signes*] remain natural by virtue of their spontaneous [*volontaire*] imposition by a wise man who imposes on each thing the name that suits it. The etymological feats with which Plato amuses himself are not successful in convincing the modern reader. One remains as skeptical when confronted with them as in reading the astonishing etymological word play which Joseph de Maistre marveled at: *cadaver = caro, data, vermibus.*

There, as elsewhere, Aristotle remains content to describe things such

44

as they are. He invented almost all the sciences considered as disciplines at once distinct and at the same time bound by connections which bind their distinct objects in reality. Today one feels a bit embarrassed by having to recall that, for him, the sciences are specified by their objects. Aristotle therefore describes first physical bodies, comprised of celestial bodies; then living or, as is said, animated bodies; next he comes upon that particular animal, man, distinct from all other known animals in that he exercises intellectual functions. A particularly important chapter in the description of the biological functions of man is devoted to the operations of the intellect. This, what is called today the *Organon*, is arbitrarily extracted from its place in the Aristotelian anthropology. It is the biological description of the functioning of the human intellect, to serve as a sort of methodological preface to the collection of the other sciences. All that remains to the Philosopher is to describe the human animal as moral and political, and to crown the entire work by a treatise on the poetic [*poietiques*] activities of the human being.

There is no distinct linguistic science with Aristotle, nor even a philosophy of language, precisely because human speech [*parole*] is a fact like other facts and because it is appropriate to speak of it as is necessary each time that its presence poses a problem: in the science of the human being, an animal endowed with reason; in logic, where the definition of the object of knowledge requires some information on the language which expresses it; finally, in political philosophy, since society is impossible without language, which allows men to communicate. Each time the Philosopher contents himself with saying what is strictly necessary, that which moreover he holds as evident and which remains today for us as it was formerly for him. The reason for this permanence is simple. In the very brief time that separates us from Aristotle, about twenty-three centuries, which are but a moment in the millions of years which today are attributed to man, nothing tempts us to think that human nature has sensibly changed. Today we know, we reason, in brief, we think, if not what he thought, at least as he thought. His description of the syllogism, taken in itself, has retained for us all its validity. Our knowledge has increased immensely since Aristotle. Mathematics has come to complete logic and to bestow on science a form which Aristotle has not foreseen: he classified, A. N. Whitehead said, even though it was necessary to measure. But the whole field of the real and of knowledge which he had the means of exploring has remained such as it was in his times. Developments, and there have been some, have remained homogeneous in the course of their "diachronicity," or continuance in time.

It seems that Aristotle speaks of language for the first time, in any case before speaking of it in the *Organon*, in the *De anima*, and within this work itself, in the part devoted to sensible knowledge, II, 8: the sense of hearing and its object.

This manner of proceeding can surprise us, for we think of speech [parole] as something that man produces rather than as a class of sounds which he perceives. If one opens de Saussure one finds as early as the first chapter of his appendix, Principes de phonologie [sic: Appendix to "Introduction"; "Principles of Phonology"], a description illustrated with a diagram of "the vocal apparatus and its functioning." Likewise, in the Éléments de linguistique générale Andre Martinet naturally approaches the study of signifiers (the components of what he calls secondary articulation) by means of an analysis of articulatory phonetics, that is, of "organs of speech": air in movement which the glottis and its vocal chords transform into speech [voix], then the pharynx with the roof of the mouth, the soft palate, the nasal cavities, etc. In brief, modern linguistics is founded principally on phonology and places in the first rank of its preoccupations the production of speech [voix], of the word [parole], of the sound which the speaker produces.

Aristotle treats of speech [voix] above all as an understood sound, that is to say, as an object of the sense of hearing. The reason for this is simple and, moreover, has far-reaching consequences. Treating of the soul in general in the De anima, he first considers the vegetative soul, then the sensitive soul, and, in order to study the latter under all its manifestations, he examines in succession its different senses. Now, the senses distinguish themselves first of all by their organs, the eye for seeing, the ear for hearing, the nose for smelling, etc. But there is no specific organ for speech, so that following his method, Aristotle would never come to it pursuing to its conclusion his study of the sense organs and their functions. There is an organ for perceiving language because there is an organ for perceiving sounds in general. It is consequently solely in connecting the study of speech [parole] to that of hearing that the biologist Aristotle can find a place for it in his description of the soul and its functions.

Even though they approach the problem from the other end, modern linguists cannot avoid perceiving the fact. For them also speech [la parole] is an "acoustic impression: resulting from articulatory movements which produce distinct words."[1] Saussure never speaks of an organ of speech, but of the vocal apparatus and of the vocal organs, which he states "are as external to language as are the electrical devices used in transmitting the Morse code to the code itself." Going further, he makes the observation that one cannot prove "that speech, as it manifests itself when we speak, is entirely natural, i.e., that our vocal apparatus was designed for speaking just as our legs were designed for walking."[2] But it appears that Sapir may have been the first to discern, with a totally Aristotelian aptitude for perceiving the evident, that there is no organ of speech [*parole*]. One sees with the eyes, one smells with the nose, one hears with the ear, one walks with the legs, but one speaks with the mouth, teeth, nose, and many another organ no one of which has as its specific function to speak. One can, moreover, speak without putting in play any of the various organs whose concourse constitutes the vocal apparatus. Sign language used by the deaf is the proof of that. "There are, properly speaking, no organs of speech; there are only organs that are incidentally useful in the production of speech sounds."[3]

Since Aristotle nothing as important has been said about language: "Speech [*parole*] is not a simple activity exercised by one or several organs biologically adapted to that function." The metaphysician, naturally persuaded that language is exercised by an incorporeal intellect, cannot refrain from remembering at this moment that according to Thomas Aquinas and, in a sense, Aristotle the intellect acts "without a corporeal organ." One even dreams of the soul such as the Platonists, including Augustine, conceived of it: an immaterial substance *utens corpore* [using a body]. This is not at all what Sapir says, but it is what he suggests without intending it when he says: "Physiologically, speech is an overlaid function, or to be more precise, a group of overlaid functions. It gets what service it can out of organs and functions, nervous and muscular, that have come into being and are maintained for very different ends than its own."[4] The appropriate function of teeth is to masticate, that of the palate is to taste; yet language superimposes on their natural functions that of contributing to the articulation of speech. One could truly say that a transcendental power "uses" the body for ends of a transcendent order akin to itself.

We return then to Aristotle's point of departure and to what Saussure called an "acoustic image," which is in fact a sound. "The voice," says the Philosopher, "is a sound proper to animated beings. Nothing inanimate has a voice."[5] It is only metaphorically that we speak of the voice of the flute, of the lyre, or, generally speaking, of that which can produce a series of sounds different in duration, pitch, and timbre. All animals do not have a voice, but everything that has a voice is animated.

We shall not reproduce here the chapter of the *De anima*, II, 2 [probably II, 8; but II, 2 is not irrelevant]. It can be read in the Greek text or in translation, and even in the excellent literal commentary which Thomas Aquinas gave of it, *In De anima*, II, 8, lect. 18.[5a] Let us note, however, that returning to this point in his treatise on the soul, which covers the vegetable and animal kingdoms as well as man, Aristotle has gone no further in the matter than to speak of the sensitive soul. Consequently he only speaks there of the voice, which many animals possess, but not all, since, for example, almost all the fishes are mute. There is no question further of speech, or language, which only appears indisputably with man.

Aristotle specifies therefore that voice already has meaning [*signifi-cation*]. This is not the case with all the sounds produced by the vocal apparatus of animals. A cough, for example, is a noise caused by air strik-ing the trachea, but it is not voice. A simple physical effect produced by an organ, a cough has no meaning. It is an indication, not a sign [*indice . . . signe*]. The cry of animal and man is something different: crying often means something for him who cries, and always has meaning for him who hears it. This is why voice presupposes some imagination. It is produced, Thomas Aquinas comments, *cum imaginatione ad aliquid significandum* [with the imagination for the purpose of signifying something]. The voices of animals do not have any *meaning* [*sens*], but they are not devoid of *signification* [*signification*].

There could be no language, such at least as we employ it commonly, if there were no voice. The description of the vocal apparatus in Aristotle is naturally incomplete and erroneous in certain respects, but it occupies with him the same place as that which we find today in treatises on pho-nology, a necessary introduction to linguistics. Voiceless animals are all those which are bloodless and, among those with blood, the fishes. In fact, voice being a movement of air, animals which do not breath air cannot have a voice. That which appears to me to be most interesting in the de-scription Aristotle gives of the matter is that, so many centuries before Saussure and Sapir, he had observed that in order to speak, living beings must put to work certain organs of the body which are already endowed with determinate biological functions. For example, inhaled air has as its primary function to maintain life. It is a supererogatory function that it is of use also in producing voice. So, too, with the mouth, the tongue, and the teeth. "Air once inhaled, nature uses it for two different ends, just as the tongue has two uses, to taste food and to articulate words. The two functions are not of the same nature: taste is necessary to the survival of the animal and is the more widespread of the two functions, while voice is a sort of luxury without which life is possible. Thus, there are mute animals."

Aristotle has not had recourse to an artifice devised to fit the cir-cumstances. He noted in his *De partibus animalium*, II, 16, that nature often causes the same organ to be used for different ends, but here she causes several organs to be used for one single and same end which differs in nature from each of their own particular ends. One could say that na-ture has devised an ingenious arrangement of biological organs which di-rectly exercise clearly defined biological functions in order to procure for thought a means of expression. Likewise, again: "nature employs respira-tion as an indispensable means of regulating the interior temperature of the body," which is a vital necessity, but she uses it at the same time for a supplementary activity, since she uses it "as material for the articulation of voice, which concerns the well-being of him who possesses it."[5b] One is really quite close to the remark made by Saussure and brought to its perfection by Sapir: the vocal apparatus is a utilization of organs destined by nature for other ends, all vital. Voice, and even less still articulated language, has no organ of its own.[6] One could perhaps make an exception for the vocal chords, which do not appear to serve anything else than speech, but they themselves do not speak.

The passage from simple voice to articulated language already presented for Aristotle, as it does today, an almost insurmountable difficulty. Animals have an imagination; one understands then that they could have a voice because they have something to express. But it appears that man alone has something to say and that the power of pronouncing an intelligible word may be connected in him to the presence of what we call an intellect. This power is not a scientifically observable fact because if it exists, it is immaterial. Consequently physicists, biologists, and many a modern linguist try to explain human language as if the intellect did not exist, or simply speaking, without recourse to that hypothesis. This attitude entails, among other consequences, the desire to be able to maintain that animals also, or at least certain among them, are endowed with language. If this conclusion were demonstrated—for example, that apes or bees or dolphins could pronounce sounds or articulate gestures and intelligible attitudes—then, since we do not attribute any intellect to them, one ought to be able to conclude in the matter that language is explicable without that presupposition.

This attitude is legitimate. No science is charged with explaining its own possibility. Physics is possible because nature exists. Of how it comes about that there should be nature and how it could be intelligible, physics knows nothing. Let us render this justice to the mathematician Descartes that if he was not a very great metaphysician, he at least had a quite exact sense of the limits of intelligibility that physico-mathematical science itself takes as given. The universal mathematics of which he dreamed, and which included a biology, a psychology, and even an ethics, would have been a universal mechanical explanation of everything except pure thought and the will. Science could, with time, explain everything with mathematical evidence, but it could not explain to him why or how the mathematical evidence was true. He wanted a metaphysics and gave us one only in order that the certitude of science, which was in his eyes a fact, should not remain, as might be said, in the air. Thus the costly detour of the *Meditations* where we find demonstrated the existence of a completely truthful God, the creator of thought, of nature, and of the laws which rule it: in brief, creator at one and the same time of science and of a world of science as free from all finality as the divine thought which created it. He knew that only a metaphysics could intelligibly establish science on the creative liberty of a perfect God. The scholars, his successors, have preserved this Cartesian world without finality by simply suppressing the unconstrained God who created it. They are then today in a world of universal mechanism, as purged of all finality as that of Descartes, and without anything to explain it.

No reason obliges them to explain it, but, to begin with, what they hold to be a *modern* position is in reality what Aristotle already considered as ancient and definitively superseded more than two thousand years ago. This is exactly the question that the Philosopher posed at the beginning of his treatise *On the Parts of Animals:*

> Ought the writer who deals with the works of nature to follow the plan adopted by the mathematicians in their astronomical demonstrations . . . or ought he to follow some other method? And when these questions are answered, there yet remains another. The causes concerned in the generation of the works of nature are, as we see, more than one. There is the final cause and there is the motor cause. Now we must decide which of these two causes comes first, which second. Plainly, however, that cause is the first which we call the final one. For this is the Reason, and the Reason forms the starting-point, alike in the works of art and in the works of nature.[6a]

The Ancients (in respect to Aristotle!) who only concerned themselves with the material cause without bringing in the final cause therefore lacked the most important part of reality. Today one is surprised to see Aristotle next posing questions which, transferred from biology to linguistics, retain their sense. About what ought we to concern ourselves, "that with which the ancient writers concerned themselves, namely, what is the process of formation of each animal; or whether it is not rather, what are the characters of a given creature when formed?"[6b] This is what we have seen the linguists call the diachronous and the synchronous, and Aristotle gauged "that there is no small difference between these two views."[6c] Always for Aristotle the two points of view are necessary, but one is subordinate to the other: just as becoming exists in view of being, it is from the point of view of the end that one must explain change. All mechanical explanation of the structure of the present "given" ought to be understood, as a matter of fact, as a hypothetical necessity, which is only necessary if one presupposes the final cause. There would be a place in a complete Aristotelian system for all of modern mechanism inaugurated by Descartes, subordinated to the finalism which Descartes eliminated. "There are then two causes, namely, necessity and the final end. . . . It is plain then that there are two modes of causation and that both of these must, so far as possible, be taken into account in explaining the works of nature, or that at any rate an attempt must be made to include them both; and that those who fail in this tell us in reality nothing about nature."[6d] The difficulty of explaining how the "end" which does not yet exist could be a cause before existing comes from falsely thinking of the final cause as an anticipated motor cause. That is not the case at all. The final cause is already present in the agent as an orientation of change toward its end. If I decide to betake myself to some place, I am, in the moment of my decision, the cause of my future presence in that place, but it is my future presence in that place, thought of and wished for by me, which is the final cause of my decision.

The form, unself-conscious, but oriented naturally toward its end, is the seat of that finality. The animal constitutes itself by its form, which we call its soul because it is living, as a house could build itself by itself, could grow in some fashion completely by itself if it were a product of nature instead of being that of an art, architecture. Everything is mechanical in a house except the idea of building it and the plan of its construction. A house is an infinity of hypothetical necessities caused by the freedom of the architect who imposes on them his idea of the house as their common final cause.[7] The animal is itself also a quantity of mechanical necessities required by the form which leads the living body to its perfection according to its kind. That is why this form can endow it with voice, groan, call, or simply a cry. Man appears to be engendered by a form capable not only of bringing him to birth, causing him to grow and act like every other animal, but also of utilizing a rather great number of organs necessary to a life which enables him to produce the sort of luxurious activity, if it can be called that, which is speech [parole]. Mute men could live and even, if need be, form sorts of embryonic societies, as some bands or troops of wild animals do. But these could not create societies like those that man forms thanks to the use of speech. Now it is only in such societies that man attains the biological perfection of his species. Aristotle does not doubt that the form proper to man, the intellectual or rational soul, ought to be the cause of the faculty of speaking that man possesses. That soul sees that he acquires this faculty in order that he can fully realize his end.

Any modern biologist, any linguist solicitous that what he teaches be characterized as *scientific*, would not admit a similar point of view. Insofar as he is a *scholar*, he ought to object to it. He has the right, and, as a scholar, perhaps even the duty, of doing so. But it is doubtful that it would be good reason to deny what he forbids himself to affirm or simply to take into consideration. Aristotle affirmed the existence of souls in living beings because he ascertained in them the presence of achievements and of operations that simple mechanism did not suffice to explain. The biologist could say that this so-called supplementary explanation is not an explanation, and, in effect, it is not a scientific explanation. One ought, however, to say in its favor that if we object to it, there is no further explanation whatsoever. That which authorizes us to have no recourse to it does not authorize us to deny it.

Now it is manifest that in a purely mechanistic explanation of life an enormous mass of obvious facts remain unexplained and, what is more, inexplicable. Not only is it that mechanism still has not explained the elementary properties of animated matter, but what modern biology teaches us about the structure of living matter makes it more and more improbable that we could find for it an explanation of the mechanistic type. When we recently consulted a renowned physicist about the probability of seeing a living cell, the simplest possible, appear from matter governed by the physics of *quanta,* he replied: "For the physicist life is a colossal improbability." A sentiment of this sort appears in the book, quite suggestive in so many respects, by the biologist and biochemist Walter M. Elsasser on a new approach to theoretical biology. Like all scientists, he also admits that all the conclusions of quantum physics hold for living matter as well as for inanimate matter. Further, he has no desire to restore the old vitalism in biology. Even more, he does not believe it necessary to resuscitate finalism in order to explain what mechanism manifestly does not explain. His intention, if I am not deceived in a matter which is foreign to me, is to make it obvious that the traditional opposition between mechanism and finalism in biology is a false problem because the facts are not of the same nature in the realm of inorganic matter and in that of life. Mechanism can be applied in the realm of inorganic matter, in physico-chemistry, because all the series considered are made up of homogeneous elements. It is inapplicable in the domain of life because the series considered there are composed of nonhomogeneous elements. Resuming his thought in a clear formula, Elsasser concludes: "We shall go so far as to say that we consider physics as the science dealing essentially with homogeneous systems and classes, and biology as the science of inhomogeneous systems and classes."[8]

This scientist has the great merit of having pushed the analysis right to the very root of a centuries-old conflict [*conflit séculaire*]. Insofar as one not competent in the area can judge of it, he is right. In the actual state of science, particularly quantum physics, such is indeed the reason that, up to the present, we have not succeeded in setting up a satisfactory physics of life. There is not a single domain in the heart of biology where one could not show that the vital phenomena are produced in accord with the laws of quantum physics, but the existence of these phenomena themselves is not explained by these laws alone.

This is not the position of an isolated individual. Bohr had already concluded from the results of his analysis that "life is a primary phenomenon which can only be observed in its manifestations, not, as such, analyzed."[9] In a valuable philosophical digression Elsasser rightly recalls the remarkable lucid view of Claude Bernard (1878), according to whom we do not know how to search out the causes of life, which is before all creativity, without engaging in research of first causes, which are not in the domain of science. "Bernard most emphatically states that there can be no deviation at all from the laws of physics and chemistry in the organism. He tells us again and again that physics and chemistry must ultimately be able to explain every detail in the functioning of the organism, but at the same time that they cannot explain its existence."[10] One last citation seems irresistible to me, since it witnesses so well to the exceptional interest of this position for the philosopher. One must cite it literally, as much for the sake of the explicit reservations it imposes on the thought of the scientist as for its indifference with regard to the powerful intellectual conformity so formidable in scientific milieus: "the problem lies at the confluence of several special sciences. Specialists, by their very nature, tend to be selective. Philosophers on the other hand have always considered it their particular business to counteract the tendency of mental selection to which the practitioners of the concrete sciences are often more exposed than the public realizes." If therefore we wish to speak of the relationship between organic and inorganic matter, we ought to some degree put ourselves in connection with philosophy and maintain the contact with the tradition of the philosophical thought of the past. And here is the conclusion which appears to me to be of decisive importance, for we shall see that it concerns the present state of linguistics:

> We could suitably apply an old maxim of the philosophers: After everything is said and done in philosophical analysis, the end result should not differ too violently from the short-cut solution offered by common sense, otherwise it might be philosophy rather than common sense which is suspect. Similarly here, we would do well to remain in touch to some degree with traditional philosophy. If the outcome of our inquiry is too much in contradiction with the somewhat intuitive results of traditional philosophy, it might not ultimately be tradition which is wrong. Bernard's view that neither vitalism nor mechanism can win a complete victory in their long drawn-out struggle seems only rational in this light.[11]

Before returning to the particular problems of the philosophy of language, it is of great use to us to know that a certain linguist of our time holds analogous concerns relating to that which can preserve as permanently valuable certain traditionally received philosophical views, views which are moreover in accord with what Elsasser so appropriately calls the "shortcut solutions" of common sense. For all induction is a shortcut, and the intellect proceeds in the same fashion from the sensation which delivers to it enough to conceive the species in the initiation of principles. It is not surprising that philosophy should return at times to the data of common sense because, readily subject to the illusions of the sensible, common sense is, in the order of the intelligible, philosophy in the unworked state.

Certain recent developments in the philosophy of language confirm this view. The philosopher can only respect the work of the scholarly linguist Noam Chomsky. His name also invokes a novel idea, which could prove by itself (but we also have the witness of Sapir and Benveniste) that discoveries of philosophical import remain possible in fields already developed for centuries. Like all important philosophical ideas, even when they are new, this one proceeds from a very ancient intuition, one that we will come across again when speaking of the theology of the Word, but which, totally preoccupied with God, theologians have neglected to apply to man. The Aristotelian idea of the intellect as act (*intellectus agens*) named it, however, but Aristotle did not see it. His philosophical disciple Thomas Aquinas did not see it either. He knew, naturally, that the Divine Word is creator, but he did not develop any corresponding philosophy of human language. Like every Christian theologian, he often coasts along this territory to explore it, but he never moves inland. St. Bonaventure, whose expressionism can so easily develop in this sense, gives evidence of the same reserve. The idea that the Cartesians could have attributed a creative activity to thought is not assuredly false, but one can not conclude in the matter that they have attributed the same power to language. The experience of Geraud de Cordemoy/Malebranche shows, on the contrary, that they simply rendered it inconceivable and impossible. The first person who, to my knowledge, may have recognized in language a poetic activity, or, as is said in a broad sense, a creative activity, is Wilhelm von Humboldt,[12] whose positions I know only through Noam Chomsky.[13] This linguist and philosopher of language would not have brought them to our attention through the precise details and developments with which he has enriched them if they had not corresponded to some personal intuitions already formed. Moreover, the sole fact of reaffirming this is remarkable in a time when the dominant tone of linguistics invites us to ignore them.

The essential notion proposed by W. von Humboldt and restored to life by Noam Chomsky is that language is not a product (*Erzeugtes*) but primarily a production [*Erzeugnung*]. In order precisely to state his thought, Humboldt restores the idea of form to dignity, understanding by that a constant and invariable factor for each language [*langue*] which subtends each particular linguistic act. It is not sufficient to think of language as that which produces this or that particular given word, but the complete idea of language ought in addition to make room for the ever-open possibility of producing an illimitable quantity of words of this sort, and that under all the conditions that thought imposes on it. The idea of "form" does not designate here a thing but rather a force always at work in language. It affects, then, or ought to affect, our view of the nature of every given language [*langue*]. "The word [*parole*] is not a thing placed before us that we could embrace with a glance in its entirety, or communicate progressively by pieces. It is rather necessary to conceive of it as an eternal producer of itself (*ein sich ewig erzeugender*), where the laws of production are determined, while the extent, and, to a certain measure, the very mode of the production remain entirely undetermined."[14]

Noam Chomsky's recent views are inspired by a similar spirit and offer this particular interest that they were suggested to him by the inherent difficulties of the linguistic positivism dominant about 1950. The taxonomic methods of structural linguistics, the ideas put to work by the theory of reinforcement, by the mathematical theory of communication, or by that of simple automata run aground in the attempt to give an account of the most simple linguistic facts. "The investments of time, energy, and money made in the use of calculators in linguistic research, and which for a field as restricted as linguistics are very important, have not led to any notable progress in our understanding of the usage or of the nature of language."

In order to get out of the difficulty, Chomsky proposes to have recourse to the new idea of *linguistic competence*, which might be rendered approximately in French as *capacité linguistique*, a cognitive method [*systeme*] acquired in earliest infancy, which subtends linguistic behavior and makes it possible. We feel immediately that our linguist is oriented toward something completely different from explanations in the mechanist spirit. It is not for him simply a matter of appealing to elements of a higher degree of complexity in order to understand language, but rather "to a complexity different in *quality*." We know indeed, since the *Données immediates la conscience* [trans. into English as *Time and Free Will*], how much and why the notion of quality is suspect to the holders of a truly scientific attitude in all domains. To hold language to be a specific activity not entirely reducible to the order of mechanical changes of the action/reaction type is more or less to return overtly in this matter to positions which structuralist, probabilist, or any other "scientific study of human language" thought definitively to have disqualified. Chomsky knows this well. He gauges, however, that far from having lessened the distance between what we know of language and what we still do not know of it, the methods put to work by positivist and "scientific" linguistics have rather increased it. One perhaps would not misrepresent his thought in saying that, as was formerly the case with Bergson at grips with the difficulties of pure mechanism and determinism in psychology, Chomsky considers that what is truly scientific is to take reality such as it is and, if that demands it, to pay a renewed, rejuvenated, and naturally better informed attention to ideas which we perhaps had wrongly despised. "Finally, it has become quite clear," he declares firmly, "that the assumptions and approaches that appear to be productive today have a distinctly traditional flavor to them; in general, a much despised tradition has been largely revitalized in recent years and its contributions given some serious and, I believe, well-deserved attention." He concludes: "It seems to me quite appropriate, at this moment in the development of linguistics and psychology in general, to turn again to classical questions and to ask what new insights have been achieved that bear on them, and how the classic issues may provide direction for contemporary research and study."[15]

We retain from these notions the idea that language, as Humboldt said of it, is *production,* or, rather, as Chomsky strongly insists in the matter, that we must recognize in language an inventive aspect, and we call this idea that of "the creative aspect of language use." We shall understand by that "the distinctly human ability to express new thoughts within the framework of an 'instituted language', a language that is a cultural product subject to laws and principles partially unique to it and partially reflections of general properties of mind."[16]

We see immediately what the fruitfulness of this view can be for the study of the very structure of language. What passes beyond the foreground is the obvious fact, usually unperceived, as such facts often are, that, far from being a storehouse of formulas and models learned by repetition, held in reserve, and applied without other innovations than those due to analogy, the language of each person is an incessant, personal invention at the heart of a given structure. In any case,

> The fact surely is, however, that the number of sentences in one's own native language [*langue*] that one will immediately understand with no feeling of difficulty or strangeness is astronomical; and that the number of patterns underlying our normal use of language and corresponding to meaningful and easily comprehensible sentences in our language is orders of magnitude greater than the number of seconds in a lifetime. It is in this sense that the normal use of language is innovative.[17]

These are immediately obvious facts. Each person is aware of them as soon as he reflects the least bit upon the nature of language as he himself speaks it. What is novel and important for the philosopher is that a linguist is saying it, and, above all, that he affirms it under the pressure and, as it were, under the restrictions of his own observation of language, that is to say, as a linguistic truth. We all have at our disposal a mother tongue [langue maternelle] which we come upon completely developed, with its structural and syntactical rules, and even its rules of literary composition; but every man invents in part the language which he uses. Whether it be a question of speaking a tongue [langue] or simply of understanding it, one must invent. Every slightly reflective mind has often been aware of all that his interlocutor needs to invent in order to understand truly the meaning of his words, just as he himself feels how many of the words he uses are far from completely expressing the meaning that he wishes to give them. He says it again, therefore, in a different manner, "he repeats himself," he succumbs to verbosity, or if he is a writer of genius such as Charles Peguy, he gives way to the need of inventing twenty different ways of saying the same thing. This is still to invent and marks perhaps the summit of verbal invention. The high virtuosity of a Shakespeare is not of any other nature than that which each of us scarcely ceases to give proof of. It is the same faculty used to the supreme degree.

But it is one thing to notice these facts, another to make of them a directive principle in the study of language [langue], and if Noam Chomsky looks for a predecessor, it is to be feared that he will find none. In any case, the generosity which he shows toward Descartes and the Cartesians is not merited if it is true, as I have said and think, that they have only rendered the existence of human language philosophically incomprehensible and its possibility even inconceivable. Swallowing all sense of shame, one must go back further still in the past until one returns to that scoundrel Aristotle. He is a predecessor unacceptable to science, but he is always in possession of an immense philosophical domain of which, despite his ambitions, Descartes has not yet succeeded in dispossessing him. For Descartes took possession of mathematics, of mechanics, and of everything which, in any order whatsoever, is dependent on the one or the other domain. But he paid for these magnificent conquests with a profound misunderstanding of what living matter can possess in its own right, including therein man insofar as he lives and thinks, thought being no doubt only the furthest reach of life. And there, perhaps precisely because he was less of a scholar, Aristotle has given proof of an exemplary fidelity to reality, such at least as we know it.

The Philosopher seems to hold as given that man is the only talking [parlant] animal. Herein he only restricts himself to the judgment of common sense, confirmed today further by the near-unanimity of linguists.

I shall dwell on this all the less to demonstrate it since the enterprise has just been carried out so well with a precision, an exemplary rational rigor, and a sort of dialectical relentlessness of which one could say, in a familiar metaphor in the language [*langue*] of its author, that it "leaves no stone unturned."[18]

I shall content myself with adding only one single remark. The question is of great scientific and, if one can say so, zoological interest, but it does not offer any properly philosophical or metaphysical interest. Those who try desperately to demonstrate that certain species of animals have a language appear to be animated by the hope of proving that since some animals speak, it is superfluous to have recourse to the hypothesis of a rational soul and of an immaterial principle of intellection as an explanation of human language. That would be in their eyes the indisputable triumph of materialism and scientific mechanism.

That, it appears to me, is an illusion. The proof that certain animals are capable of speaking would perhaps pose a new problem to Christian theologians, precisely insofar as they are Christian; but if the fact were positively *demonstrated*, that is to say, at least as solidly proved as are the laws of physics or the most indubitable biological facts, there would be nothing else for believers of every religious persuasion to do but to reconcile themselves to it. We can be sure that they would find the means of doing so without taxing their imaginations greatly. Nothing would change with respect to the philosophers. The existence of a talking animal would not be for them a novel hypothesis. This is exactly what the dualism of Descartes left the Cartesians at grips with. Since the mechanical man [*l'homme-machine*] of Descartes can speak without his soul having anything to do with it, there is no a priori impossibility that some beasts might do as much. Evidently, then, it would remain to explain how such a thing is possible. The recourse of the great Cartesians to the occasionalism of Malebranche, to the attributes of Substance and their parallelism as with Spinoza, to Leibniz's preestablished harmony, would be an absolute impossibility for those who hold to linguistic positivism. Theological or metaphysical, such hypotheses are essentially *antiscientific*. Today, to be antiscientific puts any idea whatsoever in a position analogous to that occupied by the heretical in the Middle Ages. Thus would one find oneself again at grips with the incomprehensible phenomenon of a talking machine, that is to say, in short, of mechanism explaining an activity of which one says that it is essentially inventive and in a way creative. There would remain, therefore, the modern descendants of Aristotle and of some vitalism or animism adapted to the data of current science. I fear indeed that they would have then no other choice than to attribute to animals who can speak an intellectual capacity proportionate to the extent and the degree of perfection of their knowledge. There would be difficulties in that, but no impossibility. In any case, animal psychology remains mysterious to us. There are not wanting cases in which the observer of their behavior would love to be able to say that, in short, certain animals have a sort of faculty of thought. We say therefore that in the present state of animals known to us, and within the limits of observations already made, man is the only animal of whom one could have the right to say that he speaks if human language implies the power of forming concepts and communicating them by means of signs which are associated with them.

It is thus that Aristotle already understood the nature of language, and one need not be astonished at the fact that he waited until his *Politics* in order to explain its existence. Still proceeding to that point as a biologist, it is at the moment when the nature of man as "an animal who lives in cities" (*zoon politikon*) is introduced that it becomes inevitable that he mention at least the fact that without a language political and social life, and therefore human life, would be impossible. Aristotle naturally does not ignore the fact that there exist animals who live in troops, or in herds. In this connection he speaks, almost prophetically, of bees, whom so many modern biologists want to say speak, but he finally draws a line between animals and man:

> Now, that man is more of a political animal than bees or any other gregarious animal is evident. Nature, as we often say, makes nothing in vain, and man is the only animal whom she has endowed with the gift of speech [*langage*]. And whereas mere voice is but an indication of pleasure or pain, and is therefore found in other animals, (for their nature attains to the perception of pleasure and pain and the intimation of them to one another, and no further), the power of speech [*de parler*] is intended to set forth the expedient and the inexpedient, and therefore likewise the just and the unjust. And it is a characteristic of man that he alone has any sense of good and evil, of just and unjust, and the like, and the association of living beings who have this sense makes a family and a state.[19]

The example of the just and the unjust cited as an initial example by Aristotle in this passage is attributable to the fact that the idea of the social and human group is in question at the beginning of his *Politics*. The question of knowing *how it comes about* that man speaks does not pose itself for him. He says a hundred times that nature does nothing in vain. Man speaks, therefore, because he must have the power to speak in order to be a man, that is to say, in order to be the political animal that he is, capable of living as a family as one observes him to live, and thus to found the first element of a society. Aristotle's finalism deploys itself here in all its ingenuousness. Every state is a community of a certain type, "and every community is established with a view to some good; for mankind always acts in order to obtain that which they think good. But, if all communities aim at some good, the state or political community, which is the highest of all, and which embraces all the rest, aims at good in a greater degree than any other, and at the highest good."[20]

Here we are immediately borne beyond the controversies over the origin of language. That is natural, for the state is as natural as are the most elementary forms of human grouping. "And therefore, if the earlier forms of society are natural, so is the state, for it is the end of them, and the nature of a thing is its end. For what each thing is when fully developed, we call its nature, whether we are speaking of a man, a horse, or a family. Besides, the final cause and end of a thing is the best, and to be self-sufficing is the end and the best."[21]

One thereby understands why in his treatise *On Interpretation* Aristotle will apply himself above all to the study of sentences which are "propositions," because they are the only ones that articulate truth or falsity, good or evil. They are therefore also the only ones which directly contribute to making possible the perfect form of society outside of which man would not know how to attain his complete development and his end. "Yet every sentence is not a proposition; only such are propositions as have in them either truth or falsity."[22] Language contains many other sorts of phrases, and consequently one ought to study them in treatises of a different nature, such as rhetoric or poetics. We are as far as possible from modern linguistics, which is determined to study language as such, independently of its truth and, even more, of its origin. As Aristotle understands it, its end, which is its cause, is such as it is by the very nature of language in order that it might have meaning.

Let us not dwell on Aristotle's logic but retain of it only what directly concerns our purpose. Propositions are made of words, and words differ from simple voice in that they offer meaning. What do they signify?

> Spoken words are the symbols of mental experience and written words are the symbols of spoken words. Just as all men have not the same writing, so all men have not the same speech sounds, but the mental experiences, which they directly symbolize, are the same for all, as also are those things of which our experiences are the images.[22a]

The situation as Aristotle sees it is therefore simple. There are first of all things, which are the same for all. Next, in the minds of men there are images produced by things. These are the same for all. Finally, there are vocal signs, and then writings, which are not the same for all men. The mental image of "horse" is the same with all men who have seen horses, but there are as many different words signifying the image of "horse" as there are different languages [*langues*]. If the word were as directly caused as the image it signifies, language would be as natural as the image itself. It would then be as universal as the image, and just as there is only one sole and same image of "horse" in all minds, there would be only one sole and same word to name it. There would be in that case one language [*langage*], and not many tongues [*mais pas de langues*]. This is why the word, or noun, is defined as "a sound significant by convention," and not by nature. "The limitation 'by convention' was introduced because nothing is by nature a noun or name—it is only so when it becomes a symbol; inarticulate sounds, such as those which brutes produce, are significant, yet none of these constitutes a noun."[22b] This is so because no one of them is the sign of an image, itself representing a thing.[23]

Everyone holds to this doctrine, and what is more important, everyone agrees with this primary evidence, which we call common sense. If this is not necessarily the truth, it is often a first approximation of it which it is imprudent to contradict, even if we ought not remain content with it. No modern linguist would dare to adopt a point of view as overtly finalist as this, and not without reason, for what science looks for is the "how" of things, not their "why." Now, even if one accepts the final cause as an explanation of the "why," its own "how" remains inexplicable or, in any case, unexplained. The only difficulty is that in abandoning finality scientific linguistics has put nothing in its place. Linguists continue, moreover, to express themselves as if it existed.

With some minor variations, Whitney and de Saussure agree in saying that "language [*langue*] is a social institution," not the only system of signs expressing ideas but the most important of them. Saussure envisages therefore, under the name of *semiology*, "a science which studies the life of signs in the bosom of social life."[24] The study of speech [*langage*], therefore, by virtue of its essential feature, calls for the study of language [*langue*], "which is social in its essence."[25] Now, it is difficult to attribute a social function to language without falling back upon the vocabulary of finality. Speaking of language [*langue*], Saussure estimates that as distinct from simple speech [*langage*], it is a social product "and a collection of necessary conventions that have been adopted by the social body to permit individuals to exercise that faculty."[26] But could we not suppose that, with Aristotle, the very faculty of language appeared millennia ago (in fact, with Aristotle, from all eternity) in the species "man," raised up so to speak by his vocation as a political animal and as required by his nature in order that it might be fulfilled? Everything takes place as if this were true, but how can we know it? If we admit it, we must at the same time admit the presence, in this special animal which is man, of a power of thought, whether we call it intellect or something else, which cannot be exercised fully outside of a social body tied together by language. For, finally, there being no lack of species of gregarious animals who live in herds without speaking or experiencing the need of forming what we call a "society," properly speaking, one does not see why men could not content themselves with living in troops, without language [*langue*], writing, books, and journals. This would not be without its advantages and, more or less, would not hinder man from showing himself to be, by virtue of his intelligence, his sciences, and his techniques, the most depraved, the most ferocious, and the most destructive of known animals. We say it again: to look for why man is as he is, is not a scientific question. But because man is essentially a speaking animal [*un animal parlant*], one is exposed to the danger, in deliberately setting aside philosophical problems which pose themselves in connection with language, of speaking of him as if science had already resolved these problems.

However these problems may exist in connection with language, those which present themselves to the philosopher in language itself cannot remain indefinitely ignored by the linguist. This is particularly evident with the meaning [*sens*] of the nevertheless inevitably mysterious term, the word "meaning" [*sens*] or "signification." We have already come across it many times. It is the linguists' turn to ask themselves about it.[27] It will be quite interesting to see if linguists of the strict scientific observance who announce their intention of doing so are able to succeed in keeping themselves free from all philosophical contamination. The case is that in order to know *what* the word signifies, it becomes almost inevitable that one will ask about the nature of knowledge and, consequently, about that which it is agreed to call intellect or mind. This inevitability is the principal philosophical constant of language. At the beginning of his *Essai sur l'origine des langues* Rousseau still maintained it firmly: "The invention of the art of communicating our ideas depends less upon the organs which serve us in that communication than upon a faculty proper to man, who causes his organs to be used in this fashion and who, if they were absent in him, would make others serve the same need." Imperceptible in itself, has this "faculty" recently ceased to exist?

4

The Word and the Concept

I want to speak. I want "to say something," for in truth and strictly speaking it is impossible to speak for the purpose of not saying anything. Whether it be an illusion or not, he who would "begin to speak" has the sense of the presence in his mind of something that he wants to say or that wants to be said. One can speak for the purpose of saying insignificant things, nothings, but not really to no purpose, for the only way of saying nothing is to hold one's tongue, to remain completely silent.

What one says, whatever its nature may be in other respects, is the meaning of the words pronounced. To say something implies that the word said has a meaning and that this meaning may be conceived, or thought. Whoever does not have in his mind any meaning he is trying to formulate "has nothing to say," and if he insists on speaking nevertheless, "he doesn't know what he is talking about," "he doesn't know what he is saying."

To know what one says and to know what one thinks are therefore one and the same thing, for the only way of knowing what one thinks is to say it. I ought to be able to say to myself, initially, what I think so as to be able to say it to others. The two operations can be distinct. They are so for the writer, who is his own initial public, for the professor, and generally in all cases where the problem of thinking is distinct from that of communicating one's thought; but even the professor and the writer, or the speaker in general, ought themselves to perceive the meaning of what they say or are going to say. What is called "thinking aloud" is to speak to oneself aloud, and inversely. Finally, there are things that we say to ourselves and keep to ourselves for a long time before saying them to others. Some of these "secret thoughts" can be among those that are most important to us, and for that reason alone they will never be said, they will never be "revealed."

This brings us back to the classic distinction of the Stoics between "the interior word," which consists of verbal images, and "the spoken word," which consists of words pronounced by the voice and constitutes speech

63

[*langage*] properly speaking. The distinction is evident. That which is called "thinking" consists of a sort of silent speech [*parole*] which one addresses to oneself. But if thinking consisted solely in this interior discourse, there would be no difference between thinking and speaking. Thought and speech would be one and identical.

Reflection allows us to see that this is not true. The illusion is born of a hasty identification of speech [*parole*] with thought when in fact, although all interior language may be speech thought [*une parole pensée*], it is itself born of another thought or mental activity anterior to speech [*langage*]. This is the very kind of thought for which we are looking.

But how can we speak of the signification or meaning of a language such as it is precisely before it is spoken? Doubtless, one can get in touch with this thought through simple consciousness, but that immediate experience of thought by itself is, by definition, mute. One cannot speak about it. In order to take hold of this thought in itself, one would have to be able to reascend the flow of thought even to its source as a countercurrent, that is to say, even to the point where thought begins to descend into language, but where thinking and speaking are still not completely identical. But there is an asymmetry between the two elements of the experience, for if there exists a form of thought anterior to language, we cannot say anything about it, even to ourselves. It is evident that what takes place anterior to communication cannot be communicated.

However, the existence of unspoken thought appears to be attested to by interior observation. Thought is anterior to speech with an anteriority at once temporal and causal. The anteriority of time can be more or less long. Quite often it is so short that we could take it to be almost simultaneous. But even then, what I want to say to myself or to others is something which has not yet been said. We speak of it as something, although it really cannot be a thing. We say therefore, if you will, that this *x*, which has not yet been spoken, ought to be in some fashion present to my thought, for otherwise I could not try to say it. If I try to do so prematurely, I am immediately aware that "that is not what I wanted to say." This is what we call "trying out an idea." The idea in question can be a remembrance which momentarily escapes us, or it can be an idea that we feel present to thought even though for the moment it refuses to surface and emerge from the depths of the mind. At any rate we know that it is already there. It is there so assuredly that we will recognize it immediately as soon as it shall have appeared, and until that moment we reject all other remembrances which might try to be accepted in its place.

This sort of thought anterior to all even interior *logos* is what we think of as "yet to be spoken," be it because up to the present it has not yet been said or because we feel the desire to say it once more, more explicitly or under a different form, in order better to assure ourselves of what we think.

What, then, is this first thought anterior to all language? Until recently one could get rid of questions of this sort through recourse to the notion of the unconscious. But nothing was really gained by that artifice, because the unconscious was conceived of as conscious knowledge without conscious recognition of it. Such is particularly the case in the Freudian school, where everything that takes place in the depth of the unconscious can be brought to the light of consciousness without undergoing substantial modification. The Freudian subconscious is of the same nature as the conscious, with the sole exception that in its first instance it evades consciousness. Hence the ease with which Freudian psychology reconstructs the operations of the unconscious in terms of clear and distinct knowledge. One sees this in the celebrated *Traumdeutung*, where, concerning whatever dream is at issue, a Freudian is never at a loss to reconstitute its meaning, or lacking an interpretation.[1]

In fact, if anything in unconscious thought could be spoken about (meaning by unconscious thought simply operations occurring in the mind without our being aware of them), in this respect reflection reveals us to be against an impenetrable wall. Unconscious human thought is as inaccessible to observation as are, for example, the psychological activities of the higher animals. Many of them, on the sole basis of their perceptions, show themselves capable of forming inferences appropriate for guiding some of their behavior. For example, when a mature cat learns by itself to open doors latched by a levered door handle, what psychological operation can lead it to act *as if* seeing people repeatedly opening doors in this way were able to "give it the idea" that it might obtain the same result by leaping up from the ground and landing with joined paws upon the handle? To invoke the association of ideas explains nothing: that is what must be explained, all the more in that the cat does not have hands or people paws. Again, infants think before speaking. Every parent knows this, and, moreover, no linguist contests the issue. But can we imagine thought devoid of words — those resistant nuclei, or at least those sorts of floating buoys — to which thought fastens itself, about which it organizes itself, and upon which it depends in order to develop? It is impossible even to conceive of a method of recording facts of this order of things, but our ignorance of their nature does not authorize us to deny them.

There is nothing further that can be done, in speaking of mature thought anterior to language, except to suppose that it is of the same nature as the mute psychism of animals and infants. That which the *in-fans*, the nonspeaking, thinks is probably related to what the same infant continues to think after having learned to relate it to the disciplines of a language. I say "probably" in order to point out that I *know* nothing about it, but also because concerning two consecutive states of a being of the same species (indeed, of the same individual simply continuing to live and develop) there is no obvious reason to imagine that the psychism that it manifestly displays in the first of these states ceases to be exercised in the other. The sole difference would appear to be that the concealed energy which manifested itself in the first state through acts manifests itself additionally in the second through language. It is not arbitrary to think so; rather, it would be arbitrary to think otherwise.

These remarks apply to what thought might be before language. It comes down, for us, to the experience of a presence whose nature escapes us and whose reality is attested to only by its effects, which are however material, audible, visible, and objects of a particular science, phonology. All that we are able to try to think of the not-yet-spoken is conditioned by the impossibility of doing so without having recourse to language. The only chance of observing thought in itself would be to get a glimmer of it at the fleeting moment when it descends into language, like the green ray that the setting sun sends out at the moment of sinking into the sea. But thought becoming language is already language, and, moreover, even if the experience of pure thought were possible, it would be necessary to use language in order to communicate it. One can only, therefore, return from spoken thought to that which speaks, striving to distinguish future thought from the subsequent language in which it is in the process of being incarnated. This is at least difficult, for that which is dimly conceived cannot be clearly expressed; but there would be no language whatever if that could not be conceived at all.

When one tries to describe it, the experience of a thought-not-yet-spoken is that of a sort of "all-at-once," which, however, it would be impossible to express other than by pieces of it proffered one at a time. In this regard the most scrupulous linguists do not appear to see things differently than the generality of philosophers, or even other people do. Emile Benveniste cites Saussure himself on this point:

> Psychologically speaking, and in the absence of language, our thought is only an amorphous and indistinct mass. Philosophers and linguists have always agreed in recognizing that, without the assistances of signs, we would be incapable of distinguishing two ideas in a clear and constant fashion. Taken in itself, thought is as a nebula where nothing has any necessary boundaries. There are no preestablished ideas, and nothing is distinct before the appearance of language [*langue*].[2]

Moreover, this is exactly what linguists want to say when they vouch for the immediately obvious fact that thought is impossible without language.

This is true of thought articulated into ideas approximately distinct, such as in fact language alone allows us to make use of. But language is possible only on the condition of proceeding by means of a sort of parcelling out of thought, and it is not certain that the operation can be completely successful, for insofar as it is physical reality, speech [*parole*] is in fact divisible, whether it be in space if it is written or in time if it is spoken. In both cases speech [*parole*] has *parts beyond parts*. But the thought that speech expresses, the very meaning of speech, does not lend itself to any division. *Peter's book* is composed of two words, but the phrase does not mean either *Peter's* or *book;* it only means Peter's book. If I ask someone to show me this book, one will not hesitate an instant to show it to me. For him who knows what this book is, "Peter's book" is an unique object, and the thought which conceives it is similar.

It is not necessary to be a philosopher in order to establish the fact, but it is not sufficient to be one in order to explain the possibility of it. A venerable tradition takes it for granted that language owes its intelligibility to the immateriality of the human soul, but its most illustrious representatives have some difficulty in saying what an "immaterial being" could be and how it comes about, if it exists, that such a being could be connected to a body. Plato, with his soul presiding over the body like a pilot guiding his ship, or using it provisionally as a man uses his clothes, is in this regard constantly on the frontier of myth. Aristotle, ordinarily so exact in his thought, has left his commentators in the greatest embarrassment on this subject. If one sticks to the letter of the little that he said on the matter, one can maintain, in his name, several positions: that the intellect is a separate intelligence, one for the whole human species, which is Averroes' position; that this is true of the agent intellect, but that each thinking individual has his own possible intellect, which is Avicenna's point of view; that each man has his own intellective soul and that although it is the form of the body, the intellect of this soul [sic] is an immaterial faculty whose nature is completely other than that of the body whose form it is, which is Thomas Aquinas' position; that, further, the soul, precisely because it is the form of the body, is also dependent on the body as all forms are dependent on their matter, and consequently perishes with it, which is what Pomponazzi thought, or, rather, what he thought Aristotle had thought. What Aristotle really thought no one knows with certitude, but all the positions at some time come up against the same obstacle: the nature of the relation of the immaterial soul to the material body. The several traces that Aristotle left concerning this redoubtable problem all come back to saying that the intellect abstracts from the sensible datum the intelligible element that it contains, but how this transmutation, or, at least, this metachemical purification, can take place, one cannot say. The reader [*lecteur*] of Thomas Aquinas willingly simplifies the problem in saying that immateriality and intelligibility are one and the same thing, and therefore that it suffices to admit the immateriality of the intellect in order to explain that it knows; and, assuredly, intelligibility is the privilege of immateriality.

But that does not suffice to resolve the problem, for the intellect is not just immaterial; it is "an immaterial being," and it is the relation of an immaterial being to a being which is not immaterial that reflection finds obscure. "The immateriality of a created intelligent substance [*substance intelligente*] is not its intellect," says Thomas Aquinas; "rather, through its immateriality it has the power of understanding."[3] Thus, with so many philosophers of the East, Platonists, Aristotelians, pagans, Jews, Moslems, or Christians, and right up to the proponents of French or Italian *ontologism* of the nineteenth century, the insurmountable temptation to think of thought as a light from a purely intelligible world, from a Sun of the Spirits, from pure Intellect distinct from those which it illuminates, in such a fashion that one could say that *it thinks* in us, rather than that we form the thought ourselves. It is just that immediate experience has always protested against this desperate expedient. *Ego cogito*, Descartes will say. Me, I think; therefore, even if it were true that there were no others in the world, it would be certain that I, at least I, am. The duality observed by the linguists in the words of language is but the reflex of that metaphysical duality of human nature and of the paradoxical condition of the human intellect. Man does not think without images. He ought therefore to have a body in order to be able to think. But the other animals have bodies and images; nevertheless, they do not think as man thinks. Seeing that they do not speak, their psychism ought to differ in nature from human psychism.

The easiest manner in which to approach this problem for a modern is to examine the product of the act of intellection, namely, what we conceive, the "concept." We have the habit of calling it also a "general idea," as opposed to the simple image of the particular object left in us by sensible perception. Therefore, following this terminology, it is a question of knowing what a general idea, a concept, is.

One must return here to the classic setting of the problem, for although the solutions which have been proposed to it in great number are not scientifically demonstrable, the terms in which it is posed there have at least the merit of respecting the data of experience. In whatever manner one may conceive the nature of it, there must be, between speaking subject and the things signified by language, an x of whatever name one gives it, which is a factor of universality.

On the one hand, "nothing universal is a being," "any universal is not a substance."[4] On the other, all knowledge [*science*] concerns the universal and quiddity, although all that is real is a particular concrete thing.[5] If one does not want science to be without foundation, and hence be in no way a form of knowledge, its immediate object must be the thing given in an immaterial state which is not a thing. Under these two conditions only will it be possible to have real knowledge, that is to say, knowledge which is not that of some modification of thought knowing, but rather of the very thing that it knows. It is true that put in these terms, the problem can appear insoluble, but that would not be the only problem posed by nature whose data escape from the grasp of our science. The worse fault would be to falsify the terms of the problem in order to facilitate its solution.[6]

The nature of these terms explains perhaps why a scientific solution of them is not possible. All that is physically real is material and particular. The universal, whose nature we are seeking to understand, is immaterial by definition. It is necessary therefore that that which produces it ought to be equally immaterial if one does not wish its production to be quasi-miraculous. But the order of the immaterial, of the nonphysical, is precisely that of the metaphysical. Language, therefore, involves the reality of the metaphysical by the very fact that it involves an element of universality.

Naturally, we would love to lay hold of this immaterial element in itself, this agent of universality, but it is only given to us in its effect, the concept, which, not being perceptible to the senses because of its very immateriality, is not an object of representation for thought. Our nearest access route to it is precisely language, and since language is only clearly and distinctly conceived under its material form, spoken and written, we can only make it the object of distinct scientific discipline, grammatology or phonology, but cannot hope to attain thereby to its intelligibility. This is why, as we have said, certain linguists would love to be able to deal with language as if it had no meaning, for it is truly from the meaning that all the difficulties in linguistics are born, just as in biology the most serious difficulties come from the obtrusive idea of "life," which does not explain anything, but calls attention to that without which the biologist would have nothing to explain. Such is the case here, for to eliminate meaning is to eliminate language, and a positive science could not begin by eliminating its proper object. It would be better to renounce science, should that be necessary, rather than sacrifice reality.

One can nevertheless, without developing illusions about the significance of the hoped-for results, try another method of approach in order to catch a glimpse of that fleeting object.

The great philosophies are just so many personal explorations conducted by the philosophers themselves, some of whom are obsessed by the peculiarity of these secret realities which hide themselves beneath the surface of the sensible. Obsessed without hope, for they know in advance that there are no "realities." Concerning the intellect, as concerning being and cause, each great philosophy has its message to communicate, or, we should rather say, its report to make concerning the province of the intelligible world that it has explored. It is not the personal psychology of the philosopher which is in question, but rather the nature of the domain and all the sorts of circumstances where he happens to approach it: before or after Socrates, before or after Plato, before or after Aristotle, before or after the diffusion of the religious message of the Bible, etc. Anyway, each great metaphysician succeeds in making a sort of victorious breakthrough in the assault that metaphysics perpetually delivers on the mystery of intelligible being. Plotinus is one of those whose metaphysics most resembles a view enlarged by his interior experience of being such as it is given to the intellect.

We recall the Plotinian triad of three substances and first causes: the One (who is the Good for the others), the Intellect, and the Soul. Faithful to the Platonic tradition, and at the same time to his own experience, Plotinus reserves the name of knowledge to that which deserves it in the highest degree: the knowledge of intelligible objects. In order to describe the Intellect (the *nous*), Plotinus has at his disposal no other model than his own intellect. The first and subsistent-in-itself Intellect ought to have some resemblance to the human intellect, since it is the cause of it. The principal difference is that this first Intellect, which Plotinus' French translators at times call the Intelligence [*intelligence:* understanding], *is* its own intelligible objects, of which it is itself the first, which includes all the others.

From the first moment of his meditation Plotinus comes upon difficulties. On the one hand, *Nous* is the totality of intelligibles (if one can speak of the totality of a plurality which multiplies out of itself to infinity); on the other hand, the intelligibles do not exist because *Nous* thinks them. It knows them because they are there as objects to be known: "The object of intellection ought to be there before the act of intellection."[7] Since the Intellect of Plotinus does not think the intelligibles as does ours, in abstracting the forms of the sensory data, its act of knowing cannot be called conception, or its result a concept. Plotinus therefore calls that object "Idea" which is interior to intelligence. Since these Ideas of the Intelligence are one with it, each is itself an Intelligence, and we arrive here at the point where, it appears to me, Plotinus describes the *Nous* by analogy with his own intellect:

We take it, then, that the Intellectual-Principle is the authentic existences and contains them all — not as in a place but as possessing itself and being one thing with this its content. All are one there and yet are distinct: similarly the mind holds many branches and items of knowledge simultaneously, yet none of them merged into any other, each acting its own part at call quite independently, every conception coming out from the inner total and working singly. It is after this way, though in a closer unity, that the Intellectual-Principle is all Being in one total — and yet not in one, since each of these beings is a distinct power which, however, the total Intellectual-Principle includes as the species in a genus, as the parts in a whole.[8]

This *Nous* of Plotinus resembles our intellect particularly in this fact, that it is at one and the same time unity and multiplicity, a multiplicity which leaves its unity intact, or, rather, which perpetually issues from it. This is why the idea of a language where each word would correspond to an idea, and inversely, does not respond to linguistic reality. Sapir was not a metaphysician, but I do not think that he ever cheated in his descriptions of the facts of language, a great number and remarkable variety of which he knew. But he often noted that it is impossible to make words and concepts correspond, each to each.[9] Not content to notice this lack of correspondence, he states precisely that it becomes more and more noticeable to the extent that one strives further to lay ahold of thought in itself. He sees the reason for this in the impossibility of finding a sufficient number of different words to express the infinite variety of the concrete.[10] There would not be enought distinct radicals to signify the multitude of its particular aspects. Thus the use of derivatives: *farm, farming, farmer.* And that is correct, but in following his analysis Sapir, who is not looking for philosophical problems, is led to record another fact, namely, that each word involves at least four concepts. It becomes almost impossible then for us to assign concepts to words in clearly defined thought, particularly when one considers the concepts called "relational," whether they be concrete or abstract. It becomes then evident that no "parts of thought" exist corresponding to the well-known "parts of speech." If I say "by," "from," "to," do these words, which designate no concrete object, designate at least a distinct and intelligible concept by themselves?

What is the meaning of "yes"? On first sight one can say that it signifies assent in general. But what is it to assent? This verb, formerly common, has ceased to be so, and nevertheless the act which it designates has not ceased to exist. One can, as Newman did, write a long treatise on *The Grammar of Assent* and leave us still undecided about the meaning of the verb *to assent.* Webster's American dictionary says that *yes* is an adverb signifying the contrary to *no* and expressing agreement, consent, affirmation, or confirmation. But one sees that the nuances of its possible meanings begin to multiply, and their number becomes unlimited if one admits that in spoken language [*langue parlée*], which is the true language [*langage*], it suffices to raise the voice in pronouncing this monosyllable

in order to cause it to signify Yes? Is it indeed so? Or, further, with a mim-
icry of expectation (which forms part of the sign): Do you wish to add
something? Or, more simply still: What do you want? What's the matter?
Each will find many other uses of the same word whose sense varies with
the tone of the voice: impatience (Yes, yes, yes, that will do!); doubt
(Ye-Ye-s?), which does not wish to say: "I am in accord," but rather, "I am
not sure that we are in agreement."

All that is true, but if that is what *yes* intends to say, or can intend
to say, it is not an adverb; it is a monosyllabic sentence, complete in itself.
This is what the *Petit Robert* elegantly suggests in defining *yes:* "Adverb
equivalent to an affirmative proposition which responds to an interroga-
tion not accompanied by negation." That is quite a remarkable adverb,
for it doesn't simply add a determination to a verb, or even to the totality
of a statement. It is in itself a statement. "Yes, I come into his temple to
adore the eternal . . . ," "Yes, it is Agamemnon, it is your king . . . ," as
much as to say to the onlooker: You see, this is a conversation already
begun which goes on; or, as if one of the speakers is a little surprised and
that at any rate we are not acquainted with what is happening, Racine
specifies: that's true, that's true, it is indeed I . . . , etc. Is it truly a question of an adverb?

The *Concise Oxford Dictionary of Current English* is only partially
better inspired when it writes: "YES, a particle equivalent to an affirmative sentence," for this is what this particle signifies first and most often,
but it can signify many other things. When the office secretary casts a re-
signed look upon me and asks me in an ascendent and querulous glissando:
"Yes???" she is inquiring certainly about why I am there, but she says to
herself no less certainly: "Another one! Let's find the quickest way of getting rid of him!" In any case, *yes* can be equivalent to many different sentences, therefore can be these sentences, composed of words each of which
would pose similar problems.

Thus is explained the ill-repute, in the eyes of modern linguists, of
the still classic notion of the "parts of speech." "Our conventional classi-
fication of words into *parts of speech*," Sapir observes, "is only a vague,
wavering approximation to a consistently worked out inventory of experience." To which he adds: "The 'part of speech' reflects not so much our
intuitive analysis of reality as our ability to compose that reality into a
variety of formal patterns. A part of speech outside of the limitations of
syntactic form is but a will-o'-the-wisp. For this reason no logical scheme
of the parts of speech — their number, nature, and necessary confines — is
of the slightest interest to the linguist."[11] We grant that, but that which
presents no interest for the linguist can greatly interest the grammarian,
arbiter of good usage, and still more the metaphysician, who cannot con-

tent himself with what science says if it refuses to give an account of any aspect of reality whatsoever. "Every word, every grammatical element," Sapir says, moreover, "every locution, every sound and accent is a slowly changing configuration, molded by the invisible and impersonal drift that is the life of language [*langage*]."[12] The metaphysician accepts the fact, but he simply substitutes one word in this biological metaphor. Instead of the life of *language* he says life of *thought*, and this simple substitution leads him immediately to some very ancient ideas, further away from the familiar perspectives of the linguist than they are from those of the metaphysician.

"In the beginning was the Word": after the philosopher Plotinus, let us consult the theologian Thomas Aquinas and ask of him what this mysterious revelation can signify for us who philosophize on language.

Good peripatetic that he is, Aquinas takes sensible experience as his point of departure and makes the observation that *verbum*, the "said" ["*dit*"], or word, signifies in the first place the exterior word, said or spoken. This word, because it is a sensible datum, a perception of the sense of hearing, gets our initial attention sooner or more vividly than do the images or ideas simply given in consciousness. As a consequence, the first sense of the word "speech" [*verbe*], tongue [*parole*], or word [*mot*] signifies this exterior speech [*parole*], uttered as the Stoics said, which strikes the ear. Reflection suggests, however, that the exterior word supposes another kind, the interior or mental word, which, since this is what the exterior word [*verbe*] has the function of expressing, is at one and the same time its efficient and final cause. Its final cause, since, as it comes to be said, we offer the vocal word as a manifestation of the interior word, which is its meaning and of which it is the sign. Its efficient cause, because the cause of the exterior word, uttered in order to signify what appears to it good, is a consequence of the will. In the same fashion, therefore, that there pre-exists in the mind of the artisan a certain image of the exterior object that he wishes to produce, there also exists in the thought of him who speaks a sort of interior model of the word that he wants to utter exteriorly.[13]

Thomas Aquinas appears here to think about the distinction between what the admirable Egger called "the interior word" and the language which speaks, as we say, aloud. He makes in this connection two important remarks which, if it were possible to transfer their meaning into contemporary language, would clarify well some difficulties which still divide certain of our contemporaries.

First, the interior word is "that which is expressed by the exterior [word]." It is what is understood interiorly: *verbum interius est ipsum interius intellectum* [the interior word is that very thing which is interiorly understood], and it is this understanding in its very interior act that spoken and heard language manifests exteriorly. But, second, what spoken language manifests thus exteriorly is not what it signifies. "The exterior word signifies that which is understood [*intelligé*], not the act of understanding [*intelliger*], nor the habit or faculty, as the objects of understanding, unless the habit and the faculty are themselves the things that are understood. Consequently, the interior word is what is understood interiorly."[14]

One perceives in this description a certain indeterminateness, which, moreover, is doubtless only to be found in language. The fundamental ambiguity of so many words marks particularly in Latin, even classical Latin, the substantive *intellectus, us* (sic), which can signify, strictly, a sensation, a perception: *intellectus saporum*; but also comprehension, intelligence: *intellectus sermonis patrii*; or, further, the idea: *intellectus sui esse*; then also the faculty of comprehension, understanding, intellect: *intellectus animi*; finally, the meaning of a word, of a sentence: *intellectum habere, intellectu carere*. Here is another case where a word is by itself alone several words. The meanings are rather close, for the Latin tongue is capable of the economical disposition of many words—which does not facilitate the reading of texts or, moreover, their redaction.

This is doubtless why, solicitous to eliminate all equivocation, Thomas Aquinas adds a commentary drawn from the comparison between the speaker who produces language and the artisan who produces a fabricated object. Let us allow him to speak:

> Consequently, just as we consider three things in the case of a craftsman, namely, the purpose of his work, its model, and the work now produced, so also do we find a threefold word in one who is speaking. There is the word conceived by the intellect, which, in turn, is signified by an exterior vocal word. The former is called *the word of the heart*, uttered but not vocalized. Then there is that upon which the exterior word is modeled; and this is called *the interior word*, which has an image of the vocal word. Finally, there is the word expressed exteriorly, and this is called *the vocal word*. Now, just as a craftsman first intends his end, then thinks out the form of his product, and finally brings it into existence, so also, in one who is speaking, the word of the heart comes first, then the word which has an image of the oral word, and, finally, he utters the vocal word.[15]

A notable distinction is introduced here between: (1) the product of the act of intellection, *that which* the intellect conceives and says to itself in secret, without any vocal image, even an interior one of the kind which we use when we do what we call "talking to ourselves"; (2) the interior language, or interior word [*parole*], that Thomas holds as the model according to which we think aloud; and (3) the pronounced words, which resemble these interior words in all respects, unless one would prefer to say, as many would today, that this interior language resembles them.[16] We must recognize that, at the moment at which his analysis reaches the heart of a thought, a metaphor for designating by a corporeal image the act of an incorporeal energy, Thomas Aquinas leaves us in the embarrassment we are always in when it is a question of representing psychological facts or speaking of them. Not being able to imagine them, since they are immaterial, or capable of preventing ourselves from talking of them as if we did imagine them, we have recourse to the subterfuge of images borrowed from the biological order of living bodies. The psychological domain is the domain of analogy. It is therefore not surprising that returning to the very root of all knowing, Thomas leaves us without any representation of that about which he speaks. The image of the heart has no other justification than to suggest the first characteristic, primordial and yet secret, of this first *logos* from which subsequently issues the interior speech [*parole*] composed of words [*mots*] which we say to ourselves, and the speech composed of these words spoken aloud.

Let us attach ourselves to this initial and secret word: *verbum cordis sive voce prolatum* [the word of the heart, whether vocally developed or not]. What is the nature of it and what is its connection with what we call the object known?

In the perspective of the preceding analysis, which in turn quotes as authority Aristotle *On Interpretation* (I, 16, 3), "[since] words [*voces*] are the signs of ideas, and ideas the similitudes of things, it is evident that words function in the signification of things through the conception of the intellect. It follows therefore that we can give a name to anything insofar as we can understand it."[17] The mental experience [*intellection*] of the object through the conception of the intellect is approximately what we call today the "concept," but the use of this word can be the occasion for misunderstandings of every kind. The main misunderstanding is the forgetting of the principle that what Thomas Aquinas calls the interior word does not "signify" the object but manifests it through the act of the intellect, whereas the word, which itself is a sign, signifies directly the object which the intellect knows.

The mediating function of the concept is here at the heart of the operation, since it is to the extent that it knows the thing that we can name it; but precisely in order for that to take place it is necessary that the word not designate the concept and that it designate the thing itself known by the concept. This is moreover, as is always the case in the Aristotelian tradition, what immediate experience verifies. When the infant or the adult says *a dog, a knife*, the nouns that he uses signify for him, not the idea of a dog or knife, but the very things that these nouns designate. It is because we know things that we are able to name them—them, and not the concepts that we form of them. The concept itself is not a thing; it is a particular act of the intellect, immaterial as is the intellect and, consequently, not available to direct observation. We know concepts in knowing the things of which they are the concepts.

Since the Middle Ages a tendency has developed of making of the intelligible content of the concept a proper object of knowledge, as distinct from the thing known through the concept. This is what is called the *conceptus objectivus*. This decision of some rather obscure masters remained without significance right up to the day when, deferring to the exigencies of his mathematical method, Descartes appropriated the idea of "objective concept" or "objective reality of the concept," meaning by that the very reality insofar as represented in and through the concept. The third of the *Meditations* clearly establishes this idea in distinguishing between ideas taken simply as ways of thinking, and which, thus conceived, are all equal, and these same ideas taken as representing different objects. In the second sense they are as unequal as the things they represent. The ideas of substance contain more of objective reality than those of accidents, and, obviously, the idea of God contains more objective reality than any other idea. To be objectively in the understanding is to be there "in the manner in which objects are habitually there." Thus the idea of sun is the sun itself existing in the understanding. This manner of being is less perfect than real existence outside the understanding, but it is not nothing.[18] The names which designate them then designate the ideas which represent things, and things only through them.

This position, still enveloped in an abstract mathematicism with Descartes, became quasi-popular among the *philosophes* when Locke formulated it directly in itself and as a fact [*evidence*] of psychological observation. For him man remained the only speaking animal. Animals do not have the power of abstraction: *brutes abstract not*. In fact: "It is evident we observe no footsteps in them of making use of general signs for universal ideas; from which we have reason to imagine that they have not the faculty of abstracting, or making general ideas, since they have no use of words, or any other general signs."[19]

One notices the care he takes to speak not of general ideas but rather of "general signs," for it is indeed the word itself which will in future make generalization possible. With Locke it is the capacity of the word to signify entire classes of particulars which constitutes abstraction. With words certain ideas, or rather images, are associated which are characteristic of such and such class of objects. These composite images become for us the ideas of corresponding objects, and it is they that words evoke immediately in thought. Thence the very simple position adopted by Locke: "Words, in their primary or immediate signification, stand for nothing but *the ideas in the mind of him that uses them*, how imperfectly soever or carelessly those ideas are collected from the things which they are supposed to represent."[20]

Locke explains himself abundantly and clearly. The abstraction which makes the generalization possible is a purely psychological operation, which concerns the content of thought alone without implicating any generalizable element which could belong to the thing itself and upon which the intellect might exercise its power of abstraction. One abstracts certain ideas from others in considering them separately; one does not abstract the intelligible from the sensible or, consequently, from material things endowed with forms. To abstract is simply to choose among ideas (i.e., perceptions, images) certain of them, give them a name, and use them to evoke from the mind the corresponding item. In this manner we are left supplied with "general words." "Words become general," says Locke, "by being made the signs of general ideas: and ideas become general, by separating from them the circumstances of time and place, and any other ideas that may determine them to this or that particular existence."[21]

Locke does not trouble himself with the causes of language. Regarding that he is as spontaneously finalist as Aristotle and his school. One need only reread the *Essay* at the beginning of Book III: "God, having designed man for a sociable creature, made him not only with an inclination, and under a necessity to have fellowship with those of his own kind, but furnished him also with language [*langage*], which was to be the great instrument and common tie of society."[21a] This is why in Book III, courageously entitled "Words," the first chapter of which promises as before to deal with "Words, or of Language [*langage*] in General," his attention naturally bears upon the connection of words and ideas rather than words and things. The description he makes of language [*langage*] as signs of ideas was practically inevitable from the point of view of his general project, and perhaps it was even legitimate, for if it is the nature of language [*langage*] that one wants to elucidate, it is indeed the connection of the word to meaning which is of prime importance. Ideas are the sole objects upon which the attention of the philosopher who reflects upon the meaning of words will naturally come to rest. In a course of general linguistics words signify neither real horses nor real men, but the abstract ideas of man and horse. Likewise for Locke asking himself about human understanding. What strikes him when he comes to it in language is that the only ideas which the words that a speaker uses can signify are his own. And "when a man speaks to another, it is that he may be understood: and the end of speech is, that those sounds, or marks, may make known his ideas to the hearer. That then which words are the marks of are the ideas of the speaker: nor can any one apply them as marks, *immediately* [Gilson's emphasis] to anything else but the ideas that he himself hath: for this would be to make them signs of his own conceptions, and yet apply them to other ideas; which would be to make them signs and not signs of his ideas at the same time; and so in effect to have no signification at all."[22] This is an argument that appears irrefutable in a book on language as such, for one only finds language as such in grammars and treatises on general linguistics, which concern words and sentences composed of signs and significations, grammars and treatises having abstracted from knowing whether things signified correspond to them in reality.

Linguists therefore always admit that Locke is right, for the object of their inquiry is the same: "Of Words and Language in General." But real language is not that which the linguist studies. If I ask for a pound of bread, I could do so in a study on linguistics, in which case *bread* is a noun which signifies the idea of bread. But if I pose the same question to a grocer, *bread* does not signify the idea of bread; it signifies bread, and it does not signify it through the idea of bread. That is its meaning directly and immediately.[23]

The philosopher who inquires into language as the moment of noetic activity will hesitate long, therefore, before reducing it to a two-term operation, the word and the meaning, abstracting from their connection to the extramental object to which the discourse refers in its normal usage. He returns in the matter, then, inevitably to the Aristotelian setting of the problem, not because Aristotle said it, but because it does not suffice for a thing to be false that Aristotle should have said it. Language immediately signifies, not thought, but things. It can only signify them, we might say, if there exists in man a power of knowing things under the form of universals, or general ideas, applicable to classes each of which can be designated by a name. Our understanding of these universals is what we call "concepts." That is what Thomas Aquinas often calls *verbum*, because this word is what the intellect conceives by the thing.[24] This power of conceiving of the universal ought to be as immaterial as is the universal itself. If man is the only speaking animal, capable of conceiving abstract thought and of signifying it by words, it is doubtless that he alone possesses this immaterial power.[25] This order of the immaterial, the existence of which one cannot even deny without speaking and consequently attesting to its existence, is the witness in us of the reality of metaphysics. Although entirely legitimate in itself, the existence of general linguistics raises most serious philosophical difficulties. These result precisely from the fact that one cannot make the physics of language correspond to the metaphysics of thought. Although we can hardly avoid expressing the matter so, the

Nous is not reducible even to an instantaneously presented entity of simultaneously distinct and intermixed elements. The *Nous* creates distinction through language[26] and is itself neither distinct nor confused, but anterior, as the One of Plotinus which is all numbers without being any number. The idea does not preexist language in thought, but thought is what can produce the idea. Thought preexists the idea as it does language. Its own act is to know what is, and it only uses language in order to signify it.

5

On the Customs of Language

Thought, trying to express itself, faces the initial question: In what way shall we begin?

But what does it mean to begin when it is a question of thought? A beginning only has meaning in space or in a spatialized time from which one has previously eliminated all duration. Now, thought is neither in the one nor in the other, and speech itself, if it unfolds in time, is not situated in space. The speaker is a solid in space, but his speech itself is only localizable there after the fashion of a sound wave divested of stable substance. It abolishes itself in time to the extent that it is said.

Here begins the difficulty of knowing in what way to begin in order to explain the difficulty of beginning.

I. The Loneliness of Fantasio

The status of speaker and listener, which we all are alternatively and at times even at the same time, is a phenomenon so familiar that we do not pay any attention to it. One speaks and one listens as one breathes. It is only when one is hindered from doing the one or the other that attention is aroused. The simple possibility of communication between subjects presents problems no less embarrassing and, without doubt, even insoluble.

I indulge myself by citing in support of this assertion several lines of Musset, which I trust will bring pleasure to those rereading them. Fantasio speaks:

> If I could only get out of my skin for an hour or two! If I could be that man who goes past!
>
> That seems difficult to me.
>
> That man who is passing is charming. Note: What fine silk

80

breeches! What fine red flowers on his waistcoat! The showy charms on his watchchain bang against his belly in opposition to the tails of his coat, which flutter against his calves. I am sure that that man has in his head a thousand ideas which are absolutely foreign to me: his essence is particular to him. Alas! Everything that men say to each other is of a kind. The ideas that they exchange are almost always the same in every conversation. But in the interior of each of these isolated machines what recesses, what secret compartments! Each bears within himself a complete world, an unknown world which comes to birth and dies in silence! What lonely places all these human bodies are!

There are many ideas in this little masterpiece. I wish to dwell on only one of them: each human body shelters and takes about with it a mind [pensée] which we imagine lodged in it and which is not directly accessible to us. One is only aware of oneself and one's own thought [pensée]. The always imperfect communication which can be established between two human bodies can only be accomplished through language, or, more exactly, by that which is incorporeal in language itself, which is the meaning.

At first sight that appears completely extraordinary, but a little reflection shows that this paradoxical situation, this singular connection, explains a rightful necessity. Bodies are not able to communicate because, having *partes extra partes* like the space they occupy, one of them could not coincide with the other without destroying itself or destroying the other. It is therefore necessary a priori that in order for two distinct subjects to communicate, they should do so on the plane of immateriality.

But this does not take us very far, for the problem immediately presents itself: How can bodies, which only communicate by the corporeal, that is, by language, at the same time and by that very means have access to the plane of the immaterial? The ingenious Stoic theory of "incorporeals" [incorporels] which were made of extremely subtle and fine material only poorly satisfied the imagination because incorporeality in this instance did not exclude materiality. Here one comes up against, then, what indeed appears to be the irreducible fact, however disconcerting it may be, of the intelligible borne by the material and the sensible. But this paradoxical fact reappears at each moment of our investigation.

Good Professor Egger, master at the Sorbonne about 1906–1908, had none of the Fantasio in him. His drawn visage and his speech seemed sorrowful to us, but he was intensely serious, and as in those times students loved their professors, because they devoted themselves to introducing the young to the life of the mind, we had organized a sort of alternating attendance so that the master would never find himself without some students. Egger started off by a sort of *de divisione naturae* which divided nature into three parts: the self, the not-self, and what he called the not-not-self. By the last he meant truth, which is not self since it is common to all minds, and which is not nevertheless the not-self, since I must make it mine in order to possess it. Defining the self by means of consciousness, he observed that each self is at one and the same time incapable of penetrating others and of being penetrated by them, from which he inferred a law which he called, with a shade of metaphysical respect, *the law of closed consciousnesses.*

Later on I had to rediscover this same law, set forth by the Fathers of the Church and some Scholastic theologians as a simple fact. Persuaded that God alone "probes the reins and hearts," all the theologians that I have consulted on the matter agree in saying that if one excepts supernatural and strictly miraculous cases, no person can read the thoughts of another person. It is frequently perplexing to try to know what "goes on in someone else's head," someone whose thoughts one cannot guess, although in other respects one may know him well. "A penny for your thought" (sic) translates well enough that perplexity, but this common experience receives its doctrinal justification from a teacher as thoughtful as Thomas Aquinas. The soul of Fantasio's coarse man is impenetrable even to the angels. In fact, says the Angelic Doctor, "What is proper to God does not belong to the angels. But it is proper to God to read the secrets of hearts, according to *Jer.* xvii.9: *The heart is perverse above all things, and unsearchable; who can know it? I am the Lord, who searches the heart.* Therefore angels do not know the secrets of hearts."[a] Humans as well as angels can know the thoughts of other humans by the effects that these thoughts produce, that is to say, beyond language, the expressions of the face, acts, deeds. Thomas even reckons that physicians can surmise certain affections of the mind by variations in the pulse. More perspicacious than we, angels and demons know how to read these signs much better than we do, but God alone can directly read human thoughts and sentiments.

The reasons alleged by Thomas Aquinas in support of his conclusion, notably in the *Summa theologiae,* I, 57, 4, do not appease our curiosity. The main one of them is that the thoughts of man depend on his will, and his will being free to use its knowledge at its discretion, one must say, with the Apostle (I Cor. 2:11): *the depths of a man can only be known by his own spirit.* The argument allows us to understand why, even if the thought of man were transparent to the angels or to other men, one still could not know its movements in advance; but one would love to know the reason of this simple natural opacity of thought which prevents Fantasio not only from being the coarse man who passes but simply from divining what he is thinking. The sole reason alleged by Thomas in order to explain this physical impediment is the grossness of the body: *propter grossitiem corporis.* This obstacle will disappear after the resurrection of the body. There remains then only the contrasting obstacle presented by the inalienable and unpredictable liberty of every intellectual substance. For the risen body, as is already the case for the angels themselves, thoughts will be knowable only on the condition that they communicate themselves in a language appropriate to the new condition of man. For the present the gross man is protected against the curiosity of Fantasio by his very grossness [*materialité*]. His mind is impenetrable to all other minds behind that corporeal opacity which protects it. But even if one concedes this point to Thomas Aquinas, as one must, one remains impotent to conceive the spiritual other than as the material with zero dimensions. One cannot represent to oneself that of which one speaks. Nevertheless, without an intelligible reality of this sort words would not have meaning; one could not speak.

To the extent that linguists have more resolutely faced the disconcerting nature of the object of their science, some new perspectives have opened up. The major interest of these perspectives is that they are revealed to us by scholars scrutinizing language itself and that without them the philosophers would never perhaps have perceived them. Among the discoveries of this sort we have already noted that of Edward Sapir: there is no organ proper to speech [*langage*]. One can add to it that more recent [formulation] of Emile Benveniste on certain remarkable characteristics of linguistic time.

Benveniste's demonstration is so closely woven that one is tempted to refer directly to the essay of the eminent linguist on "Language and Human Experience." This brief and substantial essay, moreover, overlaps our problem, and we will retain here only particularly instructive points touching the metaphysical element of language. Far from compromising this scholar in our expeditions into the intelligible world, we shall allow him to speak as the voice of positive science describing the reality of language, disconcerting perhaps, but such as it is. Our conclusions on this point are binding only on us.

The "law of closed consciousness" already makes it difficult to conceive how a language at least in part material can make intelligible exchanges possible. But even after admitting this intermediary, one is disconcerted by the nature of its functioning.

Our linguist begins by distinguishing three distinct senses of the word "time." The *physical time* of the world, which is "a uniform, infinite, linear continuum, segmentable at will," and to which there is opposed, in each individual, the variable duration following the personal rhythm of his in-

terior life. One must distinguish from this *chronological time* the continuity conceived by thought in order to arrange therein events in series,
for these are not time; "they are *in* time. Everything is in time, except time
itself."[1] Of this time, as of physical time, there exists a twofold account,
the one objective, which is the socialized time of the calendar, the other
subjective, in which we situate ourselves and our own history by connecting them to references in this same calendar.

We come then to the third sort of time, which is *linguistic time.* This
is another time, for although it bears the same name as the two others,
it is something else. "It is one thing to situate an event in chronological
time," let us say to verify an historical date, as we do chronologically; "but
it is something else to insert it into language's [*langue*] time," let us say
to affirm something as past or future. This operation is of a totally different sort, for in order to situate an event according to the calendar of
chronological time, as my own birth, I must make reference to some initial
moment which is the time zero of the computation: the birth of Christ
or of Buddha, or the year one of the hegira. But linguistic time is tied to
the exercise of speech [*parole*] and arranges itself "as a function of discourse." The linguistic past, the linguistic future, are that of which I speak
as past or as future. Now, as Emile Benveniste strongly notes, this time
has its center, "a generative and axial center at one and the same time" (that
from which I situate the past as past and the future as future), which is
situated in the *present* of the act of speech [*parole*]. Since this linguistic
time is organically tied to the exercise of speech [*parole*], and since each
time that speech [*parole*] is exercised, the moment of its exercise is the present, it follows that "in reality language only has at its disposition one single
temporal expression, the present," which in linguistic time consists in "the
coincidence of the event and the discourse."[2] The present of actual discourse plays, in linguistic time, an axial role analogous to those events which
provide landmarks for the calendar of chronological time. This is indeed
why in language the present tenses are generally taken for granted (because it is in the present that one speaks), whereas past or future tenses
are always explicit and situated as "points seen behind or ahead *from the
present.*" Summing up, "the only tense inherent in language [*langue*] is the
axial present of the discourse." One would not know how to shift this axis
in order to refer to it in the past or the future: "One cannot even imagine
what would become of a language [*langue*] if the point of departure for
the disposition of times should not coincide with the linguistic present and
if the temporal axis should be itself a variable of time."

The idea of the linguistic present, profoundly original and true as
it appears to me, impossible by definition to localize in some division of
chronological time "because it admits of all of them and invokes none,"

finds its confirmation in the objective analysis of language itself. Here we will leave to the reader the responsibility of informing himself about our linguist and pass directly to an aspect of linguistic temporality which is presented to us as particularly remarkable, "the manner in which it inserts itself into the process of communication."

Here are two interlocutors, Fantasio and the gross man with whom he has finally engaged in conversation. Each of them speaks in his own present, in reference to which he situates his own past and his own future, and nevertheless they understand each other as if the linguistic time of the one were the same as that of the other. Here I beg to let the words of Emile Benveniste speak for themselves. I quote an entire page, which the reader will recognize it is impossible to amend. It was born a classic:

> We have indicated the emergence of linguistic time in the bosom of the immediacy of the discourse which contains it potentially and actualizes it in fact. But the act of speech is necessarily individual. The specific instance from which the present results is novel each time. Consequently, linguistic temporality must realize itself in the intrapersonal universe of the speaker as an irremediably subjective experience and one that is impossible to transmit. If I tell what "happened to me," the past to which I refer is only defined by reference to the present of my act of speech. But since the act of speech arises from out of me, and since no one else can speak through my mouth any more than they can see through my eyes or experience what I sense, it is to me alone that this "time" relates itself and it is by my experience alone that it will be limited.
>
> But the reasoning is faulty. Something singular, very simple, and infinitely important is produced, which accomplishes that which appears logically impossible. The temporality which is mine when it orders my discourse is directly accepted as his by my interlocutor. My "today" becomes his "today," although he may not have found it himself in his own discourse, and my "yesterday" becomes his "yesterday." Reciprocally, when he speaks in response, I, becoming the hearer, convert his temporality into mine.
>
> Such appears to be the condition of intelligibility of language [langage], revealed through language. It consists in this, that the temporality of the speaker, literally foreign and inaccessible to the hearer, is identified by the latter as that temporality which informs his own speech when he in turn becomes the speaker. Both thus find themselves brought into accord upon the same wavelength. The time of the discourse is neither led into divisions of chronological time nor locked up in a solipsistic subjectivity. It functions as a factor of in-

tersubjectivity, the unipersonal which it ought to be making it omni-personal. The condition of intersubjectivity alone allows linguistic communication.[3]

Let us first note the quite rare spectacle of a linguist whom language has not ceased to intrigue, for everything in language interests linguists, but it takes a lot to surprise them. Let us next mention specifically that this remarkable page is untouched by any philosophy. The condition of the intelligibility of language, which with good right astonishes the linguist, is "revealed through language [langage]" to him. It is a matter of scientific observation, neither more nor less. But one must add further that if "wonder is the beginning of philosophy," the discovery made by Emile Benveniste provides an exemplary case of what I have called elsewhere the occasion ceaselessly offered by science to the philosopher of moving on to a metaphysical critique of positive knowledge. This exercise, which no one is obliged to indulge in, does not involve science itself at all, whose proper function is to speak of reality such as it finds it. When this reality is something "singular, quite simple, and infinitely important . . . which does the seemingly impossible," the moment has come for the philosopher to philosophize.

This time, as is usual, the philosopher's reflection will not lead him very far. In any case, it will not lead him to add anything at all to science as science, not one iota; but it will assist him at least to fix his attention sometimes on this transphysical order with a curiosity which haunts him even though he knows himself incapable of truly penetrating it.

What is there that is singular and worth noting in the fact which we have described? Essentially this: that two physically distinct subjects, each endowed with speech [parole] and each incapable of speaking otherwise than in his own present, are nevertheless capable of meeting in a temporality which is common to them. The extension of the phenomenon moreover is unlimited in time as in space. When I read Plato and he brings Socrates on the stage, the present, the past, and the future of the Platonic discourse become those of the discourse of Socrates, and at a distance of twenty-four centuries they become mine. In linguistic time I become a contemporary of Plato's Socrates, who invites me to sit down with him in the shade of a sycamore or next to the Ilissus. I am in the same time as he from the moment that I accept his invitation.

A pluri-personal temporality in the present—if the present is tied to the actual existence, hic et nunc, of the subject who exercises the act of speech—suggests the existence of an order of intelligibility in which distinct subjects can participate together. For this remarkable communication to be conceivable it is necessary that, despite the materiality of speech, the exchange should take place outside of space. The meaning of the word escapes servitude to space, for it is an act of thought, and thought exists, but in a literal sense *it has no place*. This is only, as is said, a mental perspective, but every truth is such. If one thinks about it, it was inevitable that language should lead us back once more to the threshold of the immaterial and of the meta-physical. Everything leads to it: biology as soon as it admits that there are living forms; noetics and epistemology as soon as they reflect upon the conditions required, by the object known as well as by the subject knowing, in order that science might be possible; linguistics itself as soon as one accepts language in its relations with the understanding, of which it is at one and the same time the body and the means of exchange. It is difficult not to recognize the presence of metaphysics, even if one refuses to engage in it.

II. Ideas in Search of Words and Vice Versa

Having cleared the obstacle that bodies present to the communication of minds, there remains one other, interior to language itself: its duality. Thought and its expression are not of the same nature. Language is for thought a foreign body to which it has a hard time accommodating itself. Speech [*parole*] has in time, chronologically let us say, a beginning and an end: the professor's lesson will begin at ten o'clock and will finish at eleven. But the thought that his speech formulates neither begins nor ends with the lesson, which bathes in it, so to speak, and which thought flows over on all sides. With respect to the written word, manuscript or printed, it visibly has a beginning and an end, but it only translates into material signs distributed upon the surface of a certain number of pages, a thought which itself does not occupy any surface and consequently has neither a beginning nor a middle nor an end. The well-known embarrassment of the writer who "does not know where to begin" results from the fact that thought has no beginning which one could cause to coincide with that of the written word. In whatever fashion he decides to begin, the writer could begin otherwise.

The Divine Word itself has no beginning and is not a beginning. It was in the Beginning, which itself is without beginning. Creatures have had a beginning; they began when He willed them, because, not being Being itself, they must indeed begin to be, in whatever manner that may be. Leibniz, who wants to know at least why they began in this way rather than otherwise, is firm in the contention that the perfection of God would not allow Him to proceed in any other fashion than in the best way possible; but Thomas Aquinas knows that, creating something finite, an infinite God could freely create innumerable different universes, all good and each beginning moreover in a different manner. God made everything by His Word, but His capacity allows of His having freely *spoken* creation, whether from all eternity or in a temporal duration other than that which in fact He has assigned it. God could even have begun otherwise, in time, a universe which would be nevertheless substantially the same. We find reasons for what He has done; we would find others in order to justify Him had He acted otherwise, quite certain that, by whatever manner, what God makes is just and wise. There are some necessities consequent upon His will; there are no antecedent necessities.

When thought undertakes to express itself, it could begin otherwise than it does without a change of its nature or even of its meaning. Wishing to say something, the only thing that it appears reluctant to do is to begin with that thing and to restrict itself to it. It is on the contrary a common experience to search for a beginning so lofty or remote that one ends by losing from view the point that one intended to introduce. It is not only in historical or romantic narratives that one must often remind the writer to "begin at the beginning"; the rational and dialectical exposition of any speculative thesis whatsoever seems almost always to require more or less lengthy preparations of the writer. The advice to begin *in medias res* [in the middle of things] is rarely followed, but it is perhaps only rarely possible to do so. For lack of having been forewarned of what is going to be said to him, the reader or the auditor does not notice it at the moment when it is said to him. He does not know what it is that is being said to him. The art of "preparing the reader" or the auditor is that of not beginning with the essential. It is based on the appropriate feeling that, in any fashion, what one sets out to say is not, in fact, a beginning.

One must nevertheless begin somewhere or, as is said, with an initial point. Now every point is the origin of a possible line. The initial enunciation which is "the point of departure" becomes then the origin of a possible linear order, which cannot exist under this form in thought prior to language, that is to say, when not yet spoken. Normally no one concerns himself with shaping his own thought. It is only when pressed by the need to make things explicit in order to justify or to convince that one has recourse to explicit and technically well-ordered reasoning. Then consequently, as is the case with the formal syllogism, one sees linearly ordered premises and a conclusion appear; but for the thought which forms this syllogism the conclusion is already present in the premises, even supposing that it does not engender them. If it is a question of thought left to itself, there are neither premises which precede or conclusions which follow. Thought not yet verbalized knows nothing of what we call order or disorder, for the absence of order is not a shortcoming to it. Less still is it a dis-order.

Thought in its normal state remains on this side of order and disorder, which only manifest themselves at the moment when, in order to know itself what it thinks, thought materializes the intelligible in speaking it.

There is a reason why what one decides to say initially should be so rarely that with which thought intends to end. Discourse is as justificative as it is enunciative. To speak and to affirm are the same thing, denying, moreover, being another manner of affirming. Now, affirmative discourse is without efficacy if the affirmation is not accompanied by its justifications. These being naturally other than the affirmation itself (unless this is tautological or its justification circular), we must inevitably look elsewhere for the justification of what is said. There is hardly any lesson whose content could not be summed up in several phrases. When one asks an author of an article to sum it up in several lines, he begins by declaring that it is impossible. But he does it, moreover not without the justified sentiment that presented thus naked, the message will not reach its destination. This is because what it wishes to communicate is not *one* idea. The idea is only itself when tied to others from which it is inseparable and of which it often is even composed as much as it contributes to composing. Rather than to a linear order, thought could be compared, though still grossly, to a sort of cellular tissue where that which is at present nucleus could at any moment become extended on a cylindrical axis, or inversely. What we call our ideas only exist as permanent communications when connected with other ideas, each of which is equally such. This is why everything takes place as if it were in fact impossible for the speaker to formulate his thought directly and immediately. Instead of beginning with it and remaining there, he never believes he has gone far enough in search of the necessary preparations, each of these dividing in its turn into so many elements that the speaker or the writer often asks himself when he is really going to begin.

This is also why to begin is not always "to broach the subject." How many speakers lose ten minutes in explaining how it will be difficult for them to treat in sixty minutes the immense subject on which they have agreed to speak! One reproaches certain writers, as certain speakers, with only coming so tardily to their subject. The fault would be less common if the nature of thought were not responsible for it, for thought is aware of undertaking a task at once impossible and necessary in trying to formulate itself in words. Fundamentally, what thought sets itself to say it will never say. At least it resigns itself with ill grace to recognize, at the end of its discourse, that this poor thing written or said was perhaps all that it had to say. So little! But thought does not truly resign itself, and to convince itself to the contrary, it begins again. The speaker resembles that American manufacturer of beauty products who promises to give his purchasers by means of his makeup a "natural" complexion and, in order to prove his point, prints a photograph of some young beauty such as she is "away from the lens" (*such as she looks away from the camera*) (sic). To photograph someone away from the camera is a contradictory enterprise, but it illustrates well enough the desire which motivates thought to try to tell itself what it is in itself when it is not said: *away from speech.*

It would be prudent to avoid trespassing on the domain of the literary critic, but perhaps one could find confirmation of these views in the reflections of certain writers who appear particularly lucid concerning the nature of their art. It is moreover not so extraordinary that as a result of enduring, art should become, at least with certain of its representatives, more and more conscious of what it is. We shall content ourselves here with citing the profound remark of Alain Robbe-Grillet, at the end of the introduction which he wrote for his book of literary theory, *Pour un nouveau roman:* "When one asks (of the novelist) why he wrote his book, he has but one response: 'It is in order to know why I had the desire to write it.'" In the same fashion also the painter paints his picture in order to know why he had the desire to paint it, and man speaks in order to know why he had the desire to speak.

At grips with this difficulty, the writer or the speaker look for a way out by beginning with some idea or other which they know, or believe they know, will be absolutely necessary to formulate in order to arrive at their objective. But the end itself is what they cannot be sure of in advance. To know how to end is at least as difficult as to know how to begin. One senses it particularly in the painful, at times interminable, efforts of the author who "searches for his conclusion." The fact is that between his beginning and his end he has introduced many intermediary ideas no one of which was independent of the others nor isolable as *one* idea. However he begins, he risks appearing abrupt, for it would have been necessary to provide other beginnings before it in order to "begin at the beginning." One can understand thus the American custom, so baffling to Latin minds, of beginning some discourses by telling one or two (or three) anecdotes, preferably humorous, but without any connection, so far as one can see, either among themselves or with the subject of the proposed discourse. In order to avoid the arbitrariness of all real beginnings, a violence done at one and the same time to the hearer, the speaker, and the thought which he wishes to express, the speaker begins by a refusal to begin, right till the moment when it is indeed necessary to resign himself to doing so: And now to be serious. . . (sic). One has at least deadened the shock.

It does not seem that we have discovered any simple procedure to palliate the difficulty of knowing how to conclude. No more than in the former case does the idea exist separately, and the desire to get ready for it engages the speaker in more or less lengthy circuits wherein the principal idea runs the risk of being lost. Thus it sometimes happens that the writer finishes his work without having succeeded in saying what he set out initially to signify. It is not necessarily that he lost sight of it, but rather that it was not truly what he wanted to say. In such cases everything happens as if that "idea at the back of the head" slipped away each time it was at the point of being said. Some other word comes then to insert itself in the place that this thought ought to occupy. Its turn never comes, and not unreasonably, for this thought seeks to be formulated for itself alone and in some way in total isolation, although the notion of such an idea is contradictory. Refusing even to allow itself to be introduced onto the stage, it never makes an appearance. The more important an idea is, the more reluctant it is in fact to allow itself to be uttered separately, detached from the simul-totality at the heart of which alone it has life, meaning, and truth. In the same way as, with Plotinus, the *Nous* appeared to us as being at one and the same time the totality of intelligibles and desirous of remaining such without separating itself from the One, the thought which expresses itself wants to be able to do so without separating itself from the intelligibles that it enunciates or losing its own unity. The writer who concludes without having finally said what he intended to say is not perhaps responsible for his impasse. If it is truly an impasse, he simply finds himself at grips with one among those ideas which are dear to him, which would only feel themselves intact were it possible to set them forth in a sort of solitude. They feel fatally compromised by the sole fact of being enunciated in their place in a discourse. They have no place, not being delimitable by anything else. One cuts them out of thought in the process of uttering them, their intelligible vitality there being replaced by the flux of the discourse. In fact, moreover, since there is no resemblance between the meaning and the sounds which signify it, it is when the meaning is important that thought no longer recognizes itself in sound. It is impossible that this should be the case for whatever is not said; writing and speech [*parole*] only allow for the expression of a part of a word at a time. Thought not yet expressed is already there; thought already expressed is still there because the total thought (if the expression makes any sense) is always present to itself. It refuses to recognize itself in that which detaches itself from it, just as an animal refuses to recognize itself in its stillborn offspring.

The consequence of this is that speech [*parole*] is almost always the result of a compromise between what one says and what one set oneself to say, or, rather, what one thought that one set out to say. This cannot be said better than Andre Breton has done in the *Second Surrealist Manifesto*, in a passage in which he pertinently notes that the problem is not only of surrealist interest. "No one, in expressing himself, can do more than to come to terms with a possibility of quite obscure conciliation between what he knows he has said and that which, on the same subject, he did not know he has said, but has said nevertheless." To which he adds: "The most rigorous thought is incapable of doing without this assistance, which is nevertheless so undesirable from the point of view of rigor. There is a total torpedoing of the idea at the heart of the sentence which enunciates it, even indeed if that sentence should be clear of all charming liberty taken with its meaning." Beyond all literary doctrine the observation is in fact true, of no matter what slightly sustained effort to form a series of propositions charged with the intelligible meaning. It is the profound thought of the speaking subject who knows what he really wants to say and, finally, says it.

III. A Worthy Project

One finds among the writings of Ralph Waldo Emerson an essay whose title has always seemed to me so beautiful as to incite envy: "Natural History of Intellect." One understands how this magnificent project could have seduced the imagination of the great meditator of Concord, at a time when that charming little village was still only a residential town for the use of middle-class men who had become enamoured of a nature which was not too distant from it. But Emerson imagined then that a natural history of intellect could consist in an "enumeration of its laws and its powers," similar to the description of the parts and the laws of the human body which he had become familiar with in London and Paris in 1850 through some scholarly naturalists. Why not, he asked himself? Since these powers and laws are also biological facts within the jurisdiction of natural history, it ought not to be impossible to enumerate and record them.[3a]

What particularly struck Emerson was the relationship of the life of the intellect with natural life, above all with that of vegetables. The intellect appeared to him to be a sort of plant still more than an animal. "The idea of vegetation is irresistible when one considers mental activity," he said in his long essay. "Man resembles a superior plant." The strong feeling that he had for this analogy caused him to rediscover "in mental activity, germination, growth, progress, interbreeding, withering, parasites, briefly, all the accidents which mark the life of the plant."[3b] "In fact, striking analogies exist between the birth, growth, and intellectual assimilation of ideas or works and those activities of the plant which nourishes and augments itself by means of all that it can assimilate. We say that the book has the thrust of its author."[3c]

All that is true. There is probably no one who has not been struck by the numerous and profound analogies between the biology of living bodies and that of minds, but when one tries to be more precise about the facts, they elude us. Today we are better informed about the embryology of animals and the biology of plants than were people in Emerson's time, but the embryology of works of the mind remains much less well known to us than that of animals. This is not for lack of trying. We have accumulated the research of literary history, collected rough drafts, compared successive redactions, as if the discontinuity between two redactions of the same work were not of the same nature as that which separates two different works. In fact, they are different works. The most meticulous research of this sort feels itself disarmed, without any real entrance into the subject.

A biologist as candid as Claude Bernard was could moreover tell us why. We search for the secrets of literary production when those of animal life have not yet been pried loose. Creation does not have any secrets, of any order; it is itself one. In his *Leçons sur les phénomènes de la vie communs aux animaux et aux vegetaux*[4] Claude Bernard has jealously refused admission to his general biology to the notions of final cause and of life. For him "determinism is the only possible scientific philosophy"; yet he also teaches that if biochemical explanation is the only one that has scientific value, it explains everything about living beings except their existence. We understand by that, not that such explanation does not explain life, which is a fact taken for granted, but that there should be specifically distinct and organized *living beings*. For these are not the same things. "It is important," says Claude Bernard at the beginning of the eighth lesson of his course, "as we have already said, to distinguish matter from form." Form is not explicable apart from matter. Determinism is absolute in physiology as it is in all the experimental sciences, but it comes to a standstill at the threshold of the morphology of living beings. If it can be applied there, we do not know how. The seat of determinism, protoplasm, or whatever one is to call living matter "is a causal agent [*est actif*] as regards substance and not as regards form and figure" (p. 202). The existence of organic living beings supposes that a form has joined itself to this matter. The appearance of a living thing has as essential condition the chemical synthesis of protoplasm, but in order for it to be a particular sort of being, it is necessary that to this chemical synthesis there should be added a *morphological* synthesis which shapes this protoplasm. Faithful to his ideal of scientific knowledge, Claude Bernard sees in this constitution of organic plant or animal forms "so to say, an epiphenomenon, a dependent fact [*un fait consécutif*] . . . in a word, a complexification of the essential phenomenon" (p. 203). But he does not always abide by this.

How this simple "complexification" allows for the passage from the chemical to the living, from the material to the formal, Claude Bernard explicitly claims not to know; but he holds on to the fact: In whatever manner the passage from *monomorphic* protoplasmic life to the polymorphic and structured life of living beings is brought about, it constitutes a creation. Living matter is not a living being; it is bare life, "life without special being." The living being is *shaped protoplasm*; it has a characteristic form. . . . The *form* of life is independent of the essential *agent* of the protoplasm, since the latter remains the same through numberless morphological changes. Form could not therefore be a consequence of the nature of living matter" (p. 293). This complexification which is the passage of substance to being, from brute matter to formal matter, this "morphological synthesis," in a word, is then a sort of creation.

Bernard at least understands by this word the apparition of an order of realities which are not explained by antecedent material conditions alone, although no theology enters into the thought of the scholar. The movement in question remains inexplicable to us: "Today we separate physiology from zoology because we separate living *phenomenology* from *morphology*. Living morphology we can scarcely contemplate, since its essential factor, heredity, is not an element which is within our power . . ." (p. 342). We have it a bit more in our power today than it was in Claude Bernard's time, but we are not always able to act on it except by taking for granted that it exists. Taking up again in the first lesson on the phenomena of life what he had said as early as 1865 in his *Introduction to the Study of Experimental Medicine* (p. 161) [French edition], our biologist declares without evasion: "The organic is created; it is so from the point of view of its structure, its form, the properties it manifests. . . . I shall recall on this subject the formula which I have voiced for a long time: *Life, it is creation*" (p. 40).[4a]

It is not chronologically likely that Emerson could have heard Claude Bernard in Paris about 1850. That is a pity, for he was ripe for understanding him. Perhaps this teaching would have suggested to him doubts, however, about the possibility of a natural history of the intellect, for if one calls creation every apparition of the new that cannot be explained completely from what preceded it, *noology* is still much more manifestly the domain of an incessant creative activity than either botany or even zoology are.

The embryology of literary works seems to be much less definite than that of animals. One does not bow to the problem of the birth of such work without feeling a sort of vertigo. The slow maturation which precedes the expression of the thought escapes direct observation. Everything that one knows of the idea — even if it is one of those that a poet called "*idées-maitresses*," that is to say, those ideas which direct and organize others — is that it is subject to frequent eclipses during which it undergoes modifications, a ripening which changes it without our knowledge. To the extent that it still is not mature, it returns to visit consciousness at more or less lengthy intervals. This is because it has not yet found its best formulation, or that it still lacks the intelligible supports necessary to present itself as fully warranted.

Often the germ of a new [intellectual] work sleeps for years without becoming aware of its own fecundity. There is consequently the danger that the point of maturity of the idea, that at which it is ripe for execution, passes unobserved. Certain writers thus carry about within them works which never go beyond the realm of dreams; but occasionally others also do so, in such a manner and on so many occasions already completed in their minds, that to write them would be a task as wearisome as to recopy them. They do not have the courage to inflict such a distasteful task upon themselves.

The act of writing is, however, the only way of finishing off a work, as the act of speaking [*l'acte de parole*] is the only way of finishing off a thought. This is so, provisionally at least, for bringing an idea to a conclusion in a work is not to have finished with that idea, and to speak it does not make rephrasing it under the guise of renewing it, correcting it, or retracting it, impossible. At least one is not absolutely sure of saying something until after having said it. It even is necessary to have said it in order to perceive that it was not exactly what one proposed to say. The only thing left to do then is to start out again from the thought yet unexpressed in the hope of obtaining from it finally the revelation of what it is.

The false trails are numerous. One gets involved with one of them each time that one yields to the temptation to express a thought for what it is in itself instead of in terms of the ultimate purpose toward which the entire effort one is engaged in ought to tend. But what is this purpose? And is not a lucky chance lost in refusing the temptation of what is perhaps only an apparent risk? There is no rule through which we may be assured. The pleasure of allowing the pen to run by itself, the reins loose on its neck, is initially accompanied with the feeling of liberation which one always feels when an impediment is removed. Lines readily follow lines, page flows into page. But this pleasure is soon accompanied by a difficulty: one has "lost the thread of one's ideas," one "doesn't know anymore what one wanted to say." There is peace of mind only in the feeling, illusory as it may be, that what one comes to say expresses at least something of that which one wanted to be said. But the intellect creates the thread of ideas; it does not follow it. It is through it that their order exists.

Many current facts drawn from direct observation confirm the transcendence of thought over speech. We readily speak of "free thought" and of "free speech," and to the extent that these formulations have any meaning, it is all one. But the initiatory power which reverts to thought is visibly affirmed in the experience of the writer. We think of the near impossibility of the expressed thought following the identical course twice. We know how difficult it is for the speaker exactly to repeat himself and how difficult it is for the writer to recopy his own text with literal fidelity. The ordinary copyist need provide no effort other than the attention necessary to follow the text to be copied. But the copyist of his own text finds himself once more at grips with the possibility that, in writing it, he must at every moment write it in a different way. The possible choices are so numerous and tempting (by virtue of the sole fact that they are possible) that an effort is necessary to bar the way to them. The effort to remain faithful to his first wording is not only painful in itself but is against nature. Not to compel oneself at this point, however, is to expose oneself to several risks, for giving in to the temptation to alter a text from its first formulation, or simply from a subsequent redaction, often involves more important consequences than one had foreseen. To change any part whatsoever of a coherent discourse ordinarily necessitates recasting the entire discourse. The reason for this is that the mind that chooses a new expression of its thought is not any more the author of the preceding expression. The consequence of proposing to oneself simply to say something better is that one says something else. This is why to rewrite an earlier work is a thankless task, and generally one with little fruit. At any rate it is easier to write it anew.

If one nevertheless holds to this project, some interesting phenomena are produced. In rewriting a work the writer naturally tries to conserve, in the new redaction, as many fragments as possible from the first. But some whole passages which he hoped at first to be able to conserve refuse to fit into the texture of the new discourse. They are eliminated one after another, as a living organism rejects grafts taken from another organism. Innumerable and readily observable facts of this kind ought to enter into a natural history of the intellect, a magnificent title for a book which doubtless will never be written.[5]

It is natural that writers, those artisans for whom language is at one and the same time the material on which they work and the utensil with which they work, should show themselves particularly sensible to the nature of the connections that it maintains with thought. Two recent literary movements, *Dada* and *Surrealism*, have directly descended from a quite extended reflection on the nature of language.[6]

The two movements have had in common the concern maximally

to exploit the resources of the unconscious and to force language in some way to set free its riches. From the point of view which is ours here, it is interesting to note that language appears to them to be a reality in itself, endowed with its own existence and functioning according to its own nature independently of all rational and logical rules or necessities. "The Dadas," Jacques Rivière wrote in 1920, "no longer consider words except as accidents; they let them cause themselves." They only had confidence in the spontaneity of this production, moreover, on the condition that the verbal eruption should be free from all syntax. On the other hand, their deliberate decision to free speech from all rational or simply conventional impediment added, in a quite unexpected manner, to the certainty that to place confidence thus in language in its raw state was the most certain manner of allowing thought to express itself directly such as it is. Since it is inevitable, although dangerous, to expound in order to articulate such a fleeting position, one could perhaps say that Dada wanted to eliminate from language all conventional structures (grammar, logic) which interposed themselves between pure thought and its verbal expression. The first purpose of the movement was not, therefore, in any way hostile to thought. On the contrary, the reason why it wanted to allow to language its complete freedom is that, however one should say it, it is impossible to speak in order to say nothing once all constraints are removed. "It is impossible for man to say something which makes no sense."[7]

This idea was to find its complete development with the deliberate exploitation of automatic writing such as André Breton practiced it in the first years of surrealism. According to Breton himself, "surrealism, insofar as it is an organized movement, came to birth in a widespread operation on language."[8] What the movement proposed was not at first literary and aesthetic; it was a concern to bring about the operation which we ourselves have said above was the temptation of every mind reflecting upon the use it makes of speech. "There has not been enough insistence upon the meaning and full significance of the process which tended to restore language to its true life, or . . . to bring us back with a leap to the birth of the signifier."[9]

One might doubt that automatic writing would be a good springboard for making this leap. The postulate that governs the process, that the rational disciplines of language have the result of alienating it from thought and that their elimination facilitates the leap which allows the subject speaking to reunite itself directly with the source of its speech, is, to say the least, adventurous. Automatic writing appears above all to free the automatic functions of language and, in suppressing the controls which the judgment of reason exercises upon them, to submit thought to random mechanical associations analogous to those of which dreams are made when we have not yet rationalized them in the process of describing them after our return to the waking state. But it is not our business to criticize surrealism; we wish rather to be instructed by it in putting to profit the exceptionally lucid experiments it conducted concerning the nature of language. Speaking of "torpedoing the idea" by the sentence that enunciates it, an image which grips us by its very realism, Breton adds: "Dadaism had above all wished to draw attention to this torpedoing."[10] If there can be doubt about the efficacity of the method, the intention is not doubtful. Fostered by "pure psychic automatism," Breton's pursuit of the initial intention of Dada has been haunted by the concern of attaining to "a source which it is only a question of exploring adequately, and whose course one could not claim to direct without being assured of seeing the source immediately dry up."[11]

The deliberate choice of the name "surrealism," with its transcendental resonances, is explained moreover by the desire to display the fact that this reference to something beyond the physically real was essential to the movement. In order not to appear to force his thought, we shall recall the literal words of André Breton in the *Manifesto of Surrealism* (1924), wherein, after having recalled the common design of Phillippe Soupault and himself of assuring the transcendence of "pure thought" over the material element of language, he added: ["More appropriately still, we could probably have taken over the word SUPERNATURALISM employed by Gerard de Nerval in his dedication to the *Filles de feu*." In a footnote to this passage Breton adds: "And also by Thomas Carlyle in *Sartor Resartus* ([Book III] Chapter VIII, 'Natural Supernaturalism',), 1833–34."[11a] Breton professed to be an atheist, but when it came to pure thought, he did not hesitate to speak the language of grace. Thus, in his preface to the reprint (1929) of the first *Manifesto of Surrealism* (1924) Breton speaks of the "principle of an activity" which never has disappointed [deceived] him" and in which he has more confidence than ever because, he says, "it alone is the dispensatrix, albeit at intervals well-spaced out one from the other, of transfiguring rays of a grace I persist in comparing in all respects to divine grace" [p. xi].

There we have, then, the conscience of Breton at rest. The honor of his atheism is safe, and he can still act on it. The "principle of that activity" is not "that muse which goes by the name of grace." But everything happens as if it were a grace. The consequences of grace are produced, for what Breton calls here "the passive life of intelligence" strangely resembles the state of spiritual passivity well known to the mystics; and even if it is only a matter of the transcendence of nature by nature, that to which we have access through rejoining the source of language is no less authentic for it. Certain words of Breton inspire some uncertainty about the solidity of his naturalism: "A day will come when one will no longer be permitted to use it cavalierly, as we have done, with these palpable proofs of an existence other than that which we think we lead."[12]

A sort of metaphysical piety survives in these feelings in place of that piety which has withdrawn from them.

IV. A Throw of the Dice

What the philosopher appears to neglect, poetry lays hold of. The poet makes a particular use of speech and writing, especially when, being aware of its particularity through an effort of reflection on its end and proper means, he tries to distinguish poetry from prose, which is the ordinary mode of language and, if one could say so, its normal usage.

"When one speaks, it is in order to make oneself understood," Paul Claudel ironically says; and this is true of every mode of language except poetry. The poet does not speak in order to make himself understood. That which he says may have a meaning, but those who believe they understand his poetry because they have understood that meaning fool themselves as much as they do who, because they do not grasp the meaning, believe that they do not understand his poetry. The meaning may be so bald and banal that the poet would be grateful not to have to emphasize it to us. The *trobar clus* of the Middle Ages already marked this intentional obscurity which enters to some extent into all poetry, since the latter, by the sole fact that it has recourse to verse, signifies the desire to "speak otherwise than everyone does." Preciosity, Gongorism, and other analogous schools betray the same concern. Certain of Dante's poems still call forth the insight of their readers despite the commentaries which his *Banquet* has provided them. We live moreover in a time when poetry has become aware of itself as a problem. It knows that if it defers unreservedly to one of its essential exigencies, then hermeticism is its final destiny. As a general rule, when one opens a collection of modern poetry, one expects not to understand. Boileau is therefore decidedly dead. It is difficult today for the reader to know if the writer is obscure because he is a poet or if he thinks that one can become a poet only upon the condition of being obscure.

Mallarmé certainly fled the clarity of common sense fatal to poetry, but poetry for him did not consist in the simple absence of intelligibility. As obscure as certain of his verses may be, they remain composed of words, not of simple sounds or noises, and since the meaning of the word is what distinguishes it from a simple sound, it is necessary that the language of Mallarmé continue to signify, but otherwise than ordinary language does. What, then, is this poetic meaning [*sens*]? In order to respond to this question which, more or less explicitly formulated, haunted his thought, Mallarmé often asked himself about the nature of poetic language, which presents with a particular rigor the general problem of the connection of the sign with meaning [*sens*].

Initially, the poet was troubled and surprised by noticing that to name an object consists in replacing something that exists by something else which, except by virtue of being a sign, does not exist. The real object is replaced by a word. It becomes a "suppressed trinket of sonorous inanity" [*aboli bibelot d'inanité sonore*]. Here one finds again, under the form of new poetic experience, the astonishment which inspires in many philosophers, upon the plane of abstract reflection, the opposition between the materiality of the sign and the unreality [*irréalité*] of the thing signified. We scarcely think except through concepts or universals; now — Aristotle already said it — universals do not exist.

Let us stick to poetry and take for example the word "flower." Each real flower is *a flower*, such as those which one can grow, purchase, or sell, and put in bouquets; but poetic flowers are only abstract ideas, at most images, simple varieties of *the flower* in general, which itself does not exist. To conceive it and name it is the essential poetic act, and its entire poetic being amounts to being conceived and named. That which is for the philosopher only the abstractive operation of the intellect is here the Janus-faced drama of a mental annihilation accompanied by a creation which compensates for it.

This event constitutes the entrance by the mind [*esprit*] into the distinct order that we call "literature" properly speaking, in opposition to that "universal reportage" in which, in the time of Mallarmé as already in Poe's time, "every sort of contemporary writing" participated.

In its properly literary usage the word implies, therefore, the refusal to signify a concrete reality and the deliberate will to hold the meaning of the word as the true reality. What is it, in fact, to name, that operation which was formerly called the imposition of the name, that with which God charged Adam in the terrestrial Paradise, if not "the wonder of transposing a fact of nature into its near vibratory disappearance [*en sa presque disparition vibratoire*] according to the game of speech"? *Near* disappearance, because instead of the luminous vibration caused by the object, there remains the sonorous vibration to which the sound of the word is reduced. And why bring about this disappearance if not "in order to lead out from it, without the constraint of a similarly concrete reminder, the pure idea"? And so I say "a flower," and this word alone causes every other image to be forgotten than that of calyxes in array, while (here we leave the phrasing to the poet himself) "musically it arises, the very idea and sweet, that which [is] absent in every bouquet."[13] For one does not make bouquets without flowers, but one cannot put *the flower* in bouquets, for it is a pure idea which ever had the sole meaning of a word tied to that of other words.

A second effect of poetry as creative of a world of words is to isolate speech [*parole*] at one and the same time from the real world (which takes on thereafter the appearance of being the "nonpoetic") and from itself insofar as it wants to be henceforth foreign to all care or function concerning other things than itself as pure utterance [*parole*]. It therefore refuses that which calls attention to description, teaching, information — what Mallarmé has just called reportage — in order to become as purely as possible song, speech, assertion [*dire*]: the *Dichtung* of him whom we call the poet, *Dichter*, by the very fact that he *dictates* or asserts [*dit*].

Mallarmé never got over his amazement before the quasi-miraculous phenomenon which speech [*parole*] is in reality. The "sweetness" that he found in the most simple of words was none other than that of intellection itself, whose worth he attributed to the music of the word. Is there a voice more sweet than that which says "flower"? Mallarmé, intoxicated by speech, had wanted to be able to think words directly, words which were no more than signs of their own signification without reference to any real object. He therefore obstinately struggled to sanctify language by imposing on it that nearly total poetic purification. But to push this operation to its term would have been a disaster, since that would have necessitated the elimination from poetry of language itself, which is the matter upon which the act of the poet exercises itself.

He did not think it was possible anymore totally to exorcise the memory image of the real object from poetry, but he forced himself to introduce into the poem only those images called for by the necessity of speaking poetically, and not those which the ordinary sense of the word has at its disposal. The lexicographical use of words designed to communicate information is radically foreign to the end that poetry pursues. In connection with the latter, common language [*langue*] is governed by chance, that is to say, by every signification answering to an end other than poetic. An essential element of the personal experience of Mallarmé was the desire to free himself from this chance, which, as Baudelaire had observed, always intervenes in the use of common language, so that he might impose on language a purely poetic usage. The poet himself creates a universe of pure signification, where speech is its own proper end, and where the things called real, not having any more substance than the sound of their names, are not susceptible to any other justification than a poetic one. Chance (here the name [for that which is] warranted by a reason other than the poetic) [reading "*nom*" for "*non*" in the text] is the element of speech which is not reduced to its power of signification solely within the work.

The poet, therefore, wants to eliminate it, but it is impossible, and if he persists in his enterprise, the poet assists in "the catastrophe of Therefore [Igitur]." To what degree the poet is conscious of touching here the very foundation of the metaphysics of language we do not know. But that is what is happening.

Igitur: according to the dictionaries, "consequently, therefore, thus (making a logical succession)." In the imagination of the poet who chooses this title to announce the tragic end of experience it is a question of a drama, or perhaps rather of a story [*conte*], "but this story addresses itself to the intelligence of the reader which stages things itself." We know moreover why Mallarmé wrote this mysterious text. He explained to his friend Cazalis, in a letter dated 14 November 1869, that he wrote this work in the hope of crushing the old monster of impotence which, in fact, *is the subject of it.* Once liberated from his enemy, he proposed to enter upon a great work whose nature he did not specify, but which we might suppose to be THE BOOK. Such modern criticism as passes muster as a profound interpretation of Mallarmé begins naturally by eliminating the explanation which the poet himself gives of his poem. It is too simple; but why should we who do not claim to be better informed than the poet of the meaning of his work not read it as the literary description of these efforts, vainly renewed, to attain to pure poetic speech, and of the disaster which results from it each time?

Let us therefore allow the intelligence to set its own stage, without denying the rôle of the imagination.

It is the right minute, the zero hour, already more than yesterday and not yet today, the hour of free choice that nothing in time determines. The field is free for the creative decision of the poet, who will try to create poetry out of his own substance and out of that alone. In order truly to create, he must set out from nothingness; like the God of Genesis, he wants to create *ex nihilo creaturae* and through the efficacity of his creativity alone. Thus understood, the poetic act is that of an intellect which owes its work only to itself and, in order to assure itself of that, discards everything else in order to possess itself as totally unconditional, therefore anterior to its own expression.

"Igitur" begins, then, quite classically, by following the negative method, that is to say, by emptying itself of everything given anterior to its act. It goes down the steps of the human spirit and gets to the bottom of things, into the absolute that it is. This bottom is reached at the point at which, in the spirit itself, things come to be thanks to the act that thinks them. On this side of that point there is nothing except the spirit itself alone confronting nothingness, as the poet himself is so often found before "the white worry" of the empty page. Mallarmé would call the virginity of the nothingness of being "pure" [*vierge*]. Since it is the absolute, "Igitur" remains alone. It "blows out the candle of being [*souffle la bougie de l'être*], by which all has been." Nothing more then remains. Above all, nothing more remains of "then" [*donc*] or even of that chance which still retained its own inspiration [*souffle*], for there was still chance in the initial throw of the dice of the poetic act, whereas henceforth, for this act which sets itself in the zero of nothingness, "there is and there is not chance." Yet in this absolute vacuum the creative act remains impotent to produce itself. The poet feels himself in the way. He therefore drinks "the drop of nothingness which the sea lacks" and, apparently consenting to his impotence, lies down in the tomb. "Emptiness, madness," the madness of Elbehnon is that of the poet who wished to create his work out of nothingness through a totally unconstrained, totally pure, act of speech. In fact, "nothingness having gone away, the castle of purity remains."[14]

In what is this posthumous purity distinguished from nothingness? Many an obscure image comes under the pen of the poet in order poetically to translate the act of intellect which reduces its anterior light to the state of darkness in progressively emptying itself of any object. In the purity of its own emptiness it is at once pure light and total obscurity, for if it speaks, its speech comes back to it or perishes in the vacuum. It is then that the poet "utters speech in order to plunge it once more into its emptiness." He says it nevertheless; he must do so since he is the poet. Knowing the madness of his act, his ultimate duty is to proclaim it indeed: this madness exists. One must begin again, although without illusions, for in the last analysis "all thought is a throw of the dice." We add, as the poet will: which never will abolish chance.

One cannot without emotion be present at this exemplary effort of a poetic thought to transcend itself as language, or rather, to become more purely language. Sustained over the years, this effort to make a success of an impossible enterprise was perilous for the mental health of the poet. It at least probably explains that sterility which Mallarmé hoped to exorcise. That thought did not prevent its own suicide. When one reads the perfect poems of his maturity, those which the demi-Mallarmeans prefer and whose number he alone could increase, one sees evidence that Mallarmé, in order to reduce "Igitur" to silence, had to refuse a literary success, which he knew to be accessible, in order to engage in the pursuit of a goal which he himself knew to be chimerical. Those who deplore the fact that the "servitude of the life of a professor" may have reduced his genius to silence appear to me to be misguided. Mallarmé would not have written one more line of poetry if he had had nothing else to do. That leisure would only have taken away from him the precious alibi which his trade as professor furnished him. He lost it in fact when the age of retirement came, the experience of which gives sufficient evidence that it never puts an end to any life—of work or idleness, let us say, of productivity or of sterility. It was in himself, in Mallarmé, that the origin of his silence lay, and I believe that he knew it.

The grand project of writing THE BOOK was too obviously a dream of a waking dreamer. After having said that "everything in the world exists in order to result in a book," but a book that would be THE BOOK, "such that nothing will remain without being uttered," and such that one would perceive in it "the unity of existing relations in the whole," the poet is swallowed up by a sea of stammering which is at times quite disturbing. That which he had desired, basically, had been to write a book equivalent to the *Arbor scientiae* of which Lull thought he had the vision on the slopes of Mount Randa, and which he had dreamed of writing; or, better still, of the *Nous* of Plotinus, the *locus* of all intelligibles given simultaneously in the infinity of their relations.

That was too much for a man, and he himself doubted that it could be accomplished. Mallarmé had certainly been aware, in engaging in his project, of penetrating into a realm already explored by metaphysics. It is difficult to explain Mallarmé by Hegel, who was not unknown to him. That would be to explain the obscure by the more obscure. But the poet knew enough of it to know that his personal problem was situated at the borders of philosophy, for after having said it at the beginning of the "project": "I revere the opinion of Poe, no vestige of a philosophy—ethics or metaphysics—will show through," he proceeded: "I add that it has to be present, enclosed and concealed."[15] We know the result. Concealed metaphysics suffocated poetry, not because it was metaphysics, but because it was false. For, having wished to go back up to the point where thought was sufficient to itself before sinking into language, Mallarmé was finally condemned to silence. The grandeur of this heroic and somewhat foolish destiny is no consolation for the work that a fatal error prevented from coming to realization, with no poetic compensation for anyone whatever.[16]

All this is not without its philosophic compensation for the observer, however, for the poetic passion and death of Mallarmé have made obvious the transcendence of pure thought, that *verbum cordis* without which there would have been no language, but with which by itself, in the absence of language, thought would not be able to conceive of itself before communicating itself to others. As is the case with every mystery—and all origins are mysterious—this one is, in a sense, silence; but it is the silence out of which speech [*parole*] and thought simultaneously become possible. One must consent to the mystery of being or, like Igitur, resign oneself to nothingness.

V. Language Game

All thought known to us having to express itself in a language in order to communicate itself, it is therefore contradictory to wish to philosophize about pure thought; yet philosophical reflection is inevitably tempted to do so, even if it knows itself condemned to fail.[17] This defeat is not a sterile one if with it one also places in evidence the heterogeneity of language and the thought it expresses. Thought lacks words not only to express itself but even to express the meaning of the words which it uses.

The main interest, from this point of view, which the *Tractatus Logico-Philosophicus* of Ludwig Wittgenstein (1889–1951) presents, is the straightforwardness with which the author sets the questions. The mystery of language obsesses his thought, but he grapples with it each time directly, afresh so to speak, even if he takes a backward step each time his thought comes up against the same obstacle, which is itself insofar as it uses a physical means in order to express something transphysical in the absence of possessing a common measure with the transphysical.

I imagine a French reader opening the *Tractatus*. The work is composed, it is said, of aphorisms, of which this is the first: *Die Welt ist alles, was der Fall ist.* Our reader naturally asks himself what this proposition means. The question amounts to asking what it means for a reader different from him, for whom German would be his mother tongue, and even what it signified in the thought of Wittgenstein himself who wrote it.[18]

For a French reader *die Welt* means the world, that is to say, approximately the entirety of all that exists. Of such an object we have no sensible experience nor, consequently, any representation. Moreover, Wittgenstein does not define this idea in terms of actual existence. He has recourse to the notion of totality, or, rather still, to that of an infinite series which is left open (*alles*), applied to the idea, still more indeterminate for a French reader, of "that which is the case": *was der Fall ist*. A German reader himself might hesitate over the precise meaning of these words. They intend to specify, I imagine, the object, whatever it may be, which is found to be in question or of which it is a question. Wittgenstein himself specifies that "that which is the case is fact [*un fait*]. . . ." (*Tractatus*, 2.) The world is divided then into facts: *Die Welt zerfällt in Tatsachen* (I, 2). The French translation is possible here thanks to the community of meaning of the roots *tun* and *faire*, which gives that of the substantives *Tat* and *fait*; but, precisely, it is not easy to render "that which is the case" into French as "that which is the fact [*fait*]." *Der Fall* corresponds better to the word "case" (from *cadere, casus: fallen, der Fall*), but what is the case is not necessarily a fact [*fait*] or something factual [*de fait*]. One would love to be able to rest content with the word "thing" ["*chose*"], but, precisely, Wittgenstein does not allow it. The world, he says, is the whole of facts [*faits*], not of things: *Die Welt ist die Gesamtheit der Tatsachen, nicht der Dingen* (I, 1). According to him, "that which is the case," "the factual" [*le fait*], is that which consists in a state of things: *Was der Fall ist, die Tatsache, ist Bestehen von Sachverhalten* (2). Here again the French reader (and perhaps also the German) asks himself about the precise meaning of this *sachverhalt;* to which Wittgenstein replies immediately (2:01): it is a connected whole of objects (*Gegenstanden*), of concerns [*affaires*] (*Sachen*), of things (*Dingen*).[18a]

The desire for precision could not affirm itself with greater force, but we see how uncertain the success of the operation is. Assuredly, one must be able to reason about what the words mean for a German, but nothing proves that, in this manner, one would be able to succeed in forming a firm response. The operation which consists in defining a basic idea such as "thing" is not possible in any language [*langue*]. Then, as is normal, the first question posed by the philosopher is not that which he wants to resolve. The object of his preoccupations is not "the world," but rather the relation of thought to language and their common relation to reality, or their respective relations if they are not identical. It is not the logic of language but its nature which is at first in question, and the response is given with the question itself, for all those notions of *world, things, totality of facts,* and other similar ones that the philosopher initially introduces are necessary for the very possibility of discourse about the relation of language to reality, to such an extent that language is only possible on the condition of finding itself at home directly in the midst of these notions with the power to define them and to exchange them in some fashion at will. This time, far from lacking words for what it wants to say, language has too many of them; for to say that the world consists of facts, which are not themselves things but bundles of objects, facts, or things is in reality to create words in order to speak of things; and although these words are not denuded of meaning, that to which we attribute them is not tied to them by any necessary connection. This is why so many philosophers love to create for themselves a language which would be their own, as if to speak differently amounted to the same thing as to think differently.

One would not like to think that the reality given in experience, the same for everyone, could be correctly expressed in such different terms. Reality contains all that grounds the language in which we speak about it, but it is not made up of elementary units corresponding to the terms which we use to speak of it. To analyze language is not to analyze the reality which it expresses. Wittgenstein has been reproached for speaking like the Scholastics on this point, but it is Spinoza the mathematician, not

Aristotle the empiricist, who said that the order and disposition of ideas are the same as the order and disposition of things. Things are not ideas; the order of ideas, therefore, ought to be different from that of things. Reality is composed of structured ontological nuclei [noyaux] which we call substances, endowed with properties which we call their qualities, or accidents, but that does not mean that substances need be logical subjects of which accidents would be the predicates. It is perhaps as a result of having become aware of this truth that Wittgenstein replaced the doctrine of the Tractatus Logico-Philosophicus, where speech [langue] is conceived as an image of the thing ("Den Gegenstanden entsprechen im Bilde die Elemente des Bildes," 2, 13) by that of the Philosophische Untersuchungen, where language [langage] is conceived of as the exercise of all possible verbal systems [systèmes verbaux] (Sprachspiel). Not only is it that the elements of language do not correspond here anymore to the elements of objects, but objects here are not composed anymore of elements of that sort. Here philosophy no more opens on a logic which would be as it were a philosophy of language. We no longer try to make two ontologically different universes coincide.

The present situation brings to mind another one in the first half of the nineteenth century, which was the golden age of ideology, when we saw so many philosophers, stimulated by the example of Condillac, busy themselves with the decomposition of thought into its elements, which were then called faculties, and try to see how one could next recompose it by a synthesis whose movement was the inverse of that of analysis. Neither in France nor in Italy were there two identical ideologies, and everyone always knew that there was an open field before him for adding one more to those which preceded it if he but wished to do so. Their authors did not appear to suspect that the very ease of success revealed the vanity of the undertaking.

The same situation prevails today with the philosophies of language. Wittgenstein alone found the way to elaborate for himself two profoundly different ones, without being able to say that the second dispenses with the first for other minds than his own. But we also know that from certain positions of the Tractatus, following the investigation for their own purpose, other philosophers have constructed other philosophies of language different from those of Wittgenstein. The Vienna Circle made evident many of these possible extensions, Wittgenstein taking no part in these works. And how could he not be apart from them, he who was painstakingly absent from his own?

Wittgenstein derived from Russell and Whitehead who, on their part, had each gone his own way after their Principia Mathematica. He believed himself at the end of his own research by concluding with these words the preface of the *Tractatus* of 1918: "The truth of the thoughts here communicated appears to me to be unassailable and definitive (*unantastbar und definitiv*). I also think that in essence I have definitively resolved the problem." One could nevertheless find without trouble in the *Blue Book* and the *Brown Book* overtures to still other ways, which promised other solutions than that of the *Tractatus* and that of the *Philosophische Untersuchungen*. We noted that ideology died after Taine, when instead of adding a new one to the preceding ones, Bergson illuminated the vanity of the problem that the ideologues had wanted to resolve: Into how many pieces, and which, must we cut up the unextended? Still more daring, our contemporaries persist in looking in the material of language for the explanation of structures which control the immateriality of thought. We know since Plotinus, nevertheless, that the Logos is one, but with a unity that is neither that of number nor of quantity. Metaphysics will doubtless always have the task of protecting thought against the temptation to abdicate its supreme dignity as wisdom and, in order to become science, to materialize itself.

Whatever one thinks of the detail of the two philosophies of Wittgenstein, and even if one cannot make up one's mind to grant him the reasonableness of the second, which puts forward the notion of language as a game, the fact is that, through certain of its aspects, language is a game. There is probably no one who, at certain moments, does not play with his speech as he does with his legs, arms, and hands. Those who are gifted for this sort of exercise are the virtuosos of speech, and some execute without apparent effort, or, as one says, with great ease, some veritable verbal gymnastics. He who shines in conversation plays at combining verbal signs for the pleasure of obtaining unforeseen and agreeable effects on the ear or on the understanding; if possible, both at once. One is then at one of the limits of language properly speaking, for although speech [*parole*] be a game, its end in this case is not anymore signification desired for itself and for the communication of meaning. The brilliant conversationalist, the orator who improvises while allowing himself to be borne on the wave of discourse, makes use of language as if it were for him its own end, as the acrobat uses his body, the dancer his legs, in order to show everyone what he can do with them. When he "plays with words," what the conversationalist says has no more necessary connection with the meaning of the words than the notes of a symphony have with that which one often takes pleasure in ascribing to them.

Taken in the pure state, the game of language is the "play on words." We may agree to hold such play in contempt, but there is no one who does not amuse himself thus on occasion and even succumb at times to the temptation to commit it, while excusing himself for it if necessary. Its most basic form is the pun, to which we succumb mechanically, even if we do not have the depraved taste for punning. We hold it in contempt, even in succumbing to it, precisely because it is only mechanical. The pun, or pure play on words, consists in uttering a word which is two words and may have two different meanings at one and the same time. The hearer is rarely fooled about the proper meaning of such words, but the simple fact that a second possible meaning is evoked at the same time produces a burlesque effect. Certain puns, unintended or intended, have become well known: for instance, the sick person dying at Spa and saying, with a smile: "*Je m'en vais de ce pas*" [literally "I am passing away at this pace"]. Still better known is that which is attributed to Louis XVIII when, feeling himself dying and thinking of his brother and future successor Charles X, he said to his physicians: "*Allons, messieurs, finissons-en, Charles attend!*" ("Let's go, gentlemen, let's get it over with; Charles is waiting!"). This "ghastly play on words," as it is called, fortunately bears all the marks of inauthenticity. Everyone can cite authentic ones of this sort, but he is ashamed to reproduce them precisely on account of their authenticity. The unintended pun is innocent by definition. If it erupts in the texture of a serious or even tragic discourse, its effect is only the more burlesque; but the true pun, always intended, can directly interest the mind, witness the one of Paul Claudel in his *Journal* (I, 136): "*Entre deux mots il faut choisir le moindre*" ["Of two words we ought to choose the lesser": the French pun plays on the homophones *mots*, words, and *maux*, evils]. It is hard to know if it is the accidental association of words which leads thought, that is to say, if it is the speaker who creates these verbal associations, or whether it is the words themselves which do the playing, in the absence of which he who pronounces them is there to no end.

It is the same case with the *lapsus linguae*, the simple verbal slip. Nevertheless, one can hesitate about its true nature, when, through a spontaneous displacement of letters, syllables, and a transposition in no way audially calculated, the speaker involuntarily substitutes one phrase for another. More exactly perhaps, the speaker composes one phrase out of the verbal elements of another. It appears that for some people this can be an irresistible temptation. Such a one, according to the legend at least, was the Rev. W. A. Spooner, of New College, Oxford (1930), who gave his name to the genre called in English "spoonerism." As an example of this: To say "our queer old dean" for "our dear old queen."

Some give to this phenomenon the name of "consonantal metathesis." We call it more vulgarly a *contre-petterie*. Although the *lapsus* is nature's play, the spoonerism is a sought-for discovery, one intended and, therefore, a work of art and, thus, a real game. Rabelais abounds in examples of this play of language, but it is awkward to cite them for they

are so scurrilous: "*Femme folle à la messe* . . ." [a foolish woman at mass];
"*A Beaumont-le -Vicomte* . . ."; and so on. It appears, moreover, that there
is a certain affinity between this sort of pleasantry and obscenity.[19] But
the connection is not a necessary one. Take, for example, this anonymous
spoonerism, born one knows not where, which circulated in Paris occupied
by the enemy, at a time when the occasions for laughing were rare: "*Ne
dites pas metropolitain, dites Petain mollit trop.*" The sounds [*voix*] *me*,
pe are in the same initial position, *tro* and *tain* are common to the two
groups of syllables, *poli* and *mollit* form an assonance which forces itself on the ear — it is a probably exceptional success in a genre whose examples it is often difficult to cite because their scatological coarseness ri-
vals their obscenity.

In an order more exalted but perhaps included in the same genre we
come across the *chiasma* (crossing), which consists in transposing the terms
of a proposition, as in the formula that Molière made well-known: "One
must eat in order to live and not live in order to eat." Now and then one
comes across some more exceptional ones which, by their unexpectedness
and the effort it takes to compose them, easily give the impression of profundity. For example: "The elimination of human potentialities from the
world of (alienated) (sic) work creates the preconditions for the elimination of alienated work from the world of human potentialities."[20] The impression of surprise and unexpected profundity is at times accompanied
in parallel cases moreover with a feeling of insecurity, for we may fear
that the alliterations and assonances resulting from the use of the same
words in diverse positions play a more determinant role than their meaning in expressions of this sort. At least we cannot doubt that it is here
a question of the true play of language, of him who speaks, amusing himself with words like a card player with cards and a baby with blocks. The
too great frequency of the process is always a disquieting symptom.

Finally, there exists an art of playing with words much more exalted,
for there they are named, one and another, not merely by their sound but
by their sense. These word games are language games. We owe to them
combinations of meanings ["*signifiés*" (sic)] whose unexpectedness and fecundity enchant the minds of their author as well as those who hear them.
When in an instantaneous flash it thus unveils perspectives of the imagination unexpected by the intellect, the play of language is poetry.

One example will doubtless be enough. Mobilized in Alsace in 1939,
the exquisite poet who Paul Gilson was found this verse at the tip of his
pen: "*On brodait des mouchoirs en point de jour d'attaque*" [With some
awkward literalness, "We embroider handkerchiefs on point of day of attack"]. The imagination perceives four intelligible flashes there without
discerning them.

It all begins along the thread of common discourse: "We embroider handkerchiefs on point of . . . ," but here, when one waits for the name of one of the best-known varieties of needlepoint, that of Alençon or of Brussels, the word "day" is inserted. That was unexpected, for we do not ordinarily say "point of day," but "point of the day" [*le point du jour* = *daybreak*]. In fact, that is what we believe we have heard, although the poet has not written it. That which makes us accept without hesitation "point of day" is the following words, "of attack," for when "point of the day of attack" is not said (we would say the morning, or the dawn of a day of attack), the *point of* at one and the same time supports and lays a common foundation for the two images of needlepoint, called up by "we embroider," and of "attack," called up by "day." A new perspective then becomes perceptible to the imagination which neither the "needlepoint" nor the "point of the day" preceding it provoked: it is that of the "day of attack." The meaning of the verse is not any of these images taken separately; it consists rather in the very movement of the imagination which, deferring to the associations of customary words, but only deferring partially each time, lets itself slide into rapid, almost instantaneous slippages of meaning. And the poet knew exactly what he was doing:

> Mon terrain vague de poemes
> ou trainent des echos de voix
> j'y passe partout a la fois
> un carnaval avec moi-meme. . . .[21]

> [The vague land of my poems
> where echoes of voices linger
> everywhere all at once I spend
> a carnival with myself. . . .]

It is not a question then either of chains of images such as those which Andre Breton came under the influence of in the time of automatic writing, or of games of chance with printed words cut up by scissors, shaken up in the bottom of a hat, drawn out at random, and set in line by all and sundry as in the time of Dada. It is a question of "echoes of speech [*voix*]," resonances of words often pronounced, disjointed from their customary usage and newly associated by the imagination of the poet who speaks. The poet, who offers himself this carnival, of which the words of a tongue [*langue*] are the masks, rejoins then Wittgenstein, the philosopher, who all his life was amazed at the latent inventions in each of the sentences that he pronounced.

6

The Spoken Word
and the Written Word

In all that has gone before, the word *language* [*langage*] has been principally used in the sense of spoken language [*langage parlé*], the language of the tongue [*le langage de la langue*]; but we have felt throughout the presence of written language [*langage écrit*], as if it were a question of the same thing. And indeed it is in fact a question of the same thing, since in the two cases it is a question of thought signified by signs. Besides, since speech [*parole*] is made up of words each of which is at one and the same time something signifying and something signified, writing, which is a system of signs for fixing and conserving speech, is dependent on the same philosophical interpretation.

The passage from speech to writing engenders just as many differences in the manner of thinking [as the passage from thought to speech does]. The most immediate way of coming to sense this, perhaps, would be to call to mind the distinction that every orator and every listener can make between spoken discourse and discourse read. The essential difference between the two cases is that spoken discourse is invented to the extent that one speaks it. If the orator has considered what he ought to say, he is under obligation to create his language as he speaks. He invents, and his effort at invention itself attests to the presence of an active and living thought at the core of the discourse. The pace of the delivery, the tone of voice, the gesture, the posture of the speaker, give evidence to the hearer that he who speaks is indeed the author of the thought that he expresses. Communication is established from person to person. He who reads a text written in advance puts his audience in communication with his text. The communication which existed at the moment when he wrote his text, between himself and the writing, does not exist for his audience, and it has even already ceased to exist for himself. No one can speak the thought of another, but one can read the written thought of anyone. When it is a question of his own thought, it becomes the thought of another: the thought of that person who one was at the moment when one wrote it in view of the future lecture by oneself or someone else. The hearers quickly become aware of what is happening. It is generally more pleasant to follow him who speaks to them, because the thought is alive and because every improvisation or invention attests to the presence of life; but the spontaneity of unconstrained speech is often the enemy of order. Between liberty without order and order without liberty the speaker and the hearer must resign themselves to making a sacrifice. They can hardly have both at the same time.

Modern methods of recording speech have given birth to that monster which is spoken-written language. The problem has been posed, moreover, ever since we have made use of stenography. Aristide Briand was a remarkable orator. He held his audience under a spell by the cello-timbre of his voice alone, but I have it from a stenographer of the Senate that it was necessary to rewrite his speeches almost entirely in order to be able to publish them. We doubt that Cicero delivered his speeches in the form they have come down to us. Eloquence written differs specifically from eloquence spoken, and whoever has lived through the dolorous experience of hearing the phonographic recording of a speech that he has improvised, or of a lesson which he gave without having written it, has no doubt whatever that speaking is of an entirely different order than reading aloud.

It is interesting to know that Ludwig Wittgenstein, who has spoken and written much about language, and who was a professor although he detested being such, never prepared his lessons and spoke without the assistance of any notes. He had tried, he said one day to this listener and friend Norman Malcolm, but the result had been so bad that he had renounced the effort: "The ideas which came to him appeared 'stale' or, as he had declared to another of his friends, the words he spoke appeared to have a *cadaverous appearance.*"[1] Every professor or lecturer, every preacher, I fancy, recognizes in this remark a frequent experience. It is that, in effect, sentences, alive when written, are dead when read. He must read them, then, as if they were still alive, which requires an effort of him all the less bearable because he feels it fruitless. Supposing that he should succeed in fooling others, he will not fool himself. His attention, his interest, turn themselves toward the communication of his thought rather than toward the operations of the understanding which would give it birth if he were still in the process of inventing it. The two operations, reading or speaking, are therefore generically different. It is not obvious what method one should use to measure the advantages and disadvantages of each. We know that Wittgenstein himself was worn out at the conclusion of each course. He was worn out as a result of the incessant effort to find his ideas; his audience was worn out by the effort of trying to understand him.[2] What we wish to retain of his experience is the profound difference which separates speech [parole] directly expressing thought from that which communicates the content of something written.

In order to find the thought once again in the writing, one must therefore go back up from the act of reading to the act of writing. Is it the same thing to write as to speak?

Some have maintained, and some perhaps still think, that speaking is instinctual. Saussure, Sapir, and others deny it, rightly so, I think. No one has ever maintained that writing is instinctual. It can be a need, and perhaps a natural need, with a speaking being, but he certainly does not dispose of any organ to satisfy the need. It is not even a function superimposed on the hand as articulated language is superimposed on the totality of the vocal organs. The speaker has need only of his body in order to speak; to write, the hand does not suffice. The person must have an instrument: stylus, pen, pencil, typewriter, or something else. This is not all: we write not only *with* something but *on* something: stone or brick, parchment or papyrus, paper above all today. In whatever way that the writer accomplishes his end, it is a situation completely other than that of the speaker. There is an art of oratory, but it only consists in the studied usage of a natural function of man, that of speaking. There is also an art of writing, even two arts, of which one is only bringing into play the art of speaking exercised under a new form. This is the art of the writer. The other is a manual art, so distinct that it can become in fact an end in itself, the art of calligraphy, that which the dictionaries define as "the art of forming well the characters of writing." This is why the apprenticeship to writing requires particular efforts. One begins by "making straight lines," then circles, next letters. One learns next to copy models of writing, and one ends by creating for oneself a personal style of writing, a style so personal that graphology claims to be able not only to identify it with certainty but to read in it the character of the writer. This is to say that style is so tied to the person that one sees writing change and age with him as if it fit exactly the curve of his life. Man does not, therefore, have the same relation with writing as he has with speech. An invented manual art interposes itself in writing between spoken thought and its expression.

The invention of writing is the invention of a tool, and the most astonishing perhaps that man has ever invented. Like all discoveries, it goes back to a prehistoric origin. We do not know who invented the wheel, but writing is an activity much more widespread than the use of the wheel itself. Only the invention of language surpasses it in universality, if language be supposed to be the invention of a tool. The speaker invents sounds or reproduces those that others have invented before him, but he is born with the organs necessary in order to learn to produce them. Man had to invent at one and the same time the signs themselves and the material for tracing written signs in order to mark down the sounds pronounced. Letters, the alphabet as we say, are the instrument of the most universal of instruments, which is language. The aptitude of the alphabet for universality is such that even among particular systems of writing, certain alphabets serve to translate several different tongues [*langues*], and it is not impossible to foresee a time when a single universal system of writing will suffice to translate all the tongues [*langues*] of humanity.

We leave out of consideration the history of the alphabet, and still more that of nonalphabetic writings, specialized disciplines which one must practice oneself in order to reflect usefully on them. Werner Heisenberg took pleasure in citing a passage from Galileo's *Dialogo dei massimi sistemi* where one of the interlocutors, Sagredo, eulogizes "a little book quite a bit shorter than one of Aristotle or Ovid, which contains all the sciences and of which one can have a glimpse with the least difficulty: I speak of the alphabet. There is no doubt: In arranging it as is fitting and in putting together such-and-such a vowel with such-and-such a consonant, we can obtain the most certain intelligence on each doubtful question, we can find the teachings of all the sciences, the rules of all the arts."[3] We add only that the invention of letters, by extending to infinity the conservation and diffusion of language, necessarily modifies its use. More precisely, writing created a written language different in many respects from spoken language. Only a linguist would know how to compare with exactitude the two states of language. Our remarks will be limited to noting the most prominent characteristics which set them apart, among those which we perceive.

From the lexicographical point of view written language [*langue*] is incomparably poorer than spoken language [*langue*]. It is sufficient to open the most complete dictionary of the French language to assure myself of this. I could verify in a few minutes that a number of words, or ways of pronouncing them, which are in current usage with me do not figure in this dictionary.[4] One cannot read Amyot without regretting the loss of many savory words, archaic in appearance, but which nothing forbids us to revive if it appears to us good, words which in any case exist. To restrict ourselves to our own times, the creation of neologisms is a necessity, for new things and thoughts require new names. In the United States, where they love neologisms, this becomes easy to accept, because language [*langue*] there is not the object of a cult, but rather the occasion for a game of which, in order that the party might last, no one troubles himself with fixing the rules too strictly. In France, on the contrary, the neologism is not well received, and the number of words which crowd about the door of the dictionaries seeking to be accepted therein is great. Truly, the idea of "all the words of a tongue" [*langue*] makes no sense.

No one contests the fundamental irrationality of French spelling in particular, but it is not the only one to suffer from this ill.[5] There are not enough signs to mark the diversity of sounds and meanings. If you forget an *s* or an *x* marking a written plural, that is considered a fault, when nothing, absolutely nothing, distinguishes the singulars *chien* [*dog*] and *chou* [*cabbage*] from the plurals [*chiens* and *choux*] in spoken language. All the attempts to reform miscarry, and the same Frenchman who finds it natural, as one would expect, to read *filosofo* or *telefono* in Italian will not have the courage to write *filosofe* or *telefone*. The spoken language presents an analogous problem, in the sense that there are good and bad pronunciations, but the data of the problems are not the same. A bad pronunciation is only such because it diverges from a type commonly received in certain social groups, or certain provinces, which pass for being in possession of the characteristic of speaking well. But every pronunciation is normal for him who speaks, and the sign that it assigns is not changed for that. He who "doesn't know how to spell" is aware of a deficiency to which he can resign himself, but which he regrets: he does not know how to write. Colette, Claudel never lost the accent of their respective provinces, but apart from the fact that they were probably not able to get rid of it, it never occurred to them that they spoke poorly, that they did not know how to speak.

Spelling is learned, more or less perfectly and with more or less labor. Whatever may be the case, it only opposes to the exercise of written language an exterior, so to speak, obstacle. The fact that writing is necessarily a learned art and not the exercise of an organ is at the origin of the most serious difficulties, in that they affect the very usage of language [*langue*].

The main difficulty can be illustrated by a familiar experience which we formulate variously: to be a "poor correspondent," to "have a horror of writing letters," or simply "not to like to write." I knew a philosopher who could talk endlessly of philosophy but from whom it was impossible to extract a book and extremely difficult to get the least article. Moving immediately to the limiting case, which makes the comprehension of the phenomenon easy, we have never heard it said that Stéphane Mallarmé suffered from any difficulty with words, but he certainly suffered from a difficulty in writing, such that, as a writer, he ended by being reduced to silence. Mallarmé's experience is assuredly not the common experience of those who suffer from stylophobia, but it is analogous to it and clarifies it.

"I take pen in hand" has become a rather comic cliché. "At the moment that I open my mouth" sounds nothing but solemn when Bossuet says it. It is that putting hand to pen is not a natural act as speaking is. He who gets ready to write prepares himself to constrain the easy flow of speech [parole] to pass through the narrow channels which lines printed on white paper with black ink lay out for it. Nothing agrees less with the nature of speech [parole] than to be written. It is so free that it does not willingly submit to that servitude. This is why if one would constrain it in this fashion, one ought not hope that that might be done without difficulties.

No one writes the way he speaks. The speaker uses many words which the writer will avoid using. There are some words, we say, "which belong to the spoken language [langue parlé], not to the written language [langue écrite]." That which we call the choice of words imposes a first discipline, which is a constraint and which remains such even in the decision to allow oneself at times a certain license and to let pass some vulgar, low, at times even gross, and, should the occasion arise, foul words. The speaker can allow himself everything because he can always correct himself, can try one word after another, can grope about until he finds "the right word," all of which are liberties which the writer cannot grant himself without becoming unreadable. Syntax imposes rules still more stringent than vocabulary. Assuredly, the writer enjoys an almost infinite liberty, but within rules which he can break only in utilizing them.

Writing presumes an act of preliminary submission to the code of the language [langue] which we call its grammar. There is no conversation, even among writers who are masters of their art, which does not allow many liberties with the rules of grammar which each writer, moreover, claims to recognize and respect in his writings but violates without scruple in speech [langage]. The professional writer develops early the habit of playing on the two registers. He has two languages [langues] always at his disposition: one for the practical exchanges of common life, the other reserved for written usage; and if in a novel he inserts fragments of spoken language [langage], he will use special typography in order to make it obvious that it is a matter of dialogue, that is to say, of a fragment of spoken language [langue parlé] inserted within the continuous plot of written speech [langue écrite]. This spoken language [langue] differs from written language [langue] in many respects, although the use actually made of the means of mass communication threatens to impose on all listeners, writers or not, the ways of speaking of uncultivated minds, which at least in France are monopolized by the state television and radio broadcasting, and there reign as masters thanks to the support they find in the trade-union organizations. They introduce their vocabulary, which is that of hasty translations of news bulletins in foreign tongues, particularly American. They introduce syntactically incorrect constructions which the spoken language [*langue*] tolerates, but which grammar not unreasonably condemns as equivocal or untrue to the thought which they wish to express. They even introduce there their vicious pronunciations, transforming "*-isms*" into "*-izms*," and "*-uins*" into "*-ouins*": *cataclyzms*, the month of *jouin [juin]*.

Languages [*langues*] which are only spoken have a short life, although certain words or turns of phrase which they put in circulation may one day become incorporated into good usage in written language [*langue*]. The following characteristics will subsequently allow for a text to be dated with some probability at about 1968: *par ailleurs* for *d'ailleurs*; *exclu* (*ausgeschlossen*, impossible); the pair *concertation/contestation*, imposed by political groups called "the left"; the universal adjective *valable* [valid], which in each case dispenses with the need of finding the precise adjective which it replaces: a valid speaker, for a qualified or authorized one; *Phèdre* is still a valid play, one for which there still is a public; sentiments more valid than egoism, for more noble, etc. . . . . No one knows exactly in North America why "O.K." means today "good," "agreed," "understood," or every other analogous meaning. But it is current everywhere and has even engendered a verb, *to okay*, with its past participle, *okayed*, without anyone being able to foresee if this popular invention is there just for a time or for the centuries. Written language [*langue*] finds it difficult to defend itself against the constant pressure which the spoken language [*langue*] exercises upon it. In seventeenth-century French a handful of good writers sufficed to dictate good usage. The language of the court ruled, as in England the *King's English* did. Today forty members of the *Academie française*, who do not always give good example, are set awash in every sense by the ocean of the spoken language [*langue parlé*], of which those who speak on the television and radio are the masters and which serves as a model to the journals of every sort offered as fodder to the public. After all, the French have the right to speak a language [*langue*] that suits them. The entire public has the right to play its role in the formation of usage. One must resign oneself to seeing the language [*langue*] of a country adjust itself to the intellectual level of the people who speak it. That which created in the past the admirable system of classic Greek speech [*verbe*] has naturally given us Plato and Aristotle. But the stevedores of the Piraeus probably did not speak the tongue [*langue*] of Socrates and Xenophon. Their speech was doubtless the leaf-mold through which the masterpiece which was classic Greek thrust itself. The two languages [*langues*] have need of one another, but written language [*langue*] more so than spoken language [*langue*], in which it is rooted and from which it draws its sustenance. Of those who speak as they write we say with reason that their speech [*langue*] "isn't natural."[6] Up to the present, women writers have used a language [*langue*] superior to that of men. Madame de Sévigné, Colette, always surprise us by the fulness of meaning which they know how to find in everyday words. Madeleine Gide was a better writer than André Gide. The cause was that their mothers spoke a fine tongue. The daughters whose mothers shall have learned the language through the daily and weekly press, or by hearing on the television and radio the spoken journal ornamented by its improvised commentaries, will not have the same chance.

The propositions we set forth here no longer have any link whatever with the learned linguistics of our contemporaries. For the linguist every word [*parole*] equally merits his interest. The propriety or impropriety of the grammar does not change its nature insofar as it is a datum of language [*langue*]. Such are, like the others, facts to be noted and explained. In the presence of "mistakes in French" which some speaker or other will commit, the linguist "will not therefore depart from his role if he calls attention to the protestations or railleries of certain listeners and the indifference of others; but he will refuse, for his part, to get involved."[7]

I do not know whether this scientific impartiality does justice to that part of intelligence and reason which enters spontaneously, naturally, into the formation of languages [*langues*] and into the evolution of their grammars. The preference noted by the word "customary" for certain words and certain constructions rather than for others is a fact, but it marks a choice and constitutes a privilege in favor of the verbal forms which it approves. The distinction between good usage and other usages rests on linguistic realities inherent in the structure of spoken thought itself. The first time that a shopkeeper, short of a certain commodity, gave me as the reason: "I am delivered Tuesdays" [*Je suis livrée le mardi*], I understood immediately why the received usage was better than this one. In a sentence, for example, such as "Deliveries are made to me on Tuesday" [*les livraisons me sont faites le mardi*] I do not have to ask myself by whom and to whom this excellent person is delivered, each week, the second day of the week. The desire to avoid equivocation is inherent in the structure of language insofar as it is a *vox significativa*, for to signify implies the possibility of communicating a meaning, and the meaning is communicable only if it can be set off as distinctly as possible from any other meaning. This is the source of the grammars which regulate the usage of language [*langue*] and from which it is a bit surprising that modern linguistics wants to separate itself as radically as it does. For it is true that grammar is prescriptive and that general linguistics is only the phonology upon which it rests, but all the disciplines of language are to some degree prescriptive, so that, as the science of language, linguistics has as its object the means of communicating thoughts which are inevitably prescriptive since they have as their object to teach the way of bringing about that communication. The manner in which often so ingenious, even elegant, a language [*langue*] distinguishes the singular from the plural — or various sorts of plurals, the dual, for example — calls attention directly to linguistics but also to grammar and to phonology. All that concerns the communication of thought or, as we say, of meaning has its origins in linguistics, because the function of speech [parole] is that very communication.

At least two consequences follow from that. First, writing becomes then, if not an absolute necessity, at least a practical inevitability. A grammar only becomes solidly fixed at the moment when it is codified, which can only be done properly in writing it. In this sense writing, comprising the science of letters, alphabets, and of what we call grammatology, constitutes an integral part of the science of language, because writing is a very important agent for the development of language [langue] and inevitably affects its structure. Missionaries and linguists, at grips with the tough problem of taking a census of the vocabulary and of describing the syntax of any nonwritten language [langue], cause it inevitably to undergo important modifications. In any case, they make it pass through a threshold in the history of its development. The spontaneous grammatical invention necessary to all language [langue] takes on a new aspect from the moment when, made aware of its resources by its first written codification, language can use them as it will. We ourselves see, by the gap which exists between the spoken usage and good grammatical usage of our own languages [langues], to what extent it is true to say that writing is a creative force, distinct from the simple voice, in the life of language.[8] It is so by the peculiar power which it exercises on the meaning of verbal communication.

Writing is an analysis of speech [parole] as the latter is of thought. Nothing is more striking in this regard than the autonomy which writing confers on the word. Speech proceeds by means of vocal conglomerates emitted en bloc and which the ear receives as units. We speak not by words but by verbal units of signification. "I go to the post office" could as well be written "Igotothepostoffice." Certain ancient writings were, moreover, continuous, separating sentences without separating the words within them. In making itself grammatical the study of language [langue] has intended through writing to assure the distinction of words bearing meaning. Thus words are separated from one another by intervening blank spaces. Punctuation allows this analysis to be pushed further. By means of conventional signs, writing becomes a beginning of grammatical and logical analysis. The process becomes literally visible in poetry, where the isolation of verses, archipelagoes of black words on the white sea of the page, confers on them a sort of substantial autonomy that speech alone could not give them.

Mallarmé, that exemplary poet martyred by his love of language, has left a moving confession of the hope he had of succeeding at a kind of typographic symphony in the 1897 "Preface" which he had written for the edition, in the review *Cosmopolis*, of the extraordinary poem "Un coup de dés." The "white spaces" with which versification has for a long time surrounded verse, "like silence round about," instead of framing the page as formerly, are found in this poem spread out by the poet, freely but not at random. The printed page, a unity of verso and recto which confronts the reader, offers at a single glance an entity of spacings, where "the paper intervenes" not as is ordinarily the case at the end of each verse, but "each time that an image, by itself, ends or reopens," in brief, at the places which vary according to the "prismatic subdivisions of the idea." Mallarmé himself qualifies as "literary" the advantage "of this transcribed [*copiée*] distance which mentally separates groups of words." There, in fact, writing becomes a sign [*signifiant*] as autonomous as an ensemble of words can be. But typography alone can obtain that result, the printed page becoming a sort of score where the difference of graphic symbols which distinguishes motifs into preponderant, secondary, and adjacent, governs the vocal emission and even intonation. In fact, an entire page for *plume solitaire éperdue* [bewildered, solitary pen] is not perhaps too much.

In writing itself, then, thought defines for itself its own meaning: it knows "what it wants to say"; it defines this no less clearly, at least in principle, for the one to whom the message is addressed. Thought knows what it says and knows "how to make itself understood." It provides itself with the proof, in some way material, that the words which it uses define unambiguously and unequivocally the meaning which it sets itself to communicate. It is true that no language [*langue*] succeeds in eliminating all equivocation or in always defining the meaning of sentences in a manner that precisely renders the nuances of thought, but each language [*langue*] tends to approximate this ideal, and it is in reflecting upon the structure of its written expression that it approximates it. In all the journals and weeklies, however little solicitous of their literary pretensions, one finds an article, usually weekly, devoted to questions of speech [*langue*], a "say/ don't say." These contributions to its study attest how directly they concern that of language and consequently of linguistics, but they are, inevitably, written contributions on the study of written language [*langue*]. To the extent that they are such, written language enjoys its particular stature.

A second consequence of writing is to recall to us that linguistics, or the science of language [*langage*] and of tongues [*langues*], in general is itself included in anthropology. It is an eminent or, if one prefers, a fundamental part of it, because if it is true that man, *homo sapiens*, is such only to the extent that he is *homo loquens*, all study of language, all truly general linguistics, is part of the science of man taken in his essential difference, which is language. Cicero, therefore, was not wrong in situating eloquence, the art of oratory, at the top of the hierarchy, for if man is essentially a speaking animal, the exercise of speech [parole] is the art which makes him a man, and consequently it is also the most noble art of all. Such is, to note it in passing, the precise sense which the expression *humaniores litterae* had for this master of language. "Letters" are eminently "humane" because speech [parole] attains its perfection, as a means of signification, under its written form, and because literature, letters, is the most eminently human operation of all those that man can perform. The phrase [*humaniores litterae*] had formerly a precise meaning when it designated that specific theory of the preeminence of language, spoken first, then written, as the exercise of the specific difference by virtue of which man is the privileged being that he is. The intellectual, moral, social, and political culture of man as a speaking animal is the solid core of humanism, with its ambitions and its limitations.[9]

The program had been traced out by Aristotle, for whom the biological description of man included naturally the entirety of the works of language, for, except for man, we know of no dialectical, sophistic, rhetorical, oratorical animal who is concerned with judicial, political, or formal eloquence. Nothing of all that could exist without language, and language includes all that. Linguistics of the Aristotelian sort would include, therefore, beyond a strictly scientific phonology and an objective study of language of which modern linguistics gives the example, a study of the written expressions of the language in all its principal functions, from logic to rhetoric and poetry. It is because mathematics is not properly speaking a language[10] that Aristotle did not include it in his encyclopedia, but by including in it all other disciplines of speech [parole], from the sciences of nature to poetry, he had been aware of pursuing his study of man in terms of the specific difference by virtue of which he is man. The overall plan of the work makes it obvious that it is thus, but a casual remark shows now and then that he was clearly aware of the nature of his enterprise. So, having to justify in his *Rhetoric* the use of judicial eloquence, a branch of rhetoric, Aristotle declares: "It is absurd to maintain that a man ought to be ashamed of being incapable of defending himself with feet and hands, but not of being incapable of defending himself by speech and reason, since the use of language informed by reason is a more distinctive mark of the human being than the use of his members."[11] But under whatever form it presents itself, linguistics is the written study of testimony furnished by written languages [langues], works set out [élaborées] by speaking animals endowed with hands. Now, to speak is to act, to write is to do; the written word is the fruit of a production accomplished by means of writing, a trace of that which of itself leaves no traces. It is thanks to writing that linguistics is possible, but we only write what is spoken, and the written word has as its goal reading, the interior word [*parole*] which gives back to the written word life and meaning, without which it is nothing.

It is true to say that the two fundamental forms of language, the spoken and the written, are today so inextricably mixed up with each other that we are hardly able to think without the graphic form of words being more or less vaguely present to consciousness. We are always ready to specify the word by its graphic or orthographic identification. For example, I say *mots* [and imagine in my mind's eye]: *mots* [words], not *maux* [evils: homophone of *mots*]. The two modes of language remain no less different for all that. It is not the same "way of thinking" that expresses itself in the two cases. They are not simply different but even in a certain sense incompatible. We cannot think what we write in the same way we think what we say. Every speaker has had experience of this: we must choose between reading a discourse written in advance or speaking freely, with at most some notes which only serve as written references to sketch out the general course of the speech. To read, to interrupt one's reading in order to improvise a development, and to take up again the reading of one's text, is a delicate operation and one in which it is difficult to succeed. Nothing is more easy than to depart from the written text, but it is difficult to return to it because "the thread of ideas" spoken directly is not of the same nature as that of the written word. The hearer always senses at what moment the lecturer deviates from his text and at what moment he begins to try to rejoin it in order once more to follow its course. The tone of voice changes, the speaker no longer looks at his text but at his audience, the very style becomes different, breaking with its smooth continuity in order to become more halting, varied by many an accident on the way, in brief, contrived. Bergson would say, becoming self-making instead of remaining already made, thinking, instead of already thought. Certain speakers "read well"; they are those who push artifice to its highest pitch, for they add the air of being spoken to that which is to be read instead of spoken, or, put otherwise, they cause it to appear that they are not reading.[12] Actors who accept an invitation to give public readings, if what they read is not a text written for the stage, and even if what they read is the subsequently written version of a text first created for the speaker's platform, cease to give the hearer the pleasure that they give him as actors. There only remains a fine voice and impeccable diction, which is no small matter, but this is different from the pleasure afforded by a thought which utters itself. Perhaps here we touch the very secret of good theatrical diction which, written to be spoken, can be such — even in the most fantastic arabesques of a Shakespeare — without giving the impression of a recitation.[13] The best-written dramatic text, that of Racine, is rarely as dramatic as the heroic verbal litter of Corneille. The verse of Molière, at times unreadable, always forces itself on one when spoken by the actor on stage. It is not a question of the same sort of language in the two cases.[14]

The origin of writing is unknown to us, as is that of speaking. Of all the hypotheses made on this subject, mythological, theological, or poetical, the least likely is that writing preceded speaking. That has been maintained, however, and since the hypothesis was born in Soviet Russia, therefore arrived at by Marxist materialism, one is tempted to believe that the materialization of the vocal sign in the written sign has been in some way responsible for the favor that this position has enjoyed for some time.[15] It is not impossible, moreover, that signals endowed with meaning should have preceded the use of vocal signs such as the spoken words of which we make use. When archaeologists discover ancient raised stones, as at Carnac or Stonehenge, or statues such as those on Easter Island, they cannot resist the temptation to ask themselves: What do they mean [*signifient*]? At any rate, such signals would in no way be comparable to the verbal signs which transmit to the reader, if he knows how to decipher them, the knowledge of certain facts or of certain ideas intelligible to an intellect. What we would like to know is why, with what intention or intentions, our distant ancestors have wanted to engrave inscriptions on the stele which preserved for us the code of Hammurabi, on the bricks of Babylon, the obelisks of Egypt, or the stele of King Asoka?

We shall never know that, but we know why we today write certain information or certain of our thoughts. We know particularly what the result of the act of writing is. The materialist intuition of those who maintained for some time at least that writing is anterior to the phonetic sign finds a certain degree of justification in the fact that writing completely materializes the sign. The spoken word is already physical, but it is sound: invisible, impalpable, fugitive, and almost momentary. In brief, it is material as is the biological and the living. In the case of writing, *signum signi*, the *signum* is the inanimate sign of an animate sign. Its properties are those of metal, stone, papyrus, parchment, and, finally, paper, which, though perishable, outlive by a long time the author of the book and its readers. The most immediate result of writing, the act of "putting something down in writing," is to take language out of the order of the biological in order to integrate it into the physical order by stripping it of the qualities proper to the first and endowing it with those of the second. This is, moreover, what the innumerable metaphors disclose in which prose writers, and still more poets, proclaim their ambition of producing a *ktèma eis aei*, an *aere perennius*, verses as inured to the bite of time as *enamels and cameos*. As fleeting as their speech, poets dream of immortalizing themselves in the ink and paper of their books:

Je te donne ces vers, afin que si, mon nom
Aborde heureusement aux époques lointaines . . .

[I offer these verses to you, so that my name
might happily reach to distant times . . .].

To live on in what one has written, even be it only in letters to one's daughter or friends, as with Madame de Sévigné, is not the most important thing; it is the wish to communicate oneself to those not present, known or even unknown, as seems to be the case with some authors of graffiti who take the first passerby into the confidence of their loves or their hates, when the real desire of those whose lives are written on water is not simply to leave behind a durable trace of their brief passage on earth by inscribing their name on a rock or on stone walls:

nomine stultorum semper parietibus adsunt . . .

[fools' names always appear in public places . . .].

One hardly dares to write those words, for one only does the same in having one's name engraved on one's future tomb, or upon the present tomb of others, proclaiming moreover that one sends the latter eternal regrets, that is to say, regrets which would be eternal if one were eternal oneself, in the absence of which the hard stone cut by the engraver of funerary inscriptions will confer upon them the life which we lack. In the Campo Santo of Pisa the sarcophagus at whose base a mother caused to be engraved in Greek letters a tender farewell to her dead daughter survives both, and it will communicate for a long time yet to innumerable travelers the emotion which dictated it. It is quite true, and we shall return to this, that the word endowed with the solidity of lifeless matter confers on the thought that it signifies an ability to endure and to communicate itself denied to the living word. It is necessary, but sufficient, that the reader should know the meaning of the words that the written signs signify for the thought and intention of their writer in order that wherever he may be in whatever time he becomes aware of the signs, their meaning might be immediately communicated to him. All the modern procedures of registration and reproduction of written documents conserved in archives multiply indefinitely in time and space the area of this possible communication.

Speech [parole] in becoming written changes species. Spoken, it is a being; written, it is a thing. The spoken word is not at the disposition of our needs and desires. One must be very familiar with the interlocutor in order to request him to repeat what he has just said, and he will repeat it, moreover, otherwise than he said it. One can begin to read a verse or a sentence again and again as many times as one wants, for there the speaker is set entirely apart from his own speech.

A double event is produced then, its parts connected and nevertheless of inverse meaning. If one wishes to repeat from memory there is a good chance that the phrase may be falsified. This is the phenomenon familiar in the case of inaccurate citation, which is not an accident but almost a rule of the literary memory and still more of the musical memory. I am afraid to verify my thesis by citing from memory the word of Emile Faguet: "Do you wish to make an initial citation [*une citation originale*]? Then make it exact." If it is a poet who cites another poet, the inexactitude is almost inevitable, for it is not then a question of weakness of memory but of a natural power of the word [*parole*], which causes each to take it up spontaneously on his own account and say what he intended to say again. Paul Claudel was particularly inept at citing because he was eminently suited to speaking, but who among us is not afflicted with a "poetic" memory? The activity of language, much more than the passivity of memory, lies at the origin of these apparent lapses, which are rather creations.

Inversely, the work of writing in fact has for its goal to eliminate the presence of the writer. It is only necessary for one's work to be republished twenty times for it to become sufficient to itself, to the point of excluding its author. The great books of humanity are anonymous or rigged up in imaginary attributions. It is as if their innumerable readers had become the authors of them. Particularly felicitous formulations become proverbs. In the language written by every writer worthy of the name, finally, the perfect sentence imposes itself on the mind like a resistant solid, or, better still, like a structure of which, in themselves and in their order, the elements manifest a strict necessity. This is what the writer wanted in writing it. To the extent that one feels the presence of the author, what he said could be said better. A "labored" style is not yet a good style, but the labor may be recompensed, and when it is, one does not find any trace of it anymore. The sentence is there, owing its being only to itself, evident and necessary, but at the same time easy with an ease which is that of nature itself. However the work has come about, the effort is irrelevant, for if it takes place, it works to make itself invisible by eclipsing its author. *An object so perfect that it should wipe out our imprints.* . . . "Do we not recognize in this," asks Alain Robbe-Grillet, "the highest ambition of every writer?" Yes, and that very phrase is a perfect example of it; it merits the recompense of anonymity.

The characteristic that writing has of immobilizing thought in time in conferring on it the permanent possibility of an indefinitely renewable present modifies profoundly the attitude of the subject speaking in regard to his own speech [*parole*]. The necessity of the effort and time required for the act of writing, so different from the instantaneousness of speech, gives to the writer the possibility of adopting a critical attitude in regard to his own expression. This possibility is an invitation to do so, that is to say, to take one's work up again in order to correct it. Written thought, therefore, differs sensibly from spoken thought. Neither their rhythm nor their progression nor their substance are the same. Boileau's advice "Revise your work twenty times" could not have as its counterpart the advice to the orator "repeat your words twenty times to the listener, repeat them ceaselessly and re-repeat them." Before delivering the final product to the public, the writer repeats himself in order to correct himself. In principle the reader knows nothing of the history of the work written. Speakers who "search out their words," their sentences, and their ideas soon discourage their public. Even in conversation we cease to hear them.[16]

This effort to find form for thought is exactly the same as that of *homo loquens* to invent words and fashion himself a language. Only in the case of writing, the effort becomes considerable because the resources of the signifier being inadequate, since finite, to the requirements of the signified, which are properly infinite, words and phrases naturally lag behind thought, which is more rapid than language, and do not discern exactly the meaning of it, which one never captures in the net of words and which escapes in every direction. It is thus with the most ordinary written letter compared to the direct conversation that it replaces: "I had many other things to say to you . . ."; "Time and circumstances prevent me from explaining to you properly . . ."; etc. This elementary effort to say what one thinks as simply and precisely as possible is moreover only the first of the long series which will lead thinking man to create for himself the various languages he needs: for science, which is only the most rigorous expression of thought expressing itself as knowledge of nature; for judicial and social life, without which man would not be the reasonable animal he is; for logic and mathematics, which are the sciences of the most abstract and most universally applicable methods of signification; for dialectics, or the art of displaying the probable in the innumerable matters wherein certitude escapes us; finally, for rhetoric, the art of persuading others of what we believe ourselves or desire to have believed because, true or false, we need to believe it or to have it believed. Taken in its entirety and totality, Aristotle's *Organon* presents the most perfect image that has ever been proposed of language under all its forms and in its principal applications. It is a picture of thought observed in its verbal and written expressions, classed according to their objects or ends, and described with the objectivity of a naturalist. Without writing, nothing of all that would be possible. An unwritten poetry is possible; yet as a matter of fact, any poetry is known to us only from the moment it is fixed in writing. But one can imagine that such should have existed, for a long time perhaps, from mouth to ear before being written. On the contrary, it is difficult to conceive of the development of symbolic logic [*logistique*] and mathematics, of physics and biology, without the assistance that is brought to them by books wherein the results of acquired knowledge are gathered and conserved, a kind of material collective memory of humanity, held as a common possession.

It is probably for this reason that the *Rhetoric* occupies the place that Aristotle has reserved for it at the end of the *Organon*. It is, we might say, the art of persuasion, but language under all its forms and in its most diverse uses is a particular application of that art. If thought is to speak to oneself, one thinks first of all in order to persuade oneself of the meaning of what one wishes to say and of what one says to oneself. Rhetoric perhaps enters into interior discourse most significantly, each one having the art of persuading himself of what he wishes to believe, even if he is not truly certain of it. It is not until scientific research, where each one wraps the narrow nucleus of his well-founded certainties in a thick matrix of prejudices, common, scientific, or otherwise (which he takes for granted under the name of principles and by dint of reaffirming them or simply holding them as granted), that he ends by considering them proved. Each time that one argues "to support a conclusion" in any order whatsoever, one puts scientific or dialectic method at the service of a rhetoric which the history of the sciences shows is inadequate at times to convince, even when it has truth on its side. This is why, moreover, with his customary penetration, Aristotle saw that to demarcate precisely the domain of rhetoric from that of dialectic and science itself is a difficult task, so much do they border and at times mix with each other. It is practically impossible, in the whole complex that is called demonstration, to separate out what rises from the absolutely certain, or from the more or less probable, or from the artifice of persuasion. Rhetoric is one aspect of dialectic; it is universal, as is dialectic, and neither of these two arts is the scientific study of any subject in particular.[17] But although neither the one nor the other is science, it is difficult for them not to tend to take its form, if only because the most efficacious dialectical or rhetorical argument is that which can be passed off as a scientific demonstration, or, better still, is one. "The more people correctly treat their particular subject, the more they distance themselves from pure rhetoric or pure dialectic."[18] Inversely, there are general modes of argumentation, as from the whole to the part, or from the more to the less, which apply equally to all matter upon which one could speak, the natural, moral, or political sciences. No more than one can completely describe man as the speaking animal without including in the description the logician, the mathematician, and the scholar, can one conceive him such as he is without taking account of the dialectician and the rhetorician which he obligatorily is by the sole fact that he thinks, lives, and speaks in society.

There is no question of contesting the right of modern linguistics to exist as a distinct science. It exists, and the fact dispenses with legitimation. We no longer contest its right to define itself as "the scientific study of human language." At the very most one can make the observation in this connection that insofar as the existence of a nonhuman language shall not have been demonstrated, it will suffice to say: the scientific study of language. The difficulties begin with the word "scientific." It is defined here, we have said, in opposition to "prescriptive"; therefore, as a matter of fact, linguistics is opposed here to grammar, a bit like, according to Lucien Levy-Bruhl, the science of manners would be opposed to morals. But no tongue [langue] can constitute itself without secreting its own grammar. There being no essential difference between the way in which we speak and that in which we ought to speak, the second only defines itself with reference to the first. At the very least, grammar is a fact of speech [langue]; now, it is practically inseparable from writing, which is not a discipline foreign to linguistics, since without writing and the grammar which governs written language [langue] linguistics would be impossible. The linguist as linguist can abstract from the facts of writing, but then the vocal signs which he retains as the proper matter of linguistics become a pure abstraction. The linguist then writes a book on what language would be if it were not composed in part of signs written like those of which books are composed. To print a book about language that makes abstraction of the writing which the printing reproduces would be rather paradoxical.

Writing is a fact as eminently human as the articulated word. Like the latter, it serves in support of thought, makes possible mutual comprehension and communication, and, if the final cause proper to spoken language is to make possible social and political life — the supreme form of human life — writing is directed to that same final causality as being the very type of the means of collective communication which makes possible all fully constituted society. We can scarcely conceive of a minimally extended society which does not refer itself to some written document such as a charter, constitution, or code. The linguistics which wishes to be considered as the science of spoken language [langue parlé] precisely insofar as it is spoken is therefore from the beginning of the game at grips with the difficulty of submitting an object to observation which it is impossible for it to take hold of under the precise form which it itself declares to be essential to it. As in those observations in physics where the single factor of the observer changes the nature of the phenomenon, the single factor of transposing everything spoken into written form, inevitable in order to constitute the science of it, puts linguistics in a false position, not so much in itself as insofar as it pretends to be the *science* of an object with which it cannot deal without modifying its nature. If the study of writing, then, is but one of the annexes of linguistics, all written linguistics is but an annex of itself, which creates some embarrassment.

In order to get out of this awkward position, it does not suffice, as has been proposed, to refer to the psychologist problems connected to the facts of language which refuse to allow themselves to be included in the area assigned to the linguist as such. It would be difficult to find an observer more diligent, more perspicacious of the incessantly changing relations of language and thought, than Paul Valéry was. No one using the French tongue will ever be able to exploit the resources of language in speaking of language with more mastery than did this master of our prose. We add that he detested metaphysics, or, quite simply, philosophy. Valéry had attained to philosophical blindness.[19] It is therefore with a lively curiosity that one sees him at grips with the invincible difficulty of speaking of language, which was his major concern, while using only ideas which he claims to be psychological, although all have evident metaphysical implications. Mind [*esprit*] is more or less inevitable, but the word is handled only rarely, and with many a precaution to disarm it of its explosives. Monsieur Teste is called "Head," not "Mind." His author thought of writing a "Concerto for Solo Brain," but he did not go so far as to project a concerto for the brain of a sheep or of a calf without this difference posing for him some problem. This descendant of Mallarmé was the bearer of another message, which he repeated to satiety without anyone having taken great interest in it, although its importance is considerable.

Valéry never ceased saying that works interested him less than the act of producing them.[20] He always repeated that what haunted him in the act of writing was the concern for precision, the sure mark of the state of mind of the craftsman: work of precision. Writing thus conceived, as it is its nature to be, is before all else a "work well done," or as we said formerly, "made by the hand of an artisan." That alone would suffice to foster the feeling that writing is of another species, or even of another genus, than speaking. One acts when one speaks; one makes when one writes. The activity of the poet is, as his name indicates, essentially *poietic*,[21] but every writer is more or less of a poet in this sense, for to write is to produce, and the piling up of paper blackened by scribes of every kind, by professional writers, once multiplied by the industry of publishing houses, ends by occupying a considerable space. The problem posed by the incessant swelling of the cascade which overruns the public or even private libraries contrasts with the fluidity of speech, of the "cascade of words" which flows about the world without leaving there any more traces than water does on a duck's back.

Poets are the "makers" par excellence, but every writer is such in some measure, and it is what distinguishes him from the speaker, or, as the linguists accustom us to say, the locutor. Spoken language is no more a product than is the thought which speaks. It is this thought itself in its sensible condition, the only condition in which it is directly and objectively observable to us. Written language is a product of artificial fabrication (an *artifact*) which cannot realize itself unless the spoken language submits itself to the exigencies of writing, which affect thought itself. Every writer concerned with the quality of his work and aware of its nature knows that the written thought is not a simple record of the spoken thought but is another thought, conceived with a view to writing and obedient to its own laws. This is the immense domain of literature, worked and exploited by innumerable workers who live in it more or less comfortably, but who, even when they die of it, prefer it to any other domain. The material from which it is constructed is spoken language, which must be pruned, filed down, adjusted, and tightened often, and at times extended, but always changed in view of that other collaborator who is the eventual reader for whom, other than the single writer himself, one writes. *Ego scriptor,*[22] Valéry gladly said, thus naming himself as a member of a well-defined species which follows its own ends by appropriate means.

The intervention of writing, which presupposes speaking, therefore makes something else in fact and does more than merely incarnate speaking. The second sign [*signum*], which is the sign of the first sign [*signi*], is not the expression of the same signified, for it is necessary, in order to be written, that the signified of speech organize itself in view of the new end which thus becomes its own. One cannot undergo the labor of writing without regretting at times the absence of a recording machine for thought which would save us the trouble of reproducing thought's expression. But this imagining is meaningless. The recorder of thought might go as fast as thought, but one would see in deciphering its message that it is not legible, that it is neither spoken nor written thought. Valéry noted that he spoke quickly because his speech ran after his thought. If it had been able to overtake it, it would have ceased to be speech. A machine for recording thought would not deliver to us any written message of any sort; it would have nothing to say or to write. However it may be with this fiction of a machine for transcribing thought, we must infer that since the word *thought* has some correspondence to reality (otherwise there would be neither meaning nor language), and while conceding that it does not mean a thing, the *x* that this name designates imposes on itself notable modifications of structure in order to adapt itself to the exigencies of what is written.

7

The *Seventh Letter*

The relation of the written word to the spoken word, taken in itself and as a distinct problem, is itself one of the principal constants of the philosophy of language. From Plato's *Phaedrus* to Ferdinand de Saussure some philosophers and linguists have always recalled, with a sort of embarrassment so obvious is the thing, that writing is as it were a sort of husk [*doublure*] of speech [*parole*]. If man did not speak, he would have nothing to write, and for him to write consists essentially in representation, whether it be ideas by means of hieroglyphs or words by means of letters. But there also have always been those of opposing view who observe that writing is not just the husk of the spoken word, [*parole dite*], for it [writing] does with and for language [*langue*] many things of which the spoken word by itself alone is incapable. The politician who amuses himself with Lysias by treating him as a speech writer [*écriveur de discours*] evidently thinks that a true speech is one that is spoken, not written. But on the other hand, while admitting that the most influential men of state are ashamed of writing speeches, and thus bequeathing them to posterity in written form, for fear of passing not as men of state but rather as rhetoricians, Socrates makes Phaedrus remark that in fact these politicians have no opposition to writing their speeches after having given them and take pains besides to insert in them their name and the names of their partisans![1] The problem itself is conspicuous there: "Shall we discuss the rules of writing and of language as we proposed? —Very well." Rhetoric is naturally at the center of the discussion, and with it comes philosophy, which has nothing particularly modern about it, but since the problem posed concerns spoken discourse and written discourse, it is indeed necessary that Socrates will discuss writing. Whatever he may say about it, one cannot fail to remember that the real Socrates wrote nothing, but that no one would be concerned with him today if Plato had not taken the trouble of attributing to him many an imaginary conversation and discourse, and that when Plato himself confides to us his objections to writing, he writes them.[2] The marvellous masterpiece of literary art that the *Phaedrus* is, from its plane tree on the Ilyssus right up to the final prayer, with that sovereign mastery of the conduct of a discourse sown with skillfully calculated *peripeteia* and yet springing into existence from an apparently capricious nonchalance: not only would we not hear it today if Plato had not written it, but it would not have been born without writing. With the *Phaedrus* and the *Symposium* the most skillful art of prose calculated to give pleasure to a man of taste attained a peak which can hardly be surpassed, a summit inconceivable without written language.

Like every writer solicitous for his art, Plato in his dialogue reserved the best for the end. After apparently being engaged in the quicksands of a dialectic without possible conclusion about what is the best form of language, the spoken or the written, he then arrives at the heart of the question, which is to know whether or not they are of the same nature. To the extent that a judgment of value is alone in question, Plato's Socrates does not completely succeed in convincing us. The myth of Thoth the inventor of many arts, including writing, is not without interest. To the inventor — who flatters himself with conferring on mortals the means of fixing and conserving language, and consequently of increasing their knowledge and their memory — the sage king of Egyptian Thebes [Thamus, Ammon] replies that it will be quite to the contrary. For memory will atrophy by dint of being less useful, but above all, to remember something because one knows it is completely different from remembering having read it in a book. The first of these two acts alone has its origins in memory; the second is only a sort of reminiscence whose object is a fact, not an idea.

Pushing further the intuition that he has of the real distinction of the two orders, Socrates-Plato gives as a proof of this, or at least as an indication of it, the difference of condition between spoken thought and written thought: the one is living, the other is inanimate. This is why Plato reduced writing to an image of speech. We reproach him today on this matter without always understanding it. The works of the painter have all the appearances of life, but if you pose a question to the painting, it remains mute. Likewise for books. Once written, discourses cease to speak. Question books, and they maintain the same solemn silence, or if one prefers, they continue to give the same invariable response. Plato vividly felt the difficulties of the written text, open and defenseless to the first comer, a prey to the misinterpretation of commentary, "without a father to protect it and incapable of defending itself [275e]." Therein is the difference between the two remembrances rooted in that more profound difference between two ways of knowing, for the written word and the spoken word are children of the same family, but the second one alone is a legitimate son, to wit: "The living word of knowledge, that which has a soul, and of which, properly speaking, the written word is no more than the image."[3] In order to understand Plato here, one must compare, as he does, not so much the written word and the spoken word as the speaker whom one hears and the book which one reads. A world separates them; we repeat once more that they are generically different.

Modern chronolatry is an evil so general that it is hard to discern how much of what was true in Plato's time is still true today. What, since Gutenberg, we call a book did not exist then. Plato could not have foreseen that his complete works would one day be published on India paper by Oxford University Press, in French in the Pleiade collection, and that certain dialogues would even be put in circulation as pocket books; but he knew already what the reader's attitude is. It is only metaphorically that Descartes could compare reading to "studied conversation" with the best minds of other times, for if these minds speak to us through their books, they are not there to hear our response or to respond to our questions. There is no inter-locutor in reading. It is indeed because we know that no one is there to respond that our reading is often so passive. One can "question a text" upon the condition that one give the response oneself.

"In the beginning God created the heaven and the earth." What do these words mean, St. Augustine asks himself? Then he adds: "Moses wrote that; he wrote it and he is gone. . . . he is not at present before me. For if he were, I would take hold of him. I would ask him, I would implore him in God's name to reveal to me the meaning of these words, and I would bend my ears to the sounds gushing from his mouth. If he spoke to me in Hebrew, his speech would strike my senses in vain, nothing of it would reach my mind. If he spoke Latin, I would know what he said, but how would I know if what he said were true?"[4] The modern reader has too many books to read; he is too hurried; he too often reads in order to repose his soul and to distract himself. One cannot expect from him that impassioned questioning of an interlocutor who is not the author and for whom, supposing it is done, each finally replies himself, without any certitude of giving the correct response. He therefore ceases to question. Hence what one has so well called "This unpunished vice, reading." Not so unpunished, however. It is not dangerous to read to distract oneself, to repose one's soul, to instruct oneself, but it is dangerous to read in order not to think. The danger is not imaginary. Some read so much that they do not think any more. There are those who are "stupefied by reading." Not without danger does one put oneself in a state of voluntary passivity, sought after as a resignation of the intellect, leaving it to another to think for one. Assuredly, the reader thinks also, but little, the least possible, like a man who wishes to wake up precisely so as to taste the pleasure of sleeping.

If that is the way the matter stands, why substitute an inert image for a living original? Here alone shall I abandon Plato to his critics. The true philosopher will in fact voluntarily do without writing. He will only cultivate the garden of letters, sowing and planting, for amusement. And further, "he will only write his thoughts as preserving evidence in order to protect them against forgetfulness and old age, be it his own or that of some other old man following the same route as he." To see them thus growing in some soul other than his own is a noble diversion, but how much more noble is the serious occupation of the dialectician who, coming across a soul related to his own, sows and plants there, by his knowledge, words capable of living their own life and bearing every seed and fruit [276d, 277a]!

Plato's arrow here passes above the target, and others than linguists will say that this sort of metaphysical speculation does not interest them. But this attitude may be erroneous. Doubtlessly Plato's analysis is inconclusive in reducing literature to the role of a pastime, or at the very most to a memorandum [aide-mémoire]. It is incomparably more than that, since it is the instrument which makes possible science, its conservation, its growth, and its communication beyond all conceivable limits. It is what makes the *Phaedrus* possible and, with this masterpiece, the immense treasure of literature of all sorts, the common patrimony of man. From Plato's time and place the present immensity of that "literature," multiplied as it were to infinity by the press, was not yet foreseeable. The loss of the written word would have been [eût été] an evil; it is an evil, for before printing much that was written was lost, but that was not the planetary catastrophe which it would be at present. Plato did not foresee, he could not foresee, the "serious" future of writing, which, along with reading, was a simple pastime for those who loved to read better than to party. We, who would like to emphasize it, cannot adequately imagine the *peculiar* importance of the written language [langue écrite]. To succeed in that it would be necessary to be able to portray to oneself what any page whatsoever would look like written by someone who had never read anything, living among people who had never read anything. It is simply unimaginable. We have at times the unpleasant dream of a man who would know himself to be the last and who, knowing that the totality of science, beauty, and wisdom only existed now in the little which he still remembered, would be the anguished witness of their progressive disintegration in his memory. It is a terrible nightmare, and it is nevertheless that which could happen — ought we to say will happen? — in the case of a gradual or sudden annihilation of written matter. No, Plato's disdain for the written word is not entirely justified.

The author of the *Phaedrus* was not wrong, nevertheless, to think that "the best books being only a commemoration of something known," *the true manner of writing,* for a man in possession of the principles of truth, beauty, and justice, is to engrave them, by speaking them, in the soul of those who hear them. In this sense, teaching through speech is the true art of writing, for these principles are the true possession of him who knows them, but he also possesses their legitimate offspring, first and above all else the word, speech that takes shape in his heart [*sein*] and then proceeds to take root, then to bear fruit, in the thought of its hearers.[5] A dialogue on this subject ought to have no end. When all shall have been said, we just could not deny either to Plato, or to the truth, the proposition that if thought is strictly possible without writing, writing is not possible without thought. In whatever way one might wish to conceive it, their relation remains essentially one of subordination. That is perhaps the most constant of the philosophical constants of language. No phonology or phonemics will be able to invalidate that.

In the strength of his youth, tormented by the desire to know, beyond so many things which are new to him, that one thing after which there would be nothing left to know, the future philosopher will engage in an inquiry which he foresees to be immense, but of which he does not imagine for an instant that it could be endless.

In good time he makes the acquaintance of the skeptics, but these reasonable people are not serious. Habitually making the most of the inadequacies which every expression of a difficult thought suffers, they conclude to the vanity of the efforts of all those fine minds who have preceded them in the quest for truth. There is no certitude in philosophical matters; at the very most there are but probabilities. But how are we to judge of the probable unless by relation to a certainty which, by hypothesis, we declare inaccessible?

In books and in society we come across rational positive minds who identify their ideal in matters of knowledge with that of the mathematician or the physicist, but positivism explains everything scientifically, except science. Its very possibility remains for it mysterious. Descartes decided not to accept any other than mathematical certitude, but he asked himself right away how to know if various mathematics were true. He grappled with the problem, which engaged three powerful philosophical geniuses after him, without counting many a master of lesser importance. But the net result of all that was only to end up with Hume's conclusion, alone and disheartened in a universe deaf to his questions.

There still remain religion and the mystics. But they do not offer philosophy, they dispense with it; and perhaps finally it is they who are right, but one cannot know that before having undergone the experience of it, more especially as religion itself ends by promising, as supreme blessedness, a knowledge more perfect than faith. The paradise of a Mus-

lim such as Avicenna was the ideal of a paradise for philosophers and
scholars, at least when he spoke as a philosopher. But the poet Avicenna
dreamed of a paradise beyond that.

The most disconcerting spectacle for a friend of wisdom is not nevertheless the diversity of response, in the end discouraged or hesitant, which
the history of philosophy shows him; it is rather the fact that whatever
length of life he be granted, under his own eyes new philosophies are born
and win the assent of a more or less great number of minds to the point
of making of the proselytes enthusiasts. Then one sees that blaze fall back
bit by bit like a dying fire. The idea that if truth has not yet been found
at this late date, their chances of discovering it are weak does not seem
to disquiet new philosophers. And they are not entirely wrong here, for
it has not yet been discovered by them, it has not yet become *their* truth.
It is, therefore, proper that they seize upon and aggressively affirm ideas
already discovered a hundred times, and assault if necessary those who
have known such ideas before them, but who, to hear them, have misunderstood the ideas or poorly expressed them, in brief, who have not
the right to have perceived them before the coming of minds more worthy
to discover them. It is not necessary to blame anyone. Truth is such a de-
lectable pleasure that he who finds one is excusable in wishing to sacrifice
all others to it. That makes a "system" for the philosopher the most di-
verting thing in the world to formulate and, for the professor of the history of philosophy, to "crack" in order to see "how it is made," "how it
proceeds," and "what is inside it."

That is, nevertheless, not the most interesting feature of this history.
Rather, it is the spectacle of the collective defeat which philosophical speculation is, taken in its entirety, when one compares this immense and magnificent effort to its result. It is quite far from being nothing, but it leaves
a feeling of frustration. The love of wisdom is not diminished thereby. No
regret arises within the philosopher for having consecrated his life to philosophy. He feels, quite to the contrary, that if the life he leads were to
be longer, he would consecrate it yet to the same research, as to a good
which one feels henceforth inaccessible without consenting to the misfor-
tune of renouncing it.

This experience produces another like it. The more one persists in
pushing research to the threshold of first principles, the more one has occasions of ascertaining that the ancient philosophers have proceeded properly on these ultimate questions and, without despairing of finding there
an answer, had to be satisfied with the feeling of being very close to it,
acknowledging an insurmountable difficulty in formulating it.

The "Seventh Letter" of Plato is a testimony to this. Whoever may
be its author, and no one is more worthy of having written it than Plato

himself, this letter contains a long passage which every friend of wisdom ought to meditate on at an early period of his development, if it were not so evident that a previous practice of philosophy is required for him who wishes to understand it.

Plato shows himself there at grips with the task of communicating philosophy to others after having acquired it himself. Every professor of philosophy knows the problem. The account Plato makes of his failures and of their causes will never cease to be instructive. Perhaps it is so today, more than ever, at a time when there is so much knowledge [*science*] and so little wisdom.

Of the many useful and true things that he says there, I shall retain here only that remark on the vanity of philosophical writings. "There is not," says the author, "and there will not ever be any writing of mine on the subject. For it is not susceptible of being set forth like the other branches of knowledge; but after having spoken of it much, and spent a life doing so, it happens that a light may suddenly be lit in a soul by a flame flashing out from another and that it nourishes next itself." He could not have imagined any task better than communicating to others such important truths had he been capable of it. "But are they susceptible of being written and set forth in a satisfactory manner?"[5a]

Plato does not claim to be the first to pose the question. On the contrary, he recognizes that there is a solid argument against those who venture to set down philosophical opinions in writing. He himself will only be taking up the question others have laid down.

For every object whatsoever, if it is a real object, five conditions are required in order that knowledge of it be possible.

The first is that its name be known. For example, a *circle* is first of all "a thing of which we speak," therefore a thing that one names, and its name is that which comes to be said.

The second is that we know its definition. This is composed of names and verbal forms. That which bears the name of *round*, of *annular*, or of *circle* can be defined as that in which the distance from the circumference to the center is at each point equal. Incidentally, one will notice that this necessity of beginning every inquiry into a real object with its "nominal definition" will be maintained by Aristotle and the entire scholastic peripateticism of the middle ages.

In the third place comes the image of the circle, which one can at will write with chalk on or erase from a blackboard, or pattern and cut out in circumference, then break into pieces. Not a single one of these things can attain to the circle itself. For all these things are of another order than it.

Fourth, we must possess intellectual knowledge and true opinion concerning these things: to know what the circle itself is and no longer merely the material images which one can form of it. Included in this class was all that which, concerning the circle, is found in thought and which, by that fact itself, is of a different nature from the material circle as well as its image, its definition, and its name.

Fifth comes knowing the circle itself, object of the true knowledge that we have, that which is the real being to which we give the name of circle. This is what Plato often calls elsewhere the "circle in and of itself." From all that which precedes, the intellection of the circle is what resembles most the circle itself and is the nearest thing to its true nature. The three other modes of existence of the circle remain farther from it (342a–d).

This distinction applies to all objects of knowledge, to the straight as well as the circular, to colors, to the good, the beautiful, the just, to all natural bodies living or not, to all actions carried out and all passivities undergone. Without having acquired the knowledge of the thing according to the first four ways of knowing it we have mentioned, no one can attain to the fifth, that is to say, to knowledge of the very thing, "in and by itself." Here Plato hurries toward his conclusion, whose words he makes us weigh: "Further, the weakness of language being what it is, each of these first four modes tries to show what each thing resembles, quite as much as what each thing is. This is why no intelligent man will try to formulate his philosophical views in the medium of language, and above all not in a language that cannot change anymore, as is the case with language which has been put into writing under the form of letters" (343a).

This recoiling before writing as a form of language twice removed from pure thought might invite long reflections. For why does thought fear this fixation under a form henceforth inalterable[6] if not because the vocal word [verbe] never definitely translates thought and always remains ready to begin again in order to correct itself and utter itself, perhaps better, at least otherwise? Because the fundamental inadequacy of speech to thought becomes visible and as fixed as ever in writing, thought, above all that of a Plato, rebels against this definitive and irremediable betrayal, which permits the first comer to ascribe to it the only meaning that he himself is capable of conceiving, adding to it: "He wrote it!" The most serious difficulty is that the philosopher betrays his own thought in writing it, since in each point of his discourse he appears only to have thought what he wrote down, whereas he thought a hundred other things, and even only to have thought what he wrote just as he wrote it, although perhaps, even probably, his text simply represents one of many efforts of his thought to express itself. The road that leads the writer from his thought to words is not certain, and the road which leads the reader from the words of the writer to his thought is even more uncertain. The premature silence of some philosophers is explained by that fact. That of certain theologians more so still: *Videtur mihi ut palea* . . . [It appeared to me as so much chaff . . .].

The contingency of the verbal sign in relation to thought is hardly less, and with regard to the object of thought it is extreme. Nothing would prohibit it from calling round what we call square, or curved what we call straight. For those who take pleasure in giving to things the names of their contraries, or of playing with words, nothing is less permanent than a name; nevertheless, in whatever way we name the circle, or red, or justice, the nature of that which these names signify remains the same.

After the name, we said, comes the image and the definition. But the image is of a nature other than the essence. The image of the circle is not without possible connections with that of many a straight line, whose essence is exclusive of its [the circle's] essence. The circle in itself has no tangents. With respect to the definition, it also is composed of verbal forms and of names such as those which we have come to describe. And moreover, whether it be a question of the name, of the definition, of the image, or of the essence, the same cause of error is always at work. We try to define what the thing is, its substance, and we define or name instead one of its qualities. Now, a quality can display itself, not demonstrate itself, and as the testimony of the senses can always be contested, it finally leaves him who invokes it in great insecurity.

The philosopher, therefore, will relinquish the four first expressions of thought in order to attach himself to the fifth, which is his proper object. There Plato finds himself at grips with a problem that every philosopher knows to be insoluble, and yet, nevertheless, never resolves to refuse to pose: How to think the intelligible object such as it is in itself outside of thought? One will say no doubt that the enterprise being contradictory, the question is absurd. Yes. But the contrary position is no less impossible, for to think the object as other in knowledge than what it is in reality is not to think it at all: it is to think something else in its place; and if, as idealism would have it, this other thing is a product of thought, thought then only ever knows itself and is deprived of that immediate hold upon the being of the other as other with which it nevertheless feels itself flooded in sensation.

If one refuses to hold this experience as unreal, one must admit that some knowledge of the other is possible, but the problem becomes then to know how to transmit to others the little knowledge that we have of it. How communicate? He who tries it quickly convinces himself of his impotence and, if he persists, opens himself to ridicule. Plato described the embarrassment of the philosopher who commits the imprudence of expressing himself upon any essence whatsoever in writing, in speech [*paroles*], or in responding to questions. There is no sophist who has some experience in the dialectic struggle and in felling his adversary who does not before long make his adversary appear to his audience as a man who understands nothing of the things of which he speaks or upon which he writes. Others do not always perceive "that it is not the thought of the writer or the talker which is at fault, but the defective nature of each one of the four instruments" (343d). Neither words, nor definitions, nor images, nor even intellection, which nevertheless is the closest and the most nearly related to it, realize the desired grasp of the intelligible essence which is the matter to be known. It only happens that as a necessary result of moving from one of these ways to another, the mind naturally disposed to this sort of knowledge may end by engendering in itself the desired reward. Such is the condition of the sage. Nevertheless, let us not believe that having attained his end, whatever it may be worth, he commits the error of confiding to writing the result of his efforts.

Why would he do that? The ultimate truth expresses itself in some quite short sentences, and there is no need of any memorandum to remember them, for he who has acquired the intelligible is not in danger of ever forgetting it anymore. No more could the function of writing be to communicate truth to others, for truth does not come out of books. After long efforts to press and grind to powder names, definitions, and images, truth springs up from the contact with minds made for it like a sudden bolt of lightning which does not flash in any other mind [*esprit*]. The intelligible thus seized is not transmissible, and the philosopher knows it. Taking up once more the subject of the *Phaedrus*, the author of the "Seventh Letter" concludes: "Every great mind, treating the most elevated objects, will then guard itself well from exposing them to the ill will and incomprehension of men by putting them down in writing." When one sees any writing whatsoever, such as laws, edited by some legislator, or any other sort, "one can be sure that it is not there that its author put the highest value. If he is a great mind, do not doubt that he has sheltered his treasures as much as possible" (344c).

We cannot read without emotion these disenchanting words from the greatest artist of the philosophical word that the world may have known. They illuminate certain disconcerting elements of his work. There is no "philosophy of Plato" except that which the intrepid blind man Victor Brochard constructed for him, week after week, a dialogue posing each time a question to which, eight days later, another dialogue gave reply. The myths themselves were inserted in this philosophy of ideas as if their ultimate meaning were that one must content oneself finally with images, for lack of the ability in language to grasp hold of the intelligible, which is above language. Socrates had not written anything; Plato had the skill to finish his dialogues without bringing them to a conclusion; and we have seen many a great mind, as it were consumed by the love of philosophy, retire prematurely into silence. Maine de Biran hides his writings; Ravaisson, Lachelier, Boutroux, worn out by doctoral theses, desert teaching in order to give themselves the alibi of some great office; Bergson himself, after having courageously struggled to speak of the inexpressible, and as if haunted by an anticipatory fear of what the future would do with his writings, put back from year to year the moment of delivering to the crowd his ultimate thoughts. This is because, above speech and writing, condemned to multiplicity, he searched for the intuition which makes of philosophy a "simple act," a sounding in the depths from which what he can write or say about it only delivers up what one brings back from it, good garbage for disciples and historians. This great mind knew that "the master, insofar as he formulates, develops, translates into abstract ideas what he brings [back], is already in some fashion a disciple of himself." But is it not that to the extent that he attains — even so tentative as it may be — the simplicity of philosophical intuition, the philosopher finds himself, in himself, on this side of himself, in an *abditum mentis* [absence of mental activity] anterior to language, from which one goes out as soon as one speaks of it and where one can only reenter on the condition of remaining silent?

Bergson was right to look for metaphysics, not in the philosophies, but in the philosophers. One must add, nevertheless, that it cannot be by chance that so many philosophers should have yielded to the need to express themselves in a philosophy. That which cannot be said is at the same time an irresistible urge to express itself. The Plato of the "Seventh Letter" asks himself how a lofty intellect could deliver over to the crowd, under the form of writing to be torn apart, the most valuable of his thoughts. Nevertheless, he wrote the *Phaedrus*, the *Symposium*, and the *Republic*. He even wrote *The Laws*, the perfect type according to him of the sort of thoughts which are good to think, not to write. What is this secret seething in us, which rumbles with a confused din of a crowd but which can only issue one word at a time? And why is it absolutely necessary to speak, so much so that the Divine Word Himself desired to become flesh and lived among us? One will not clear up one mystery by something still more mysterious, and, besides, the mystery is by definition that which should not be cleared up. It lives within us in the incomprehensible explosion of language, unequal to the thought which bursts out with it and which nevertheless does not cease to burst forth. Meditating on the lesson of Plotinus, who was so dear to him, as the opposite of himself, Bergson regretted that this Greek mistook a bubbling spring for a waterfall, as if a waterfall could not be a bubbling spring. But Plotinus was not wrong either to see in the manifold an inferior image of the One, or in the One, which is the Good, the unmoved source of the many. How else can we explain within us this inexhaustible spring which gushes forth in a cascade of words incapable of drying it up? All the great metaphysicians come to a standstill with Plato at the edge of this source. They are reunited there with the poets of night and obscurity, for the night and obscurity of their poetry is nothing but that of language itself in its point of origin. "There must be something of the occult in our deepest being," Mallarmé said. "I decidedly believe in something of the hidden [*abscons*], clearly intimating the closed and concealed, which dwells in the common," for as soon as this obscure mass is thrown onto paper, "it thrashes about, a hurricane anxious to attribute the obscurity to anything whatsoever, profusely, flagrantly." For having thus wished to commune with the night from whence springs language, Mallarmé plunged it back into that night again. Tired of drawing "from any inkwell other than [*sans*] Night the misleading [*vaine*] stratum of intelligibility"⁷ that all writing requires, he rejoined the Plato of the "Seventh Letter" in his haughty silence. But without language silence itself could not exist.

The obsession, always most [*plus*] insistent with Mallarmé, with the spacing between words, the "blanks" [*blancs*], and with their calculated dispersion on the printed page, corresponds to what we have noted as one of the first analytical operations of writing [*de l'Ecriture*]. That is so true that those who know how to write imagine, of course, that they speak written sentences and that they write spoken sentences, although these two systems of symbols [*signes*] differ in so many characteristics. He who learns a foreign language [*langue*] will often succeed in understanding a sentence only by representing it to himself under the form of distinct words written according to the grammar of that language [*langue*]. To "understand" it is thus for him precisely to distinguish the words in it. This analysis of the written word [*analyse scripturale*] quickly becomes necessary for each in his own language [*langue*] as soon as, rising above ostensive formulas which simply point out objects, he wishes to build sentences made up of associations and dissociations of concepts. The two modes of signification are inextricably tangled up. There is an absolute priority of the spoken over the written with respect to origination, but a relative primacy of the written in the order of the critique of the spoken.

Plato, who was never short of arguments, but who had not behind him the long history of literary history that the moderns have acquired, would have been able to reply to himself, had he lived to our times, not to contradict himself but to balance his truth with another. Orphan of its father, the written work, nevertheless, does not remain without defenders. With a remarkable perspicacity, which did not escape Sainte-Beuve,

Francis Bacon defined in advance the place, still vacant in his time, of a future literary history which we can conceive of as a response to the appeal inaugurated by Plato for support for writing deprived of its natural defender. Great literary history, constituted above all by a critique of the beautiful [*beautés*] of which, in France, Sainte-Beuve himself represents till now the summit, can be considered as the other fold [*volet*] of a diptych of which the first would be the dialectic of the *Phaedrus* and the "Seventh Letter."

It is true that, like linguistics, literary history tends more and more to constitute itself as a science. Like the ideal of a linguistics bearing on a "language denuded of meaning," which thus would be no longer a language, modern literary history tends more and more to offer as its objects "literary works, an abstraction being made of their beauty." The enterprise is legitimate; its success can even open to high literary criticism fields for examination which otherwise would remain closed. We do not have too many men of good will to assure the most tutelary affection possible to the orphan whose lot in life Plato pities.

All these friends are not always good friends, however. A law ought even forbid placing certain sorts of commentary alongside the great masterpieces which their very beauty exposes to this sort of homage. But [a similar interdiction ought also prohibit the devotion] of sincere and fervent friends, many of whom are not unworthy of being the celebrants of the more than centenary, at times more than millenary, cult whose object is the great monuments of the art of writing! This spiritual family of admirers not only protects the objects of its admiration against oblivion and death, but it confers on them a posthumous but real and always present being, living in its own way since it changes, and which owes its own perenniality to writing. Aeneas and Vergil, Beatrice and Dante, are not only all that they were in reality or in the imagination of their authors. They are also all that they were in the mind of the readers of the *Aeneid* and the *Divine Comedy*. Sainte-Beuve and his *Comedie litteraire* still furnish us today with their own substance along with that of Racine, Boileau, Moliere, and many other writers about whom we love to read. These authors furnish not only what they have written but what the reader of such rare quality has said of them.

Sainte-Beuve had a personal experience of literary criticism that was too extensive and too deep not to perceive the two aspects of the question. Like Plato, he had felt the state of abandonment in which thought is left, by the sole fact that the writer ceases to speak it himself in order to write it. He advised authors destined to become famous concerning the matter: "One of the greatest conceits of glory, even of literary glory, which of all of them appears nevertheless the most authentic, is that one of its first effects consists . . . in changing and distorting you more or less. The lofty admiration of the future is to be had only at this price. The actual writings can come to amount to nothing; they are interpreted, they are refined, their meaning is strained. You do not belong to yourself any more. . . . Each generation mints and remints you according to its image." And continuing in the same vein he concluded: "If it seems to place you so high, O spirits and phantoms of the great minds, do not be thereby more proud; for it is no longer you: it is itself that posterity salutes in you. Your name is hardly more than a token and a symbol."

But thinking no doubt of all that he had put of himself, and of the best of himself, in his tireless commentary on the writings of others, Sainte-Beuve added immediately, as counterpoint: "We well know that we become, in the course of time, cooperators with and demicreators of these time-honored types which, once handed over to admiration, are interpreted and transformed incessantly. We know that we add thereto, of our own authority, intentions that the author never had, as if in compensation for all those which he had but which escape us."[8]

One could cavil at length, but to no point, about this self-consolation of a critic inconsolable for being only that. But literary criticism, when it reaches that level, is itself literary creation. It has value in itself, and in addition to contributing to a better reading of works, it is a work which deserves to be read for itself. It even enters into a sort of general conversation among the interlocutors, some living, some dead, who, without ever being together, talk about some mighty spirit of whom the written work alone assures the presence, and which can itself only be pursued in silence, like a party game in which partners should exchange written remarks without a word being said.[9] Here each chooses freely his own company: Racine and Sainte-Beuve, Dante and Michele Barbi, Keats and du Bos, accompanying only with his own silent thought the subjects of conversation of his chosen friends. Every such company makes and unmakes itself in an exchange which is followed over the course of years, even centuries, without time being able to impose a foreseeable terminus to it, an exchange which is not conceivable outside of a civilization of the written word.

Perhaps one ought not be amazed at this much. When one reads the *Gorgias,* that masterpiece of philosophical dramatic art [*theatre*], a comedy whose intellectual vicissitudes are an incessantly renewed enchantment for the solitary reader who gives himself a picture of them, what astonishes at first is the perfection of the literary composition. But next one notices that the work exists, after more than twenty centuries, thanks to an ingenious system of mute signs whose former pronunciation we do not even properly know. The thought of Plato its father remains for us sufficiently authentically accessible so that so much profundity, subtlety, sprightliness winged from the summit of the spirit, so much spiritual emotion even, of that quite rare species which is philosophical emotion, might be reborn and communicated from his mind to ours. The thought out of which the *Gorgias* was one day born, as distant as we may be in time from its birth, *is* still today. If we could put his own child back again under Plato's eyes, he would recognize it without hesitation. Thus, born of the spoken language from which it remains inseparable, the written language confers upon it, nevertheless, a peculiar status, as of an empire within an empire, a permanent refuge of the works of the most true and most beautiful intelligence. It is a holy and quasi-divine domain, in the strict sense of the term, for in the written the spoken endures, and in the spoken the intellect lives, a witness in man of a power of creation superior to man. One has today so few companions upon the roads of metaphysics that one does not dare recall to them the word of Saint Augustine: "When you think these things, it is the Word of God in your heart."[10] But the modern man hardly thinks anymore of these things. He bathes in the divine without being aware of it.

8

Two Digressions

I. Form and Meaning

We borrow from M. Emile Benveniste, beyond many other things as shall be seen, the title of his communication to the XII Congress of the Philosophical Societies of the French Language [*Langue*] under the date of Saturday, September 3, 1966. He insisted on forewarning his audience concerning his attitude in respect to the problem: "I obviously approach this subject as a linguist and not as a philosopher." Now he ought to hold exactly to his promise in this respect. The philosopher who reads him owes it to himself, unfortunately, to begin by the contrary notice: I obviously approach this subject as a philosopher and not as a linguist. This is a difficult and even a dangerous position to hold, for insofar as he is a philosopher, he has no more competence to speak of linguistics than of physics, biology, or any other of the sciences of nature. But Aristotle thought that the metaphysician's task was to judge of principles and of particular sciences in the light of first principles. In the case of linguistics the metaphysician almost feels himself provoked to intervene, for if he does not know what language is, he at least knows how to use it, though it only be like everyone else, and that explains the illusion that he has of knowing a little of what it is. Speaking, therefore, as a linguist, without claiming moreover to represent the opinion of his confreres in that science (but doubtless with the desire to meet with their approbation), M. Emile Benveniste forewarns that speaking personally and setting forth views which are his own, he will attempt "to situate and organize the twin ideas of meaning and form, and to analyze their functions outside of all philosophical presuppositions."[1]

Perhaps the enterprise is not impossible of accomplishment, but it is difficult to succeed completely therein, for the common language spoken in Western societies in the twentieth century has been profoundly shaped by two classical languages [*langues*]: Scholastic Latin and the Greek

147

upon which this Latin was modeled. Of the two twin ideas of meaning and form the second at least comes from Plato and Aristotle. It is an essentially philosophical idea, the name of which has so passed into common use that, like an old piece of money, it is hard to see what it represents. Molière would ask, "Is it a question of the form of the word, or of its figure?" These "threadbare terms" still carry a remainder of the ideas which were their origin or, at least, which they have signified at a moment of their history.

Taking up the issue even today, is it so true that "to oppose the form to the meaning is a banal convention"? With those who interest themselves in language under any title whatsoever — grammar or style, for example — the remark in fact finds its application. And those who so interest themselves are numerous; but what is their proportion to the totality of men, all speaking animals, who nevertheless concern themselves rather little to distinguish in their language the form of what they say and the meaning that it has? And the linguist himself, when he takes this distinction for granted, or the paired entity, or that opposition as standing to reason, does he not concern himself with the furthermost edge of linguistic at the risk of overshooting it? As soon as, speaking with language, we take up that formula again in order to apply it to language, we see "that it encloses in its antithesis the very being of language, for here at a stroke it puts us at the heart of the most important problem, the problem of meaning [signification]."2

All that is quite just; it is even linguistically irreproachable, for it is natural for every science to define its object for itself. In the absence of doing so it does not know of what it speaks. We can thus continue with the same linguist and ask, as "the first question which immediately arises: What is meaning?" There, nevertheless, we must beware of the sort of response that we expect. When we ask the physicist what the object of physics is, he responds with something like: it is matter, or extension, in movement. But we must not ask him further what extension is, what movement is. What is the object of biology? Living phenomena, for example, material beings endowed with spontaneous movement. But we must not ask the biologist to say what life is in itself, beyond its immediately perceptible manifestations. Likewise with language, whose property is to have a meaning, and everyone knows what these words intend to say. Meaning is what we understand, the message which we know that the speaker wishes to communicate. As a practiced linguist, M. Emile Benveniste does better: "In a first approximation, the meaning is the idea [notion] implied by the very term 'language' [langue] as a whole of communicative procedures understood in the same fashion by a group of speakers." This first approximation already goes rather far, for it is rare that a group of speakers should understand the signs that they use in the same way. We can accept hypothetically and as an optimal case the proposed description, but we must remain with that, that is to say, content ourselves with saying what takes place when the remarks exchanged have the same sense for those who exchange them. The means of these exchanges is language, "because the property of language is first of all to signify." But we cannot try to go further without getting involved with a circle of reasoning: to signify is to communicate meaning; the meaning is what language signifies, it is its signification.[3]

The linguist's point of view is not either that of the psychologist (or philosopher) or that of the logician. Taking language [*langue*] such as it is, he begins by refusing to consider meaning [*signification*] as a function which could be added to what exists; meaning is not an activity exercised by language [*langue*]: "It is its very being; if it were not that, it would be nothing." No one will contest that point. Nor shall we contest either what the same linguist calls a characteristic of language [*langue*] "completely different, but equally necessary and present in every real language [*langue*], although subordinate (I insist on it, he says) to the first: that of realizing itself by vocal means, of consisting for practical purposes in a group of sounds emitted and perceived, which are organized in sounds endowed with meaning"; we therefore will say with de Saussure, "by virtue of first approximation" that speech is a system of signs.

Here we are brought back to Saussure, but we suspect we have not been led back to him in order to remain there. Departing from the idea that language consists in signs, we infer first of all that *the sign is the semiotic unit*.[4] In this new project of the decomposition of language [*langue*] there is a lower limit: the sign is the linguistic element below which there is no more any signification. We will then call the sign "the autonomous entity, lowest in its order, not decomposable into a lower unit which could be itself an autonomous sign." It is in this sense that we say of the sign that it is the semiotic unit of language. It is as such the object of science, not only by way of analysis into phonemes, which constitutes its phonetic analysis, but still more by discernment of the formal components of signifiers, that is to say, of the structure according to which, in each sign, the phonemes are associated.

Thus for the signifying [*signifiant*] of the sign; and what shall we say of the signified? Simply that it is the fact that those who make use of the same sign receive it as supplying meaning, "and the totality of these signs forms the totality of language [*langue*]." Moving resolutely to the end of his thesis, the linguist identifies, in the semiotic plane, the property of having a meaning with the fact of being understood in the same way in the bosom of a linguistic group. *That which* the sign signifies does not have to be defined in semiology. If a thing signifies, it is a sign; if not, not. "On the plane of signification [*signifié*] the criterion is: Does it signify or not? To signify is to have a meaning, no more. And the Yes or No can only be pronounced by those who use [*manient*] the language [*langue*], those for whom that language [*langue*] is simply *the language* [*langue*]."[5]

This position is clear. The philosopher may find it a bit severe,[6] but sentiments have nothing to do with science. If things are such, he must accept the fact. But the semiotic order is not the ultimate one. The sign can only serve to communicate thought if it is given in one of those groups of signs that we call sentences [*phrases*]. It is by means of the sentence that the "communicative function of language [*langue*]" is brought about. Now according to M. Emile Benveniste we do not move from the sign to the sentence by simple addition or extension, as if by adding signs to signs we could obtain clauses, then complete sentences associated in structured extensions. In sum, "the sign and the sentences are two distinct worlds," and they require distinct descriptions. "There are for language [*langue*] two ways of being language [*langue*] in meaning and in form. We have just defined one: language as *semiotics*. We have yet to give a satisfactory account of the second, which we call language [*langue*] as *semantics*," the supreme expression of which is the sentence, in which the production of discourse consists.[7]

For a linguist sensitive to the reality of speech [*parole*] in its actual use, therefore, the semantic function of discourse is exceptionally important. The sentence is thus equally important. Semiotics concerns the signification [*signifié*] of the sign; semantics concerns that which he who uses the sign *wants to say*, the meaning of the thought which he wants to communicate. Although the semiological meaning is that of the word, the semantic meaning is that of the speaker [*locuteur*], as linguists call the subject who speaks. To use the perfect expression of M. Emile Benveniste, semantics is the *linguistic actualization of his thought*. Consequently there is a radical change of perspective: "Semiotics is characterized as a property of language [*langue*]; semantics results from an activity of the speaker who puts language [*langue*] in action."[8]

In following this analysis with an expert in the science of language, the philosopher, who does not have such expertise, notices that he has until now ignored a capital distinction and, without knowing it, has mixed up semiotics and semantics. This is only too certain, moreover, and it only remains to him to excuse himself for it, if it is true, however, that the sign as pure semiotic admits truly of a meaning.

The question can at least be posed. Searching for a unit into which the object of his research might be decomposable, and having stopped at the *sign* in the order of the semiotic, the linguist determines the type of

unit which suits the formal structure of the most simple sentence, and replies: "We have seen that the semiotic unit is the sign. What will the semantic unit be? Simply, the word."[9]

The philosopher whom the constants of thought in all its orders interest finds himself gratified here. The word as linguistic unit is an accepted
notion, but we get uneasy in leaving behind us the sign, which, apparently in its strict acceptance at least, cannot be a word. We are uneasy
all the more in that it is difficult, be it simply for lack of habit, to conceive,
at the interior of the order of language, a sign which would not signify.
A general semiology ought naturally to make room for all sorts of other
signs, but since it is a question here of semiology in linguistic form, can
we conceive the meaning of a sign which would not be a word?

The philosopher asks himself the question in the light of common
experience, since he has no other at his disposal, and he asks himself how
one can recognize that an isolated sign exists. The linguist responds to
this, "by the fact that it is understood": "In semiology what the sign signifies has no definite being. For a sign to exist it is necessary and sufficient
that it be accepted and that it be joined after one fashion or another to
other signs. Does the entity under consideration have meaning? The response is Yes or No. If it is Yes, that is all there is to it. We record it. If
it is No, we reject it, and that is all there is to that. Does 'hat' [chapeau]
exist? 'Yes'. Camel [chameau]? 'Yes'. Chareau [presumably, a sign without
meaning]? 'No'."[10]

That is hastily said. To the last of these three questions my own
response would be: "I know nothing about it." First of all, it could be
a proper noun. In fact, I find two "Charou" in the Annuaire officiel des
abonnés du telephone de la ville de Paris, that document so exciting for
those curious about our language [langue]. If I hear "Chareau," I am unable to guess the spelling, which is unimportant under the circumstances,
and I recognize moreover my embarrassment in not finding any "Chareau"
(these linguists do not allow themselves to be caught so easily), but we
find there a Mme. J. Charo, a Charrau, two Charraud, a Charraut, six
Charreau, and how should I know, as a last chance, that there does not
exist a "Chareau" not printed in the Annuaire or even, as it is said of the
painter Degas, someone hostile to the telephone?

It will be said naturally that this is not a game. Speaking semiotically, the linguist will only take into consideration common nouns, not
proper nouns. So be it. But how define the group in whose bosom a sign
is understood or not, exists as a sign or not? Signs literally quantitatively
innumerable (not-numerable) are used by the French which do not figure
in the Dictionary of the French Academy, be it because they are technical
or because they only live among certain speakers: provincial to be sure,

but how much more French than are *locuteur, semiotic, semiology,* and so many other words whose usage is certainly legitimate (the right to invent signs anew is unlimited), but which it is doubtful that the majority of Frenchmen understand. Without contesting the legitimacy of the criterion, its use can be held as always arbitrary, at least up to a certain point.

It is true that the acceptable definition of the sign contains an ingenious clause. For the sign to exist it is necessary and sufficient that it be received *or that it be joined in one fashion or another to other signs.*[10a] Put otherwise, a sign is acceptable when we know that it has a meaning or when we can guess it by analogy with other signs. But we cannot join it in thought to other signs without creating at least a mental discourse and thus engaging it in one or more sentences. Besides, comparing the rigor of the linguistic principle involved with its concrete conditions of applicability, the contrast is striking. We recall the principle: "We therefore elevate the idea of usage and comprehension of language [*langue*] to the position of a principle of discrimination, of a criterion. It is in the usage of language [*langue*] that a sign has existence; that which does not enter into the usage of a language [*langue*] is not a sign, and literally does not exist."

Discrimination. Criterion. Our linguist here "speaks to the point." The trouble lies in the idea of usage. Usage for whom? Let us suppose that I take up again the test, imagined by M. Emile Benveniste, simply by following a section of the *Petit Larousse: "Argumenter?"* Does it have meaning [*Existe-t-il?*] Yes. *"Argus?"* Yes (probably: the "Argus" of the press). *"Argutie?"* [*"Quibble"*] Yes (probably). *"Argyraspide?"* No (not for me, but Yes, for the *Larousse*). *"Argyronete?"* No (with the same reservations). *"Aria?"*. . . . Here we ought to pause, for there are two signs *aria,* which the dictionary indicates together [*tous deux*]: the one, an Italian word which most French people accept, and which consequently exists (air, melody); the other, which is Burgundian, at least (Pierre Larousse was born at Toucy), but which few French people use, so that, for them, it does not exist: "[*Aria*] *Fam.* Trouble, worry: Such a fuss! [*que d'arias*]" In its Italian meaning *aria* is a French sign; in its French meaning I do not recall ever having heard it in the language [*langage*] of any Parisian speaking normally the language [*langue*] of cultivated persons. As it is familiar to me since my childhood, I was agreeably surprised to find it in the *Petit Larousse,* in the plural moreover, which ought to be possible, though I believe I have always heard it used in the singular at Cravant or Vermonton (Yonne): *"C'est ben de l'aria! - Oh, un' aria!"* Almost in the meaning of the Montrealais: *"C'est ben du trouble!"* or in Franco-Parisian: *"C'est bien des ennuis!"* [all expressions meaning "That's a lot of trouble"]. When M. Benveniste decides (I think of the Scholastic Latin: *sententiat*): "There is no intermediate position: one is inside the language [*langue*] or outside of it, *tertium quid non datur*,"[11] I see more clearly than ever that we do not live in the same linguistic world.

In fact, I am one of those who live as a general rule in a third semiotic domain of the nonexistence of which we are precisely assured. To understand a sign is for me to understand a meaning. In the example in question, if I hear *aria* in Paris, I shall think rather of its musical meaning, but if I am in Burgundy, I shall think of the provincial meaning of the sign. Above all, if we restrict ourselves to the semiotic order, I shall say that I do not think of anything at all, for it is impossible for me to know the meaning of this sign taken in its isolated state. Its meaning will depend for me on the sentence in which I come across it, which amounts to saying that the meaning does not arise for me at the level of pure semiotics. Semiotics as such has no meaning; it receives its meaning only in a sentence, which is in the semantic order. For the nonlinguist that I am, apprentice philosopher from the flatlands, pure semiotics is not a sign. To consider it apart from everything else is legitimate, but then one may doubt that any distinct reality corresponds to it. Concerning any word whatsoever pronounced in our presence, if we are asked: "Does the entity being considered mean anything?" the correct response is not perhaps Yes or No, but Yes, or: I do not know.

It naturally belongs to linguists alone to know what they ought to do with the distinction between the sign and the word, semiotics and semantics, which is thus set before them. The philosopher is not, moreover, without understanding or at least imagining, what concern calls forth the distinction in the mind of its author. It is a question of conferring its own autonomous regulation on that immense datum which is the body of languages [*langues*], with its own substance and life, its quite ingenious procedures — invented by what genius always immanent to the work? — which are inflections, derivatives, etc. In principle one ought to be able to study and describe this anatomy, physiology, and histology of languages [*langues*] for themselves without concerning oneself with the semantic functions of communication which they exercise, just as in biology one can study living bodies without having intervene the study of their concrete behavior or their ecological relations with their milieus. There certainly one ought to have a science of verbal forms taken in their very materiality, and one sees no reason for not reserving to them the name of "signs," if it pleases one to do so. But one sees less well how to define the signification of such semiotic units, since they ought to have some meaning if they are to be signs, without at the same blow integrating semiotics once again into semantics from which one means to distinguish it.[12]

The doctrine which is set before us demands from us, by its very novelty, an effort of which we are perhaps not capable. Introducing into linguistics a distinction which runs through all of language [*langue enitère* (sic)], it asks us, and even imposes on us, the requirement of departing from the "two domains of meaning and of form," that is to say, of recognizing that "there are for language [*langue*] two ways of being language [*langue*], in meaning and in form,"[13] these two ways being, for semantics, to communicate, and, for semiotics, to signify. What we ask ourselves with perplexity is if there can exist a verbal sign which would not be a word?

About the way in which meaning is constituted in semantics M. Emile Benveniste opens perspectives at once new and valuable in lessons with which the philosopher ought to familiarize himself to his profit. He has the sharp sense of what we might willingly call, if the word had not been put to so many usages, the existential character of the sentence as the very substance of spoken language. He recalls first of all his profound remarks about the connection, essential to language, which binds it to the present time in which it is used, but he adds immediately that since this is so, the "semantic meaning" of the word is necessarily particular. In a formulation so perfect that we can only deliver it as such to reflection, our linguist writes: "We set as a principle that the meaning of a sentence is other than that of the words that compose it. The meaning of a sentence is its idea, the meaning of a word is its use (always in the semantic sense [*sens*]). From the idea, each time particular, the speaker puts together words which in *this* use have a particular "meaning."[14]

We see thereby how that doctrine can attribute to the sign a semiotic meaning distinct from the semantic meaning which this same sign receives when it enters by virtue of being a word in the context of a sentence. The sentence always expresses a certain idea that the speaker is interested in expressing in the present by the act of speech, all of which enters into the sentence through the word; the word participates in the particularity of the idea and of the sentence which expresses it. This amounts to taking up again under another form the remark made by M. E. Benveniste on the difficulties inherent in every attempt at translation: we can always translate the idea by a sentence, but it is not always possible, in fact it is practically never possible, to find a word which can serve as the equivalent of each other word. The word assumes a particular meaning according to the idea which it contributes to the meaning of. Although the sign (semiotic) is naturally indeterminate and general, the word (semantic) is always tied to a present act of signification and, thus, particularized. The words define the message, but the message determines the meaning that the words must have in order to express it. "The *signs*, in themselves conceptual, generic, not affected by circumstances, must be used as *words*, for the ideas, always particularized, specific, affected by circumstances, in the contingent meanings [*acceptions*] of discourse."[15]

The consideration of this duality of the sign and of the word is all the more fertile in misunderstandings as, materially, it is "the same lexical entity" which functions at one time as sign and at another as word. Of the numerous consequences[16] of this we wish to retain at least one for the sake of the light it throws on the doctrine and at the same time on a situation too familiar to translators.

Every writer who has to say the same things in two different languages [langues] knows from experience that he cannot say them in the same way, the lexical, grammatical, and above all syntactical particularities of each language [langue] imposing on the writer some ways of saying things which can at any moment become ways of thinking. He who makes use of two languages [langues] is very much more free than the professional translator, for he can think directly the same work [oeuvre] in the two languages [langues], whereas the translator (who can be in that a great artist) must reinvent, in another language [langue], the movement of thought which he can only rediscover through its first utterance. We return now to the words of M. E. Benveniste:[17]

> That nevertheless it should be possible, approximately, to "say the same thing" in two different categories of idioms [idiomes] is the proof, at one and the same time, of the relative independence of thought and of its narrow modeling within the linguistic structure.

> Let us reflect closely on this notable fact, which appears to us to put in the light the theoretical articulation which we do our utmost to disengage (between signs as signs and signs as words). We can transpose the semanticism of one language [langue] into that of another, salva veritate; this is possible in translation. But we cannot transpose the semioticism of one language [langue] into that of another; this is impossible in translation. We here touch the difference between semiotics and semantics.

> Nevertheless, that translation remains possible as a global process is also an essential fact. This fact discloses the possibility that we have that in us which is above language [langue], which is separate from it, which meditates on it, always using it in our reasoning and our observations. The metalinguistic faculty to which logicians have been more attentive than linguists have is the proof of the transcendent condition of the spirit vis-à-vis language [langue] in its semantic capacity.

One cannot read these lines without feeling that quite special sentiment of intellectual gratitude which we experience toward him who "causes us to understand something." Truth is the good of the intellect; to perceive

it is a joy, profound for him who discovers it for himself, intense for those
with whom the discoverer shares his discovery. In fact, why does he feel
that intense desire, that almost visceral need, to communicate it? However
that may be, it appears difficult not to admit in fact the existence of a double point of view on language, that of semiotics and that of semantics,
semiotics organizing the discourse according to the order of signification,
semantics organizing, on that semiotic base, "a signification of the intended
product by the syntagmation of words where each word only retains a
small part of the value which it has insofar as it is a sign." A difficult distinction, moreover, for this "double system constantly at work in language
[*langue*] . . . functions so quickly, and with such a subtle play, that it requires a long effort of analysis and a long effort to detach oneself from
it if one would separate out what depends on the one and what on the
other. But at the basis of everything, there is the signifying power of
language [*langue*], which exceeds by far [*qui passe bien avant*] the power
of saying any [particular] thing."[18]

One does not feel any desire to contradict the certainties which war-
rant such a perspicacious and essentially deeply rooted observation on the
manners of language. We must nevertheless return to the sole point which,
doubtless due to our own fault, creates a difficulty in our own mind. It
dealt with, we recall, the nature of semiotic, and our purpose is only to
discern what is acceptable of the analysis which has just been made of
it, and the point about which we continue to feel hesitation.

The general distinction between semiotics and semantics does not
seem to be contestable. Nor does the description of semiotics, so it seems
to the layman which the philosopher is in the matter, to the full extent
that it deals with what, to put it briefly, could be called the body of the
verbal sign: the sound of the word and the phonemes which compose it,
more yet (a point to which M. Benveniste justly attaches great importance), the form according to which the phonetic elements of the word
are put together, which covers the universal domain of paradigms with
the declensions or inflections of every sort, the conjugations, and such.
Who studying a foreign language [*langue*] has not often experienced a
feeling of admiration for its spontaneous art of formal creation in the invention of verbal forms? When I learn that Russian nouns ending in -*ok*
form their plural in -*ki*, I experience a feeling of intense satisfaction of
which a phonetician alone could tell me the cause, but which I have still
not gotten over. It is a delight for the tongue and, if it is a Russian who
says the -*ok*, for the ear. We must again, in the third place, recognize that
verbal signs have a meaning [*sens*], since they are only signs on the condition of signifying to the mind an intelligible meaning. A fourth non-
contestable point is that the act of understanding the sign as such consists

in perceiving it as endowed with meaning and utilizable in a language [*langue*], just that and nothing more: "In semiology what the sign signifies does not have to be defined." One last point remains, the only one which still may cause difficulty in my mind: Can we distinguish, other than by an abstract view of the mind, the meaning of the semiotic sign and that of the semantic sign? In other words, is a totally nonsemantic signification conceivable?

What gives force to M. Emile Benveniste is the strictly scientific character of his attitude. He is only truly satisfied, as much as a scientist [*savant*] can be such, when he can justify a conclusion by appealing to some observable fact of language [*langue*]. It is then a matter of genuine linguistic experiences, since according to Claude Bernard an experience is an observation provoked, *or* invoked, in order to verify an hypothesis. Experimental verifications of this sort abound under the pen of M. E. Benveniste, and they are evidently what he himself values most. It is also what the philosopher leaves totally in the shade in recalling his thought in order to retain from it the most general conclusions, all naturally bordering on philosophy, which in similar cases we with delicate modesty call "psychology."

We still must go with him as far as we can in accepting the facts. Here we can only contest [the proposition] that the sign might have a linguistic status different from that of the word, it being, moreover, well understood that the same emission of voice can be indifferently word or sign. What happens when we hear an isolated word, a word consequently reduced to the condition of a sign? It is certain that we instantaneously recognize it as supplied with signification for ourselves and for the community of those who speak the same language [*langue*] as ours. It is a question here of a fact of primary memory, one that cannot be explained by another fact, of the same nature as what we call the recognition of objects. There even exists an "illusion of false recognition," which causes great trouble to psychologists and philosophers and which, under its acute form, can consist in a false impression of already having seen everything that one sees. No explicit judgment is necessary when it is a matter of recognizing a sign as such. Must we still be asked, or must we each ask ourselves individually, Is it a sign? "Does the entity considered have meaning? The response is Yes or No." There is then question and response, which situates us in the order of semantics.

Let us suppose that a man stops me in the street and says to me pointblank: "*Chareau.*" I will understand that he wants something of me, but for lack of recognizing the word, I shall think that I have misheard, misunderstood. I shall react then with a question to which I shall await a response unless, of course, the speaker insists on repeating "*Chareau,*" in which case I shall conclude either that he speaks a language [*langue*] unknown to me or that he is saying his name to me. In any other case what he says will not be for me a sign; it will not be such because I shall perceive it as bereft of meaning. There is nothing more significant than a "password" [*mot de passe*], but, rightly, it is not simply a sign; it is a word.

If the man I encounter says to me "hat" [*chapeau*], I shall not hesitate a second over the meaning of the word, but it will be necessary for me to invent upon the spot a sentence in which the word may take on meaning: "You forgot your hat"; "Your hat is on backwards"; or even, "I give in, I have lost, I take off my hat before you." Here the question is: Does "*chapeau*" mean anything for you? My response, Yes, is in the realm of semantics, just as to "Chareau" my response, No, is of that realm. The body of the sign belongs to semiotics, except solely in that it is the body of a "sign," as the body of man is of the mechanical and physicochemical realm, but is also that of a living person. Likewise for language. Every word encloses a sign, which is the body of it. Taken as the physical body of the word, the sign has its form which is answerable to the science of phonology. To know whether the morphology of languages [*langues*], incontestably subject to physiological constraints, or simply to the natural conventions of the vocal apparatus, is itself constituted without undergoing any influence exercised by the meaning of signs, is a question which neither linguists nor philosophers can settle. One might as well claim to explain the passage from general biology to zoology. It may be more advantageous for the progress of scientific research to adopt either one or the other point of view depending on the case. If in linguistics it is permitted to the *insipiens* to say his word, it is probably advisable to distinguish the two orders of semiotics and semantics as if they were really distinct. It is advantageous to research to deal with signs as if they were not words. The morphologist of language will have every interest in pushing as far as possible the study of verbal forms and of their very complex play without ever causing the idea of their possible semantic meaning to intervene. A methodologically distinct, and even separate, semiology is probably necessary to assure the progress of the science of language. There, in any case, is a point upon which the philosopher need not be consulted. For making use of expressions in which the connection of words with meaning would be interesting to analyze we will say that "he has missed the boat," "he doesn't know what's going on."

But there exist in every order opinions without scientific, logical, or philosophical value, opinions which are incapable moreover of being proved technically enough to be able to be communicated, let alone to compel recognition, and which nevertheless, *when all is said*, come back obstinately to haunt the mind. Personally I would willingly count this one in their number. The spontaneous recognition of a sign as understood is its perception as the subject of possible meaning. The sign about whose meaning I feel I can express myself, and often in many different ways, is understood by me as belonging to such and such a language [*langue*] whose vocabulary I know. To be aware of the fact and to apprise myself of it are the same thing. Inversely, the sign whose sound "says nothing to me" is for me not a sign, but simply a noise. To speak truly, nevertheless, it may be imprudent to take this sane methodological hypothesis as the expression of reality without other precaution. It is good for the linguist to push research as far as possible *as if,* even with regard to meaning, semiotics were a domain really distinct from semantics. Yet it remains doubtful that there could be in the reality of language a *sign,* endowed with meaning, whose power of signifying could be perceived without an instantaneous act of the subject outlining the act of saying it to himself. There certainly is no word which is not a sign; we are tempted to think that neither is there any verbal sign which is not a word, even if it suits the linguist, who can have excellent reasons for so doing, to consider it provisionally as outside every sentence and foreign to every act of communication.

II. In the Margin of a Dictionary

For the philosopher who asks himself about the nature of language it can be instructive to participate in the construction of a dictionary, for example, that to which the Academie Francaise devotes the last part of each of its sessions. Each academician finds at his place a fascicule of about twenty pages, each of which bears, pasted in the middle of it, a column from the preceding edition of the *Dictionnaire,* surrounded, in ample margins on the right and the left, by remarks: additions, deletions, and corrections made by the Commission on the *Dictionnaire.*

That diligent Commission, charged with preparing the work of revision of the *Dictionnaire,* works more quickly than the Academy, if for no other reason than that it is less numerous and is not distracted from its work by any of the other questions that the Academie must settle before beginning this work. This revision moves forward with extreme slowness. When I had the honor of entering the Academie, the work on the *Dictionnaire* was on the letter "B." That was in 1946. Today, Thursday, November 21, 1968, that is to say, twenty-two years later, we were engaged with the letter "C." Until now it was estimated that a minimum of seventy years was necessary to prepare a new edition, but at the rate things are going it will take quite a bit more, which is more disquieting in light of the fact that in three-quarters of a century language [*langue*] has the time to undergo numerous changes, and one comes to ask oneself if a work of this sort is still possible.

From time to time the Academie is disturbed by this situation. Concerned with finding a remedy for it, it gave then a session to discussing the means of speeding up the revision of the *Dictionnaire*. Certain of these means are not without efficacy, but I would not be surprised to learn that, deep in their hearts, certain members of the Academy, far from finding this work too slow, fear lest it be rather too fast. If one consulted them on the matter, they could perhaps give reasons for making the most of their feeling.

The object of the *Dictionnaire* is to gather together all the words which belong to good usage in the language [*langue*] and to define their meaning. In the seventeenth century good usage was that of the Court of Versailles, consequently that of the families of the high nobility and the wealthy [*bonne*] bourgeoisie. It was far from the case that this was all of France. Whole provinces spoke different dialects of the French language [*langue*], and it was not for them, then, that the authors of the *Dictionnaire* worked. In revenge, inside the restricted domain upon which they had hold, their authority did not lack efficacy. The Academie effectively dictated language [*langue*] usage. Today it is no longer they who direct the movement, and they even have trouble following it. The means of mass communication, and first of all television and radio broadcasting, impose on the public ear the personal jargon of speakers licensed without always being qualified. But they have millions of listeners who are not reached by the discreet remarks made by about forty academicians talking among themselves about the meaning of words. To find a remedy for this disorder is not an easy thing, but the difficulties begin in the bosom of the Academie, almost with regard to each word.

The first difficulty is to determine what words belong to the usage of the language [*langue*]. In the mind of the authors of the *Dictionnaire* it is a question not only of good usage but also, if one might say so, of current usage. Terms called "technical" are not accepted. How decide which words are technical terms and which are not?

Some cases are simple. Thus the Academie des Sciences works on its side to make up a French lexicon of terms of which the scientist [*savant*] makes use. The Atomic Energy Commission publishes a *Dictionnaire des sciences et techniques nucleaires*, filled with magnificent words of surrealist resonance but divested of meaning for those who are not specialists: *anticoincidence, antimatter, neutrino* and *antineutrino*, and such. But the question often presents itself whether a certain word is of current usage in the common language [*langue*] or only in the technical language [*langue*] of some science or another, and the response can be difficult to ascertain.

To speak truthfully, nothing is less precise than the line which separates the two domains: that which is common language [*langue*] for some can be technical language [*langue*] for others and inversely.

Let us take as an example the word *concept:* Is it a technical word or not? I recall the day when we came across it in the revision of the *Dictionnaire.* It was already there. Our predecessors, therefore, had already taken it to be a word of current usage, which was a presumption in its favor. Being myself of that number who have often used it, I found it natural to keep it. I did not foresee, moreover, any opposition, and there probably would have been none had we not had the unfortunate idea of re-reading its definition:

> CONCEPT (The "P" is pronounced), Masculine noun, didactic term: mental view, idea which one makes of a thing in detaching it from its real object. "The concept of time." "The concept of space."

There is one incontestable point in that description of the word: the "P" is pronounced. For the rest, that will vary according to the taste of each. The word *didactic* would be more justly called "philosophical," for the word is not only used in teaching; a *mental view* is better called an intuition (unless one wishes to say: "that's only a mental view"), *idea* is more often opposed to concept than standing for it; what one makes of a *thing . . .* but many concepts do not refer to things (for example, the concept of concept) and, appropriately, the examples chosen prove it, for time and space, incontestably abstract ideas, are not detached from real corresponding objects in the same manner as the concepts of horse or tree are. To know *what it is* that we call space or time is not easy. In fact, Kant would not admit that we could speak of an idea of space or time, these two ideas signifying for him "*a priori* forms of sensible intuition [*sensibilité*: intuition, sensibility],"[18a] whatever may be moreover the meaning of this celebrated formulation.

That is why, that day, I was a bit surprised, but not shocked, to hear one of our confreres say that *concept* being a technical word, we ought to remove it from the dictionary. I was at first surprised that the remark came from someone whose philosophical competence was known to me. In fact, however one defines them, one can hardly philosophize without speaking of concepts; but, precisely, the word has passed into current usage with the meaning, or absence of precise meaning, which the *Dictionnaire* attributes to it: what the mind *conceives* is a *concept.* This is why the definition of the *Dictionnaire* is quite acceptable from the point of view of usage. It is right in this respect because it is philosophically contestable, and that is indeed why it was a philosopher who contested it. One can only contest examples of it which, although applicable by virtue of the definition given, refer to cases where the definite object is almost inevitably an object of philosophical speculation and tied to some particular doctrine. The concept of oak (or of plant), that of horse (or animal), would be exempt from this objection, but one says the idea of oak, not its concept.

The objection of our confrere was then reasonable, and he saw the propriety of it because he was a philosopher. It is impossible to give a definition of concept which in philosophy would not be tied to a particular philosophy. Now it is by this characteristic that a technical term is recognized. The *Petit Larousse illustré* (1952) gives this excellent definition of "technical": "Adj. . . . That which belongs properly to an art, a science, a trade." Concept is incontestably a technical term insofar as it is a philosophical term. Taken in this sense, it ought not figure in a dictionary of common usage, except by virtue of the fact of being a technical term fallen into common usage where it became practically synonymous with idea, a term, moreover, of no less technical origin and victim of the same fate.

One can then ask oneself if it is possible to delimit with exactitude the domains of common usage and of technical usage. The *Dictionnaire* does not try to do so. On the same page I read: "*Copulative:* Grammatical term. . . . *Copula,* logical term. . . ." The fault of *concept* is, not that it is a technical term in philosophy, but rather that it is a term originating in a technique whose definitions are rarely accepted by all. There always will be, therefore, and in practice inevitably, a varying proportion of technical terms in this dictionary of common usage. The most general reason one can give for this fact is the number of words whose scientific definitions are generally recognized. The proportion of these technical words admitted to the *Dictionnaire* varies according to the composition not only of the Academie but of the assembly the day when the word is examined in session. The general rule followed then is that each Academician qualified to speak for a particular technique insists on obtaining for each word relevant to the area of his expertise as precise and exact a definition as possible. The more the science concerned is precise, the less do its representatives in the Academie insist on introducing its terms into general usage. They know that their own technical language [*langue*] — that of mathematics, physics, biology — is not that of common usage. On the contrary, the less the language [*langue*] in question is strict, the more do its representatives have the tendency to introduce its definitions into the *Dictionnaire.* To the extent that they succeed in this the dictionary runs the risk of degenerating into an encyclopedia, a work in which the entirety of knowledge, principally in the order of the sciences and the arts, is dealt with. Encyclopedias are technical by definition.

The Academie is very conscious of this danger. It could not avoid noticing this, for the technical character of a word is recognized quickly by the impossibility of defining it without engaging in numerous and complex scientific details. The discussion is hardly begun when it gets bogged down. This is the case at once in medicine, science, and art, which have always been represented on the French Academy. When common usage shows itself altogether too vague or inexact, the representatives in the assembly always propose the necessary rectifications for bringing such inclusions to a stop with the minimum necessary to avoid encyclopedism. It is inevitable, moreover, that the most general definitions be also the most stable. All that can be introduced that is technically precise in a definition runs the strong risk of being scientifically out of date when the revised and corrected edition of the *Dictionnaire* shall appear. The greatest discretion is therefore recommended in the introduction of provisionally technical terms and of their provisional definitions. "Atom," which at first meant *uncuttable*, no longer figures today with this meaning even in the usual definitions of the word. Thereby one can see, at one and the same time, that technique invades the realm of the usual and that it continues there only by losing its technical qualities.

This absence of precise frontiers delimiting the domain of common usage has as a consequence that the often-posed question of the number of words of which a language [*langue*] is composed cannot receive any precise or even reasonably approximative response.

In the first place, each time that we introduce into usage a new word it enters there with its whole family, which may be numerous. If *concept* is admitted into usage, nothing prohibits our receiving also *conceptualize, conceptualization, conceptualism, conceptual,* and perhaps still other words. This is not a necessary consequence, and each case would demand a particular discussion, but it is not impossible.

Besides that, there are no fixed limits to the number of new words, or of new meanings to old words, which it is advisable to introduce into the *Dictionnaire*. That same Thursday, November 21, 1968, which we take as an example, after *cooblige* [n., legal term for one bound with others by a contract], someone proposed the new word *cooccupant:* "someone who occupies a place with one or more other persons." The Academicians present inquired among themselves. No one appeared to have read or heard the word, but someone made the observation that co-occupants are unfortunately not always cotenants [joint lessees], that some occupying powers are only too often co-occupants, and that strictly speaking, in terms of ecology, all the inhabitants of the same earth are co-occupants, including the undesirable guests that it shelters. The word was therefore at first rejected, then, upon reflection, admitted, although for the most part we had not ever spoken or written the word, or heard or read it.

Next there was proposed a new usage for the adjective "cooperative" disposed to cooperate: *he did not show himself to be cooperative.* I fear that after an exchange of confused remarks the new meaning was not adopted. That makes one more word to say, in another way, what was said formerly and even recently in French by means of the phrases: to demonstrate good will, give evidence of good will, throw oneself fully into some undertaking. Since it was a question of a simple translation of the Anglo-American ("you are not very cooperative"), we shall come across it further on with innumerable cases of the same sort.

After "cooperation" it was proposed to introduce *cooperatism:* "theory of political economy which advocates the development of cooperatives." Why not? Between "cooptation" and "coordination" someone proposed "coordinator" [in French, *coordinateur*] with, as its meaning, "the same meaning as *coordonnateur.*" If the meaning is the same, why add this new word? No doubt it is to correspond to *coordination,* n., "action of coordinating or the result of this action." Assuredly, if the coordination *coordonne* [coordinates], we do not see why he who coordinates would not be a *coordonnateur.* Thus the entry in the *Dictionnaire* as [*au titre de*] a new word: "*coordonnateur/trice:* adj., coordinating. 'freely coordinating'." No objection to this, with the single exception that if the word is an adjective, no academy in the world would ever keep me from using it as a noun: he who is charged with coordination is certainly a coordinator [again, *coordonner, coordonnateur/trice*]. Cut on the pattern of *coadjutor,* the word is legitimate. But if each loudly spoke out the remarks which came to mind, the slowness of the work on the *Dictionnaire* would only increase, at the same time also as its interest.

Two of the following proposals call attention to another order of questions. Although the *Dictionnaire* strives not to move toward technical considerations (to which it nevertheless often succumbs, as it did moreover that day in keeping the word *coordonnées* [coordinates]: "in geometrical terms"), it shows itself on the other hand very indulgent toward the category of the "familiar," providing that this "familiar" be not either vulgar or even excessively common. Thus, finding the word *copain* [pal or companion] (one of the oldest nouns in our language [*langue*]) already in place, on that occasion the Academie gave to it as "companion" the feminine *copine.* That was well done, for the development of coeducation having created the thing, it is appropriate that the word should follow. It did not seem that *copie* [copy] ought to hold any surprise in store, and in fact there was none, except that we wanted to make mention of copies made by machine and above all to take account of the growing importance of journalism as regards language. Hence the addition of the following examples: *The* [newspaper] *writer [redacteur] sent in his copy. The copy is already in press. The printers do not have enough copy to fill the sheet.* Nevertheless, another example suggested, "a bad but prolific journalist" [*un pissecopie*] was not retained. It is a pity.

It is hard to speak of method in connection with a work of this sort. It rests on the postulate that some thirty writers, whether they be from the fields of pure literature or represent besides diverse competences, can be held as qualified witnesses to the good usage of the common language [*langue*], meaning by that the words that a cultivated man of our times is supposed to know and that he in fact does know most often in their principal meanings. In the margin, so to speak, of this compilation the *Dictionnaire* therefore receives also a great number of technical terms whose knowledge makes part of the intellectual baggage of the modern man knowledgeable about the most general scientific ideas and in possession of the corresponding vocabulary. From Littré to Robert, without counting the encyclopedias and specialized lexicons, there exist excellent dictionaries. They are present on the table which is opposite the desk in the hall of sessions of the Academie. Periodically one of us gets up to go look at one of these volumes in the course of a discussion. Certain of us have it in mind continually to check the work against one of these dictionaries in order to assure ourselves that no new word is neglected, no important new meaning omitted. When all is said, the feeling persists that nothing is sure in these matters. Rather, there is moral certitude that even within the modest limits to which the *Dictionnaire* of the Academie professes to restrict itself, the idea of a "complete dictionary" makes no sense.

There remains one last problem, the most serious for the destiny of the language [*langue*], the most difficult to deal with in its concrete reality, and with which the Academie is constantly at grips: that of neologism. When, under what circumstances, is it proper to integrate a new word into the family of French words?

Two principal reasons contribute to the difficulty of the problem: the exceptional influx of foreign words at the present time and the repugnance which French writers feel for neologism.

It is natural that peoples speaking different languages [*langues*] should reciprocally borrow words if they have commercial, industrial, athletic, artistic, and literary relations. Such exchanges are constant, and their normal manner of taking place is easily observable. Every land exports its language [*langue*] in exporting its products. There are no words less American than automobile, chassis, chauffeur, which nevertheless are currently used beyond the Atlantic because, it seems, they were imported there with the first automotive vehicle coming from France. Inversely, innumerable terms used in sports have come to us from England at the same time as the games which they indicate: tennis (*court de tennis*), football (*balle au pied*), rugby, basketball (for *balle au panier*), set (*manche*), game (*jeu*), and so on. The multiplication of these exchanges has been considerably intensified since international communications were themselves multiplied: exchanges of persons, of books, of journals, of press releases hastily translated by more or less competent translators making the greatest possible use of false cognates [*faux amix*] in order to get on with their business. One can often guess the words of the original dispatch from the faulty translations that the journals print. Often even, if the foreign word has a French equivalent that sounds like it, it is preserved as such. Time is gained, and it is easier. No censorship being practiced over the usage of the language [*langue*], a jargon spreads out over the public. Since it is written in the journals and spoken over radio broadcasts, it must indeed be correct. It is repeated, and its usage progressively imposed, and no one can do anything about it.

The French Academy is nevertheless disturbed by this, and at any rate it sees certain of these foreign words returning for consideration at each revision of the *Dictionnaire*. Depending on the composition of the assembly on the day of the discussion, certain of these words do not clear the hurdle, although others pass without difficulty, at times even receiving a triumphal welcome.

Finding myself in Quebec to participate in a conference, and having a free day at my disposition, the desire seized me to see once again the Ile d'Orleans and to revisit its charming parishes. I therefore hired a vehicle and a chauffeur who, after taking me across an arm of the St. Lawrence, drove me to that isle so evocative of a France which we soon will no longer find in France itself in this pure state. Breaking the thread of our conversation, I suddenly asked my chauffeur, pointing out to him an edifice situated at some distance: "What then is that structure [*bâtiment*]?" Turning his face to me, he replied with all the seriousness in the world: "We do not say 'structure' [*bâtiment*] anymore; at present we say '*building*'; it is the French Academy that says so. It is in the journal."

I must acknowledge that my Quebecois did not seem to be either scandalized or surprised by that, but I was both, to receive this information in this land so jealous of its language [*langue*], in this town where I was scolded one day by a waitress at an inn for having asked for *grapefruit* juice: "We do not say grapefruit here, we say *pamplemousse*." And I suddenly learned that my illustrious colleagues had established an English word in the French language [*langue*] which in Quebec defends itself so vigorously against this sort of intrusion! "My illustrious colleagues do not lack audacity," I said to myself, "but this time how could they have gone so far?"

Returning to Paris, I indeed had to find the evidence. The Academie had gotten this far in its work. In the session of Thursday, January 17, 1957, it had incorporated in the *Dictionnaire* the following paragraph:

> BUILDING: Word of English origin designating premises of large dimensions made up of a great number of floors, used as offices or for housing.

The incident is not without some interest for the linguist, for it casts light on the mechanism which brings about the transfer of a word from one language [*langue*] to another.

In English *building* is a noun regularly formed from the present participle of the verb *to build*, which *bâtir* means. A *building* in English is therefore in French a *bâtiment*. The *American College Dictionary*, which I have in my hand, thus notes about *building:* "n. 1, anything built or constructed. 2, the act, business, or art of constructing houses, etc."[18b] The case is therefore clear: a *building* is either what we call a structure [*un bâtiment*] or what we call the structure [organization, construction: *le bâtiment*], in the sense of: "The structure determines all." There is not moreover any other French usage. We live in houses [*maisons*], which are structures [*bâtiments*] or the main parts of structures [*corps de bâtiment*]. In barracks, for instance, the various *bâtiments* are designated by numerals; in apartment buildings they are often designated by letters: stairway A, D, E. But we do not get the impression that the English word has passed into French usage. I find a sign of this in the fact that its pronunciation has not been Frenchified. It is not one of those English words really incorporated into our usage, such as *redingote, boulingrin* [bowling green], or *bifteck* [beefsteak]. We still do not say *bildaingue*. It is easy to count the number of American enterprises established in Paris which, installed in a *bâtiment* which is their own, give to it quite naturally the name of *building*, which is its correct name in their own language [*langue*]: "*Building*," says my American dictionary, "connotes in general a useful purpose: houses, schools, commercial offices, etc. . . ." Perhaps one must add, for this is the meaning which appears to have kept the attention of certain Frenchmen: "of related professions: *medical arts building*," in which all occupants are physicians more or less specialized, passing their patients between themselves mutually if possible. This is what in France we call a "house" [*maison*]: "House of Chemistry," "Radio-Broadcasting House," that is to say, a *bâtiment* or edifice where certain activities are "at home" and where those who practice them are "at home," as if in their own place of residence. Neither in the provinces nor in Paris do we speak of a school or of any public *bâtiment* as a *building*. Why claim that the word has become French since that is not the case?

It is, I believe, because the English word corresponds to something, precisely to that notion of a specialized place of residence for a certain trade or skill, destined for a certain end. The Americans, for whom every construction is a *building*, produced by the act *to build* (sic), have not had the need of making a new word for such an ancient thing: they have acted like we should do if we were satisfied in French with *maison: les maisons de la culture, la maison commune*, and so forth. Perceiving the difference between this sort of *maison* and the *maison* of Pierre, Jacques, or of Bertrand, some people find it satisfying to give it a particular name, in such a fashion that following their example, we use a particular noun, borrowed from the English, to designate what English-speaking people themselves designate by as undifferentiated a name as possible. The process does not make sense.

Why do certain people feel the need to do this and contribute by their example to its becoming general? I do not know the answer to that question, which arises from collective psychology, and in connection with which, beyond the basic generalities, we quickly enter into merely formal explications. The most vague of these generalities, which I mention only because it has haunted my mind for a long time, is, paradoxically, that the cause of these borrowings is our hatred of neologism. When we feel the desire for a word because we think we have a need for it, we prefer to borrow a foreign word already existing and known rather than create a new word or use in a new sense some French word already in the dictionary.

That is so much the case that we at times see a French word adopted into a foreign language centuries ago become French once more with its foreign pronunciation rather than simply putting it back into usage or making a new use of it and pronouncing it correctly.

A typical case in this respect is the recent vogue of the rather ridiculous word *suce-panse* [something that sucks on a pot belly, but the play here will be on the pronunciation]. Those journals which formerly watched over their language, such as *Le Monde* (offspring of *Le Temps*) or *Le Figaro* (self-generated), today print the word *suspense*, which is only the French word *suspens*, with identically the same meaning, but pronounced henceforth *in French* like the English themselves have come to pronounce it in their own language [*langue*] since they borrowed it from ours. If he wants to say *suspens*, a speaker of English will naturally say something like *seusspence*, but it is indeed the French *suspens* that he uses. The same American dictionary indicates the etymology: "Old French, *suspens*, in the phrase *en suspens, in suspense*." The English meaning of *suspense* is that of mental uncertainty in expectation of a decision or about an issue, ordinarily with a shade of apprehension or anxiety. In French it exists with the particularized meaning of "suspended, forbidden, an ecclesiastic suspended from his functions, a priest *struck with the interdict* [*frappé de suspense*]." But we call him, therefore, a suspended priest [*prêtre suspens*]. Beyond this case we still use the word in the adverbial locution *en suspens*, to be in suspense, to be in uncertainty. It is true that the rapid multiplication of detective novels familiarly called in America "whodunits" (for *who has done it, quilafait*) has created the need for a substantive to designate the state of uncertainty and expectation that the authors of detective novels exercise their wits to create, since it is for the pleasure of feeling this that the reader reads their books. Nothing was easier. It was enough to say *du suspens*. We must indeed use this in order to be within the language. The horror of the Frenchman for a neologism is precisely such that he *prefers to borrow a foreign word rather than modify, as slightly as it may be, the use of a French word already existing. Du suspens* is not said, so then we speak of *suspense*, although *suspense* is the same as the French *suspens*, retaining the same meaning and being written in the same manner except for one letter.

These reflections have no other object than to translate into words the perplexity of the philosopher in immediate contact with the specific complexity of the language within its own reality. It ought to be easier for a single man to make a dictionary than for forty to do so, but, more rapidly produced, the result is not necessarily better. The uncertainties and irresolution concerning details inevitable in every collective work come from the fact that a group is already a society, and if that society gathers together for the purpose of the solemn function, literally as old as Adam, of the Imposition of Names, the language which seeks itself through the words and meanings in the thought of its members will carry out this function in more natural conditions, conditions closer to those which prevail at its birth, than if we imagined it as the work of some divine Littré free to decide matters according to the inspiration which may guide his personal choice.

A dictionary so constructed is more real than any other. It translates better the difficulty inherent in the very essence of language. He who finds himself called to take part in this work tells himself at times that he is collaborating in the erection of a new tower of Babel. But it is the contrary that is true, for language *is* in fact a tower of Babel, the confusion of language [*langue*] *is* language [*langue*], and the work of the lexicographer is an attempt to come out from that confusion rather than to augment it, and to do so, moreover, without drying up its source, which is the creative vitality of language [*langue*]. If a living cell were conscious of being such, a unit among millions of others in the structure of a living being, it would doubtless have trouble in assigning to each of them a function unique and rigorously defined once and for all. The *Homo loquens* who each of us is cannot be unaware of the fluid elements which the living structure of language has. To let these waverings appear in the inventory that he makes of it is perhaps for the lexicographer the best way to respect the nature of his object.

A language [*langue*] is a social, therefore a collective, fact. Its social character is recognized by the fact that, according to what we could call Durkheim's Law, every infraction of the rule that it establishes is visited by a sanction, even if it only be that of ridicule. When at a circus a clown amuses himself with speaking improperly, children laugh. But each thought moves with ease at the center of that domain which, completely collective as it is, depends on it. At each instant there is born somewhere some new locution. At any moment each of us can invent one of them without even knowing that we do so. To claim to stop the growth of the vocabulary at any point is an enterprise contrary to the nature of its object.

The neologism is a particular case of this rule. In his excellent *Lettre sur les occupations de l'Academie française* the purist Fenelon pronounced a vigorous eulogy of it. We do not have the impression that the author of *Telemaque*, who invented a new French prose, often had recourse to the use of new words. Saint-Simon showed himself more daring in this regard, but, precisely, when Saint-Simon innovates in matters of vocabulary, he does not borrow; he creates, which each of us has the right to do and even is invited to do at his risk and peril. Like creating, borrowing is also a right, and often a necessity. Nothing, therefore, is more legitimate than to do so, on two conditions however.

First of all it is desirable that this adoption of a foreign word be spontaneous, that it come about by a natural evolution of language [*langue*], and not as the result of a bludgeoning of the hearer by the occupying powers of the means of mass communication, or as the result of a raging epidemic of offhanded writing on the part of journalists forgetful of their letters, or perhaps even illiterate. When the evolution is natural, the pronunciation of the word and its spelling change, to the point of making it lose its original appearance. Contrarily to what the French Academy decided in the matter, *building* is not a "word of English origin"; it is an English word. To the extent that we do not pronounce and write it *buildaingue* it will remain one of those marvelous nominal present participles which make for the richness of the English language [*langue*], and which we can well envy them, but not borrow from them. There are no French words ending in *-ing*. Those which we are tempted to acclimatize — *building, footing, shopping, caravaning,* etc.— remain in our language [*langue*] as foreign bodies: we know neither how to write nor pronounce them. A living language [*langue*] gives witness to its vitality by inventing, often by analogy and metaphor (which testifies to the poetic essence of the language), words which satisfy at one and the same time both the mouth and the imagination of those who speak it. *"Faire du léché-vitrine"* [window shopping: to lick shop windows] is a creation of genius. I recently heard from a young student the word *"dragueuse"* [literally, a female dredger, dragger: figuratively, a woman looking for a pickup]; the word could be ancient. The students perhaps have borrowed it from the vocabulary of the oldest profession in the world. At any rate it is excellent. In my time there was only a *"drague"* [literally, a boat equipped for dredging; also, figuratively, a streetwalker]. We saw them often on the Seine at Paris, but my father, whose language was however chaste, called the dredging barge a *"marie-salope"* [mary-slut], which was also a linguistic success. If *"dragueuse"* still exists when they get to the letter "D," the Academie will be able to consider sympathetically the meaning that this word receives in the language of modern university coeducation. This is a point upon which, for once, male and female students have a right to be consulted.

The second condition for a foreign word being admitted to our language [*langue*] is that we should not already have at our disposal a French word to say the same thing. Except to amuse ourselves, which we always have the right to do in playing with language, it is superfluous to say *"faire son shopping"* [do one's shopping] when we can say *faire ses achats, faire ses emplettes, faire ses provisions, faire ses courses, faire les magasins,* or even *trainer dans les magasins* [do one's buying, make purchases, get one's supplies, do one's errands, "do the stores," or even "loiter about the stores"], about all of which the Parisians understand each other wonderfully.

This once said, each one ought to feel beyond constraint. It is impossible to know how many words make up a language [*langue*], to decree dogmatically that a word does or does not make part of a language [*langue*], because in fact there do not exist, in the same country, two persons whose vocabulary is identical as regards the number of words and the shades of their meaning. We must nevertheless note that "to speak as one wants" does not exclude the requirement that one be able to give an explanation, at least to oneself, of one's own language, which is nothing other than "to know what one is saying," "to know what it means to speak," or to know how to speak, "that which is called speaking."

Notes

1. THE MYTH OF THE DECOMPOSITION OF THOUGHT

1. On this Cartesian aspect of the thought of Condillac see E. Gilson and Thomas Langan, *Modern Philosophy: Descartes to Kant* (New York: Random House, 1963), p. 279.

2. Emile Benveniste, *Problèmes de linguistique générale* (Paris: N.R.F., Éditions Gallimard, 1966), p. 40: "Saussure après un demi-siècle." Cf. Ferdinand de Saussure, *Cours de linguistique générale* (Paris: Payot, 1968), p. 24. See note 1, Introduction, for texts the translator used. Where not specifically stated otherwise, texts are Gilson's or Saussure's French.

3. Condillac will be cited after the collected edition of his *Oeuvres* (Paris: Édition Georges LeRoy: Presses Universitaires de France, 3 vols., 1947, 1948, 1951). In order not to multiply needlessly references and notes, we shall generally indicate the reference to the place cited in the work then in question by the use of parentheses in the text.

4. Concerning what Condillac thought of Scholasticism and of the Middle Ages see his *Discours de réception a l'Académie francaise*, in *Oeuvres*, ed. Georges LeRoy, I, 390.

5. Condillac, *De l'art de penser*, I, 1: ed. cit., vol. I, p. 719. Concerning this too often neglected part of the doctrine see the study of Roger Lefevre, "Condillac, maitre du langage," in the *Revue internationale de philosophie* 21 (1967), pp. 393–406.

6. The best introduction to this problem remains the work of Martin Grabmann, *Die Entwicklung der mittelalterlichen Sprachlogik*, in *Mittelalterliches Geistesleben* (Munich, 1911), vol. I, pp. 104–146.

7. Stephane Mallarmé, *Oeuvres complètes* (Paris: Pleiade, 1945), ed. H. Mondor and G. Jean-Aubry, pp. 902–903. On the notion of "word," "this disparaged and irreplaceable term," see Emile Benveniste, *Problèmes de linguistique générale*, pp. 123–124, in particular: "The word could then be defined as the smallest free signifying unit capable of effecting a sentence, and of being itself effectuated by phonemes" (p. 124). On the notion of phoneme, p. 121. Its simplest notion is that of a sonorous element of language, a sound.

8. One can in any case hark back often, if not always, to Ferdinand de Saussure's *Cours de linguistique générale*, ch. VI, "Representation de la langue par

l'ecriture," pp. 44–54. ["Introduction," ch. VI; de Mauro, ed., pp. 44–54.] Saussure is far from minimizing the role of writing, but he justly maintains it in the subordinate place which it deserves: "Speech and writing are two systems of distinct signs. The unique reason for the existence of writing is to represent speech. The object of linguistics is not defined by the combination of the written word and the spoken word. The latter by itself alone constitutes that object. But the written word is mixed in so intimately with the spoken word that it ends by usurping the main role. One comes thereby to give as much and more importance to the representation of the vocal sign as to the sign itself. It is as if one believed that in order to know someone, it would be better to look at his photograph than at his face" (p. 45). Cf. further on, ch. VI.

9. In their celebrated *Grammaire générale de Port-Royal* Arnauld and Lancelot build upon this observation in order to recommend a reformation in the teaching of reading. They advise to set out, not from the artificial pronunciation which makes up the names of letters, but from their actual sounds. In the case of consonants, the only letters concerned in the reform, instead of teaching infants to say "Bee," "Cee," "Dee," "Eff," etc., one ought to teach the sound of the consonant followed by a mute semivowel, "b," "c," "d," "f," etc. I personally know of only a single master who may have followed this method: Monsieur Jourdain's philosophy teacher in *Le bourgeois gentilhomme* (1670. The *Grammaire générale* dates from 1660). The most recent pupil of this master is Tristan Tzara, creator of the Dada movement: "Da, Da. Oui Ah! The pretty things! The pretty things!" These words have been chosen by M. Michel Sanouillet to serve as the epigraph to his *Histoire de Dada à Paris* (Paris: L.-J. Pauvert, 1965).

10. Paucity: smallness in number, from the Latin *paucitas:* a small number, a rarity. Still used today in such compounds as *pauciflore*, that which only bears a few flowers.

11. André Martinet, "Le mot," *Diogene* 51 (1965), p. 51.

12. Ibid.

13. Ibid.

14. J. Vendryès, *Le langage: Introduction linguistique à l'histoire* (Paris: Albin Michel, 1923), pp. 133, 417.

15. E. Benveniste, *Problèmes . . .* , p. 45 [sic].

16. Ibid., p. 16.

[16a. Gilson uses *travailler, travaillerons*, and *-ons*.]

17. A. Martinet, *Éléments de linguistique générale* (Paris: A. Colin, 1967), pp. 15–16.

18. Ibid., pp. 33–34. The author does not see any theoretical impossibility to the execution of this scientific project. On the contrary, one feels that he sees in it the putting into operation of the only method that might be theoretically irreproachable. It is only its great difficulty of application which keeps him from "recommending" a method which makes "total abstraction from the meanings of the significative units" (*loc. cit.*, p. 34). Still, it is necessary, in order to be a language [*langue*], that that which one is ignorant of should have meaning for someone.

19. Emile Benveniste, *Problèmes de linguistique générale*, p. 25.

20. "The word *symbol* has been used in order to designate the linguistic sign,

or, more exactly, what we call the signifier [*signifiant*]. There are disadvantages to admitting this, precisely on account of our first principle [the arbitrary nature of the sign]. The symbol has as a characteristic that it is never completely arbitrary. It is not a vacuum; there is a rudiment of natural connection between the signifier and the signified. The symbol of justice, the balance, could not be replaced by just anything, a chariot, for example" (F. de Saussure, *Cours de linguistique générale*, p. 101). [The distinction sometimes made in English between *sign* and *symbol* is not observed in French apparently. For us *sign* does have some analogical resemblance to the thing signified, e.g., the color red as in a "red stop light" meaning danger. A symbol, on the other hand, has its connection with the thing signified only by convention, e.g., the word "red" with certain segments of the visual spectrum. We speak of language as symbolic, not *signal*, communication. But see the translator's "Introduction".]

    21. E. Benveniste, *Problèmes. . .* , p. 26.

    22. Ibid. The least practiced ear perceives immediately under such enunciations the presence of problems which, under the names of realism and nominalism, agitated the schools of the Middle Ages for at least three centuries. Today one is satisfied with holding these philosophical problems as resolved by virtue of a simple preliminary decree: do not philosophize. It is not sufficient, however, that a solution should not be philosophical in order that it might become scientific. What is the "concrete object" which can only be an "exemplar" of the concept? Plato, Aristotle, Abelard, and Ockham immediately call for the word, and today one can only hold one's peace or take up the problem at the point where they left it.

    23. E. Benveniste, *Problèmes. . .* , p. 26. The author immediately gets involved with the problems of knowing if "this essentially symbolic capacity for representation which is at the base of conceptual functions only appears in man." Response: Yes, it is the characteristic of man. Could one conceive of man without language? Response: No. "The emergence of man . . . is due before all to his faculty of symbolic representation, the common source of thought, language, and society" (p. 27). There, then, is this "symbolic capacity" positioned as the source of thought, but in the following paragraph it is thought itself which explains this symbolic capacity, for according to the word of H. Delacroix (*Le langage et la pensée*, p. 602), "symbolic thought is simply thought" (cited by Benveniste, p. 28, note). One harkens back thereby to the initial remark: "Such is language, a double-faced entity" (p. 28). Every attempt to explain one of its faces by the other or to reduce it to the other ends in a verbal dialectic which does not allow reflection to advance a single step.

    24. E. Benveniste, *Problèmes . . .* , p. 25. In return the same linguist says: "The content to be transmitted (or, if one prefers, the 'thought') is thus decomposed according to a linguistic scheme. The 'form' of thought is configured by the structure of language [*langue*]" (ibid.). I do not see anything to be objected to. I understand that a scholar should have scruples, or even embarrassment, at writing a word as impure as "thought," but, finally, if the form of thought is configured by language [*langue*], by what is the structure of language [*langue*] configured if not by thought, or what we designate by this word?

25. "Der Satz ist ein Bild der Wirklichkeit," L. Wittgenstein, *Tractatus logico-philosophicus* (Suhrkamp Verlag, 1966), 4.01, p. 30. It is thus that his interpreter Justus Hartnack understands it (*Wittgenstein und die moderne Philosophie* [Stuttgart: W. Kohlmanner, 1962], p. 22): "Nach der Affassung von Wittgenstein ist die Sprache eine Abbildung der Wirklichkeit. Eine Vorbedingung dessen, dass sich die Wirklichkeit so abbilden lasst, ist es, dass das Abbildende und das Abzubildende in ihrer Struktur ubereinstimmen. Die Struktur der Sprache ist daher die gleiche wie die Struktur der Wirklichkeit."

26. Walter M. Elsasser, *Atom and Organism: A New Approach to Theoretical Biology* (Princeton: Princeton University Press, 1966), pp. 58–59.

27. Ibid., p. 59.

28. Ibid., p. 38.

2. WORD AND MEANING

1. A suggestion noted by Noam Chomsky, *Current Issues in Linguistic Theory* (The Hague: Mouton, 1964), p. 21.

The present essay holds itself excused, by its very subject, from extending beyond the domain of the word [*parole*] and taking into consideration other kinds of signs. It is even more difficult to ignore their existence since St. Augustine stated precisely a long time ago that the word was only one of a number of known means of signification. See the remarkable chapter in *De doctrina christiana*, II, 3, 4. After having recalled that animals use signs and that one could ask if the cries and groans of humans are or are not signs (II, 2, 3), he observes that certain signs (or means of communicating thought) address themselves to others audially. Motions of the head, actions of the hands, some stage performances of actors, military ensigns and flags, appeal to the sense of sight: "All these signs are in some fashion visible words." But Augustine adds that the signs which appeal to the ear are incomparably more numerous, that words are for men the principal means of communicating thoughts, and he concludes that moreover, "I have been able to describe all these signs with the assistance of words, whereas no matter what effort I might make I could not describe the words by means of these signs." The problem of the relation of linguistics to general semiotics [*sémiologie*] is one of the constants of the philosophy of language.

2. F. de Saussure, *Course de linguistique générale* (Paris: Payot, 1968), p. 115. [Gilson's reference is somewhat erroneous. Ch. IV of Part II is indeed called "Linguistic Value." The passage cited, however, is in Ch. III of Part I, "Static and Evolutionary Linguistics." I have translated Gilson's French. Baskin's translation varies only slightly from this. For the French see de Mauro, ed., p. 115.]—The distinction of sign and meaning is not introduced between two "things." The sign, vocal or written, is a physical reality, then, a sort of thing. The meaning is not a thing. It has no physical reality distinct from the act by which the word signifies. It is what makes possible the normal polysemy of the word. One ought doubtless understand in this sense the remark of Paul Valery: "The illusion of philosophers is to believe that words have a *meaning*, whereas they only have a particular usage."

Edmée de la Rochefoucauld, *En lisant les Cahiers*, t. III, p. 205. The *meaning* of the word is precisely the *use* that one makes of it.

3. Ibid., p. 116. [p. 80. Again, I have translated the French. The differences between my translation and Baskin's is slight.]

4. *Le petit Robert*, p. 1873, at the word valeur, IV, 3: "Ling. 'Meaning (of a word) limited or made precise by its function in a structure (associative field, context).' 'In language [*langue*], each term has its value through its contrast to all the other terms.'" (Saussure). [p. 2062, 1978 ed.]

5. F. de Saussure, *Cours* . . . , pp. 125–127 [pp. 88ff., 110, Baskin.]. Saussure elsewhere uses this comparison less to clarify the nature of language than to illustrate the distinction that he even calls an opposition (p. 127) [p. 89] between the diachronic and the synchronic; cf. p. 43. Moreover, he takes up again later on (p. 153) [p. 110] the comparison with chess in order to make intelligible that which he calls *values*.

6. While in the *Tractatus* the function of language [*langue*] is to provide an image of reality, it becomes in the *Philosophische Untersuchungen* word play, a *Sprachspiel*. There is much of this in it, and there might even be an unlimited amount of it. The class of *Sprachspiel* does not possess a distinguishing characteristic in all its members. The concept of language [*langue*] cannot then be defined. Fundamentally, it is the same with the idea of play. Play has not any precise, specific distinguishing characteristic, but only a "family likeness" (*Familienahnlichkeit*). See James Hartnack, *Wittgenstein und die moderne Philosophie*, pp. 62–65.

7. F. de Saussure, *Cours* . . . , p. 127 [p. 89].

8. Ibid., p. 23 [p. 8].

9. *Le petit Robert*, p. 1116, at this word, 2: "Ling. Sound or group of articulated sounds (most often) constituting a semantic unity and maintaining a certain formal consistency in discourse. Remark: For modern linguistics, the word is not a precise unit (except in written language [*langue*]: a series of uninterrupted signs)" [I do not find this in the 1978 edition of the *Petit Robert* (p. 1232)]. The reserve that accompanies each term of these descriptions is certainly noticeable. Other reservations could be added, for "pull" [*tire*] is a word written uninterruptedly, and "plug" [*bouchon*] is another, but "pull-plug" [corkscrew: French, *tire-bouchon*] is at one and the same time interrupted and rendered interrupted by the hyphen which makes of these two words a single compound word. The meaning of it is not moreover that of "pull" or that of "plug." It means the small instrument which one uses to open a bottle. It can signify in addition a spiral, like that of some staircases, or a lock of hair curled spirally, or a vicious way of reasoning "*en tire-bouchon*," etc. . . .

10. In the same language [*langue*] differences of pronunciation originate from province to province, at times from family to family, a number of different names. The Canadians are disturbed, almost indignant, that some of their number say *joual* instead of *cheval*. *Joual* is a pronunciation as legitimate as is *juene* for *chevesne*, a form one has come across frequently over the past fifty years or so, and which offers the advantages of substituting an easy dipthong for two syllables separated by a "v," which takes an effort to pronounce.

11. In his translation of the *Nicomachean Ethics* the lamented J. Tricot notes:

"We translate *mégalopsukhia* as is ordinarily done (by magnanimity), but this term expresses rather the dignity of the person, the just sense of his worth." Following in that Aristotle and his definition of *mégalopsukhos* in the *Posterior Analytics*, II, 13, the same translator understands the word *mégalopsukhos* in the sense of "proud." One is aware of how the passage from one meaning to the other is possible, even easy, but the meanings are different nonetheless.

[11a. The difficulty of choosing the appropriate English term for the French words listed, particularly *coeur*, is an illustration of the problem M. Gilson addresses.]

12. de Saussure, *Cours . . .* , p. 145 [p. 103. Again, I have translated from the French].

13. I take the liberty of referring on this point to an essay which I formerly published on the matter in *Études sur le rôle de la pensée médiévale dans la formation du système cartesien* (Paris: Librairie Philosophique J. Vrin, 1930).

14. This point of view is developed in *The Unity of Philosophical Experience* (The William James Lectures) (New York: Scribners, 1937).

15. Geraud de Cordemoy, *Discours physique de la parole* (Paris: Bibliotheque du Graphe, no date). Reprinted in *Oeuvres philosophiques* (P.U.F., 1969) with a biobibliographic study; critical edition, presented by Pierre Clair and Francois Gorbal.

16. *Discernement de l'âme et du corps* (Paris, 1666).

17. Cordemoy, *Discours physique*, "Preface." See, further on: "And in this entire discussion, I refute so many new arguments in order to show the distinction of body and soul, that it does not seem to me that one could know anything more obvious than that."

18. Ibid., pp. 16–17.

19. Cordemoy is clearly aware of this articulation of his thought: "And as I have shown that a body never gives movement to a body, but only that their encounter is an occasion for divine power which moves one of them in order to apply it to the other; one must also conceive that as soon as a soul wants to make known to another what it thinks, that comes about, because God makes it so that, following the will of the first, the second knows it. And in the same fashion that the will we have that our body should move does not move it but is only an occasion for the First Power to move it in the way that we wish it to be moved, so the will that we have that a mind [*esprit*] should know what we are thinking is an occasion for this Power to bring it about that this mind should perceive it." *Discours*, p. 83.

20. Facts are always anecdotal and never prove anything, but they state things precisely. About 1903 or 1904, as I was reading an ancient French text, my mother taught me the meaning of the French verb *echarnir*. She knew this old word since her early childhood at the School of the Daughters of Cravant (Yonne): "*Madame, elle m'a echarnie.*" This very day (July 25, 1968) a minister announced on the radio that the time has come for the University of France, "*as we say presently*, for dialogue and planning together [*du dialogue et de la concertation*]." Indeed, these two words with their new nuances ought to become part of the next edition of the *Dictionnaire* of the Academie Francaise. *Concerter* [to concert, arrange, plan] is pri-

marily used under the reflexive form, *se concerter* [to act in concert, to counsel together]; but one can also "plan [*concerter*] a common enterprise." It will be necessary then to introduce "concertation" into the dictionaries with the meaning "the action of concerting." The word is already in the language [*langue*], synchronically, like a young infant in a family, and those who use it today know that it is young. The synchronous is given *in* the diachronous.

21. J. Vendryès, *Le langage. Introduction linguistique à l'histoire*, pp. 193–194. The remark on the word, or the words, *fille* is found on p. 208. The only element common to the three words is that they all signify a feminine individual. But France, eldest daughter [*fille*] of the Church, has no other sex than the gender of her name. A "*filette*" means a small girl or, on occasion, a half-bottle: a half-bottle of white wine, etc. . . . .

22. An evolution predicted by de Saussure, *Cours de linguistique générale*, p. 111 [p. 76].

3. LANGUAGE AS A HUMAN ACHIEVEMENT

1. "Many phonologists limit themselves almost exclusively to the phonational act, i.e., the production of sound by vocal organs (larynx, mouth, etc.), and neglect the auditory side. Their method is wrong. Not only does the auditory impression come to us just as directly as the image of the moving vocal organs, but it is also the basis of any theory." F. de Saussure, *Cours de linguistique générale*, p. 60. [Ferdinand de Saussure, *Course in General Linguistics*, trans. Wade Baskin (New York: McGraw-Hill, 1966), p. 38.] This is why "the linguistic sign unites, not a thing and a name, but a concept and a sound image." Ibid., p. 98 [trans. p. 66].

2. Ibid., pp. 25–26 [sic] [trans., pp. 18, 10].

3. Edward Sapir, *Language* . . . (New York: Harvest Books, 1949), pp. 8–9. French translation: *Le langage* (Paris: Payot, 1967), p. 12.

4. Ibid., p. 9.

5. Aristotle, *De anima*, II, 8, 420 b 5 sv. ["Voice is a kind of sound characteristic of what has soul in it; nothing that is without soul utters voice. . . ." McKeon, ed.; trans. J. A. Smith.]

[5a. See *Aristotle's De Anima in the Version of William of Moerbeke and the Commentary of St. Thomas Aquinas*, trans. Kenelm Foster and Silvester Humphries (London: Routledge & Kegan Paul, 1954), pp. 293–299.]

[5b. Despite the intervening citation of the *De partibus*, the quotations are from Aristotle's *De anima*, II, 8, 4206 16–23 (McKeon, ed., pp. 572–573). I have translated from Gilson's French.]

6. In speaking of the various senses, Aristotle gauges that he ought to speak first of the objects proper to each of them (*De anima*, II, 6, beginning). Voice is therefore studied in connection with the sense of hearing. In defining it as "the sound produced by an animal, and with a special organ" (II, 8, 420b 10–15), he means not to say that there exists an organ whose productions are the specific object of hearing, but that the production of the voice by the animal requires an or-

ganic cause, air striking against the lining of the trachea and articulated by various organs. Aristotelians will follow the method inaugurated by Aristotle. See the ample treatment of the question in Albert the Great, *Summa de creaturis*, Pars. II, q. 25, art. 1–4. He notes that the animal only perceives in the voice of another animal a generic desire, such as that of feeding or mating, the pain caused by a wound, or any sort of a call. Art. 2, q. 25 is important. The question is: "How can the intelligible species" which is in the intellect descend into words? Response: signifying discourse (*sermo significativus*) is a relation with two other things. First, with something outside the soul. This is why in his *Sophistical Refutations*, I, 1, Aristotle says that "As it is impossible in the course of a discussion to introduce the very objects of which we speak, we replace them by their names as by symbols; after that we reason as if that which proceeds from their names proceeded also from the things in reality, exactly as those who calculate do with their accounts." Second, signifying speech (*sermo significativus*) is in relation with the sensible species in the imagination and the intelligible species in the intellect. At the time of its initial institution, meaning [*sens*] came to speech [*parole*] from the will of him who instituted it. Likewise today, the power of signifying comes to the word from the *intention* present in the thought of him who speaks. Albert then engages himself courageously in a detailed scientific explanation of the central difficulty: *How does signification join itself to voice?* Tied to the presently outmoded notion of *species* (which we have not moreover replaced by any other), this laying out of the problem has become an archaeological curiosity, but it is remarkable that the medieval problematic of the problem remains and, it appears to me, that the responses have still not been found.

[6a. Aristotle, *De partibus animalium*, I, 639b 8–16; in Richard McKeon, ed., *The Basic Works of Aristotle* (New York: Random House, 1941), p. 644. Trans. by William Ogle.]

[6b. Ibid., 640a 12–13, p. 645.]

[6c. Ibid.]

[6d. Ibid., 642, 1, 15–17, p. 650.]

7. This detailing is only a very free paraphrase of the great text of Aristotle, *De partibus animalium*, I, 1. What we retain serves only as an invitation to read it. Our intention in using it freely is to separate out the connection which links up the problem of language, as it poses itself presently, with the old Aristotelian ideas of life, form, and soul. This connection, implicit with Aristotle, ought not lose any of its force for being made explicit.

8. Walter M. Elsasser, *Atom and Organism: A New Approach to Theoretical Biology* (New Jersey: Princeton University Press, 1966), p. 35.

9. [Paraphrased in] Ibid., p. 19.

10. Ibid., p. 20. On the complex position of Claude Bernard see further on, ch. V, III.

11. Ibid., p. 21.

12. Wilhelm von Humboldt, *Uber die Verschiedenheit des Menschlichen Sprachbaues* (Berlin, 1836: cited by Noam Chomsky, *Current Issues in Linguistic Theory* (The Hague: Mouton, 1964), p. 17; also, anastatic reproduction, Bonn, 1960 (Chomsky, op. cit., p. 116) (sic).

13. Chomsky, *Current Issues . . .* , pp. 17–19.

14. Ibid., pp. 19–20. [I do not find this passage as cited and have translated from the French here.] In this perspective a tongue [*langue*] is no more conceived as a reserve of concepts, themselves considered (as de Saussure appears to have done) as a store of well-defined objects, but is a productive capacity always at work not only to create them anew but even to recreate, or revivify, old ones as each act of perception or conception requires it. Ibid., pp. 20–21.

15. All these remarks are inspired by a very stimulating article of Noam Chomsky's, "Language and the Mind, I," in *The Columbia University Forum*, Spring, 1968, pp. 5–10. This essay is adopted from a book presently announced (1968) to be published by Harcourt, Brace and World under the title of *Language and Mind*. The essay allows one to predict that the book will be of extreme interest to philosophers. [For these citations see Noam Chomsky, *Language and Mind* (New York: Harcourt Brace Jovanovich, 1972), 2nd printing, p. 5.]

16. Ibid., p. 8 [1972, p. 6].

17. Chomsky, ibid., p. 9 [1972, p. 12. Gilson has at the asterisk I have inserted in the text, "or even, when everything is said, than the number of seconds in the history of language." I have no access to the 1968 article or the 1968 text.].

18. Mortimer J. Adler, *The Difference of Man and the Difference It Makes* (New York: Holt, Rinehart, Winston, 1967). The demonstration is conducted with an entirely scientific precision, and the conclusion is only reached at the price of a rigorous critical analysis of the facts and arguments upon which adverse positions are founded. I do not see the use of repeating in an abridged and less exact form what M. J. Adler has said so well: Man is the only talking animal actually known.

19. Aristotle, *Politics*, I, 2 [1253a 8–18, in McKeon, ed., p. 1129; trans. Benjamin Jowett]. Aristotle's thought does not contradict that of Darwin, for the position of the problem is entirely different in the two doctrines. They are irreconcilable, but Darwin does not reply to Aristotle. His position is antitheological, therefore theological. Considering the mass of facts that he has accumulated (analogies of structure between different species), he concludes that "the great principle of evolution stands up clear and firm. . . . ." "He who is not content to look like a savage at the phenomena of nature as disconnected, cannot any longer believe that man is the work of a separate act of creation." Charles Darwin, *The Descent of Man*, ch. XXI, "General Summary and Conclusions," *Great Books*, 49, p. 590. The high level of our intellectual faculties and of our moral disposition "is the greatest difficulty which presents itelf, after we have been driven to this conclusion on the origin of man," [591], namely, that "man is the co-descendant with other mammals of a common progenitor" [590]. How overcome this difficulty? Darwin candidly replies: "But everyone who admits the principle of evolution, must see that the mental powers of the higher animals, which are the same in kind as those of man, though so different in degree, are capable of advancement" [591]. Chapters III and IV of the first part of *La descendance ou origine de l'homme* (sic) are devoted to the comparison of the mental faculties of the lower animals and of man. This has nothing to do with the question of knowing whether "each species has been created independently of the others" (*Origin of Species*, "Recapitulation and

Conclusion"). It is solely a question of knowing whether, as Max Muller objected to Darwin (*Descent of Man*, ed. cit., p. 299, notes 62, 63): "The use of language [*parole*] implies the power of forming general concepts; and that as no animals are supposed to possess this power, an impassable barrier is formed between them and man" [*Descent*, p. 299]. Whether or not there is an evolution of animal species, in the sense that some are descended from others, is a purely scientific question. The fact that some analogies and almost indiscernible gradations exist between species proves nothing: the law of continuity of order (the "great chain of being") is familiar to Aristotle, who believed, however, in the eternity of species. That there is an animal psychism is evident, and also that it exists in degrees. Aristotelians, moreover, have always known that (cf. their theory of the "estimative"), but no known animal displays vocal behavior attesting to the presence of concepts. Darwin only says, after having read the arguments in a contrary sense: "I cannot doubt that language [*langage*] owes its origin to the imitation and modification of various natural sounds, the voices of other animals, and man's own instinctive cries, aided by signs and gestures" (*Descent of Man*, ed. cit., p. 298). Naturally, if one sets out from the "principle of evolution," all the continuities of order become continuities of origin, but one does not then get out of the realm of possibility, or, more so, from that of probability, which here moreover comes up against the [im-]probability, not less scientific, that the inferior should be able *mechanically* to engender the superior. On that matter the thesis of Emile Boutroux, *De la contingence des lois de la nature*, has posed, since 1874, conclusions which have not yet been refuted and which the subsequent development of physics has rather confirmed.

20. Aristotle, *Politics* [I, 1, 1252a, 1–5, in McKeon, ed., p. 1127].

21. Ibid., I, 2, 1952b–1953a [1252b–1253a, in McKeon, ed., p. 1129].

22. Aristotle, *De interpretatione*, I, 11 [I, 4, 17a, 3–4, in McKeon, ed., p. 42; trans. E.M. Edghill].

[22a. Ibid., I, 16a, 3–7, p. 40.]

[22b. Ibid., I, 2, 16a, 27–29, p. 40.]

23. Language is always more or less inadequate to the thought it wishes to express. The word "arbitrary," which is assuredly as imperfect as would be every other word in its place, is only justified in the sense of "nonnatural." Now, to the category of the natural and necessary there is opposed only that of the voluntary and the free. The arbitrary character of the imposition of names does not, therefore, necessarily signify that there is not any connection, any conformity of any sort between the word and the meaning. It only signifies that where such conformity is noted, it does not result from a natural necessity but from a voluntary choice. If, with Plato, we admit that this will is that of some sage legislator, there is no problem. His wisdom manifests itself in the very choice he made of names appropriate to their objects. Every man charged with "finding a name" for a product strains his ingenuity to find some conformity of this sort: *conveniant rebus nomina faxo suis*. Not believing much in the existence of this name-giving legislator, we are reduced to the notion of "convention," although no explicit convention presides over the acceptance, diffusion, or rejection of most names. It is rather a question of a sort of spontaneous accord which comes about regarding the satis-

factory quality of vocables cast up by one-does-not-know-who and little by little accepted by the great number of people. The only certain thing is that verbal epidemics take their origin in some sort of a concourse of wills. These observations do not contradict any of those of Roman Jakobsen, "A la recherche de l'essence du langage," in *Problèmes du langage* (Paris: Gillimard, 1966), pp. 22–38. His remarks, often accurate, about the sonorous motivation of certain words in certain languages [*langues*] do not change anything about the fact that in other languages [*langues*], and sometimes in the same one, other words with totally different resonance have the same meaning. In the origin of vocables there is often a choice, some taste, a sympathetic ear, a secret comprehension. It is not that which we deny in speaking of the arbitrary in the choice of vocables. We only affirm that this choice always has its cause in spontaneity, in liberty. Once the usage is established, that usage then comes to act as a sort of nature for the individual thing. That is obvious. But here it is the word "nature" which is not altogether suitable any longer, because there is no speaker of a language [*langue*] who does not fashion it to his own usage and is incapable of creating words if there is need of doing so. Usage would be better respected if it were not free. One will find further on some significant remarks on the regrettable lack of adaptation of certain words to their senses.

24. F. de Saussure, *Cours de linguistique générale*, p. 33 [trans., p. 16. I have translated from Gilson's French].

25. Ibid., p. 37 [trans., p. 18, perhaps. Baskin has: "[language] which is purely social. . . ."].

26. Ibid., p. 25 [p. 9]. Cf. A Martinet, *Éléments de linguistique générale*, p. 9: "Human institutions come about from life in society; this is indeed the case with language, which is conceived essentially as an instrument of communication." "The essential function of that *instrument* which is a tongue [*langue*] is that of communication" (p. 9). "In the final analysis it is indeed communication, that is to say, mutual comprehension, which must be retained as the central function of that instrument which is speech [*langue*]" (p. 10). Compare this with the actual development of the idea, still so ambiguous, of information: "the principal instrument of communication bearing information is language [*langage*]." Roman Jakobsen, *Essais de linguistique générale* (Paris: Editions de Minuit, 1963), p. 28.

27. Summing up the works of a conference of anthropologists and linguists held at Indiana University in 1952, Roman Jakobsen stated: "Finally, one of the most symptomatic traits of this conference will have been this: we have long and passionately debated questions of meaning. Certain speakers have remarked that only a few years ago that would hardly have been thinkable." *Essais de linguistique générale*, p. 38. And, further on: "There are still people to say that questions of meaning have no meaning for them, but when they say *no meaning*, one of two things follows: either they know what they want to say and by that very fact the question of meaning takes on meaning, or else they do not know what they want to say, and then their formulation has no meaning whatsoever" (ibid., pp. 38–39). The well-known linguist speaks golden words, but he would do well to be on his guard, for his reflection on *the meaning of meaning*, if it does not change directions quickly, threatens to lead him where he does not apparently want to go.

4. THE WORD AND THE CONCEPT

1. It appears impossible to me to recount a dream without rationalizing it simply by virtue of speaking it. I ought at least to confess an almost total personal incapacity of retelling one of my dreams without conferring on it, by the use of speech [*parole*] alone, a precision that I am aware of conferring on it in describing it. But it could be that Freud, who scarcely gave evidence of such scruples, had been endowed with an exceptional aptitude to do so. What makes me doubt this, and has always restrained me from taking the *Traumdeutung* seriously, is the violence of the rationalizing passion that he puts at the service of his interpretation. Dream symbolism presents for him a rigor of which few conceptual and completely rational thoughts would be capable. The more "absurd" are the dreams that he analyzes, the more are they rigorously construed and connected. For example: *Traumdeutung*, VI, 6, "Absurd Dreams: Intellectual Activities in Dreams," where it is shown that "the absurdity of the content of the dream is only apparent; it disappears when the dream is completely examined." We do not object to anything in the distinction between the preconscious, the subconscious, and the conscious; we deny still less that *psychisme* ought to be of the same nature under all three forms (or at these three levels), but it is doubtful that what we can observe of the functioning of conscious *psychisme* allows us to form an accurate picture of unconscious or preconscious *psychisme*. On this point we can only call upon Freud himself in the last chapter of his *Traumdeutung*. We need not grant to Freud that "the unconscious is the true psychic reality"; all psychic activity is the true psychic reality. But he is right to say that "in its intimate nature, the unconscious is to us exactly as unknown as is the reality of the exterior world, and it is also quite as imperfectly communicated by the data of consciousness as is the exterior world by what is related of it to us by the sense organs." This is precisely why it is imprudent to rationalize the unconscious overmuch. It is indeed the same thought which, at first unconscious, becomes conscious, but it comes to consciousness only by incarnating itself in language. It is therefore natural that we should not be able to represent it to ourselves such as it is without language.

2. Emile Benveniste, *Problèmes de linguistique générale*, p. 51, citing Saussure, *Cours de linguistique générale*, first edition (Paris-Lausanne, 1916), pp. 51–52. [The passage is to be found on p. 111 of the English translation. I have translated from the French, which is to be found on p. 155 rather than where Gilson places it.]

3. Thomas Aquinas, *Summa theologiae*, I, 79, 1 ad 3m [should be ad 4m: *Basic Writings of Saint Thomas*, ed. Anton C. Pegis (New York: Random House: 1945), I, 746].

4. Aristotle, *Metaphysics*, XIII, 10, 1087a 2; X, 2, 1053b 17 ["for the universal is not a substance"; "no universal can be a substance." McKeon, ed., pp. 911, 838 (trans. W. D. Ross)].

5. "A further difficulty is raised by the fact that all knowledge is of universals and of the 'such,' but substance is not a universal, but is rather a 'this'—a separable thing. . . ." Ibid., XI, 2, 1060b 20 [McKeon, trans. Ross].

6. Mortimer J. Adler, *The Difference of Man and the Difference It Makes*

(New York: Holt, Rinehart and Winston, 1967). Following his own dialectical line and his own problem, which is not exactly ours although in more than one point the two coincide, M. J. Adler sums up his noetic in four propositions which appear to me to be incontestable: a) "Our concepts are that in us whereby we apprehend the universal aspects of the things we think and talk about. b) To perform that cognitive function, our concepts must be actual universals (*actual universals:* real existing in fact and at present, in opposition to imaginary or simply virtual ones) [sic: Gilson]. c) But for anything to be an acutal universal (*acutal universal*), . . . its mode of existence must be immaterial. d) Hence the existence in man of conceptual thought cannot adequately be explained by the action of a material organ, such as the brain, but requires the presence and operation of an immaterial factor." Ibid., pp. 346–347. The prudent utterances of M. J. Adler happily avoid the always menacing danger in these matters of misplaced metaphysical realism. All that can be said about this "universal aspect of reality" on the basis of the objective observation alone is that it is what is grasped by the concept and signified by the word. Our philosopher therefore says of the universal, with perfect precision, that it "exists actually in the knower as that whereby he knows individual things in their universal aspects" (p. 347). One could not protect oneself from the metaphysic of universals better, but it is there anyway. In what do these universal aspects which are *in* things (*in their universal aspects*), consist? This potential universal has exercised over the centuries the ingenuity of excellent minds. M. J. Adler speaks of it in terms which recall those which Peter Abelard used ("common characteristics or traits in virtue of which they [the individual things] belong to classes or kinds," p. 347). But Abelard knew well that, things being individual insofar as they are real, universals cannot signify them as real things, since insofar as they are real [*réelies* (sic)], things signify nothing. As a philosopher of language, therefore, one does not know upon what real element the community of universals and the names that signify them rest. Names, Abelard says, are corporeal in themselves, but incorporeal as regards meaning: *incorporea quantum ad modum significationis;* literally, as regards their manner of signifying. But why? Aristotle and Thomas Aquinas would probably say: because things, even as material, have forms. In fact, with Aristotle even the corporeal is not totally material. But one enters here into the metaphysical order of the nonmaterial which, if hylomorphism is true, is a constitutive element of physics. For any form taken in itself, including the form which is inseparable from matter, we do not have appropriate language, because we are not able to think without images nor imagine an immaterial being. [I have taken Adler's own words here rather than translate Gilson's French. Cf. Mortimer J. Adler, *The Difference of Man and the Difference It Makes* (Cleveland: World, 1968). The page numbers are the same as in the edition Gilson cites.]

    7. Plotinus, *Enneads* V, 9, 7. Cf. I, 2, 3, and IV, 3, 18.

    8. Ibid., V, 9, 6. [Plotinus, *The Enneads* (London: Faber and Faber, 1956), p. 458. The French text Gilson cites does not apparently agree in all particulars with that used by MacKenna, the translator of the English edition.]

    9. Ed. Sapir, *Language* [New York: Harcourt, Brace, 1949), p. 32. Note in this passage the chronic and generalized mistrust of linguists toward the idea of "word." It is precisely that "our first impulse, no doubt, would have been to define

the word as the symbolic, linguistic counterpart of a single concept. We now know that such a definition is impossible."

10. "As the necessity of defining thought solely and exclusively for its own sake becomes more urgent, the word becomes increasingly irrelevant as a means. We can therefore easily understand why the mathematician and the symbolic logician are driven to discard the word and to build up their thought with the help of symbols which have, each of them, a rigidly unitary value." Sapir, *Language* [p. 33]. It goes without saying that symbols of this sort only signify themselves and the possibility of certain operations, which is entirely different from every concept properly so called.

11. Sapir, *Language* [pp. 117 and 118].

12. Ibid., p. 171.

13. Thomas Aquinas, *Quaestiones disputatae De veritate*, q. IV, art. 1, Reply. [*The Disputed Questions on Truth*, trans. R. W. Mulligan (Chicago: Regnery, 1952), vol. I, p. 172.]

14. Ibid.

15. Ibid.

16. Thomas Aquinas thinks about the connection of the two languages in the perspective of discourses completely constituted. After that we think the words that we wish to say: "*et haec est dispositio interioris sermonis, ex qua procedit exterior locutio*," *Sum. theol.*, I, 79, 10 ad 3 m.

17. "*Dicendum quod, secundum Philosophum* (I, *Perihermeneias*, lect. 2) *voces signa sunt intellectum, et intellectus sunt rerum similitudines. Et sic patet quod voces referuntur ad res significandas; mediante conceptione intellectus.*" *Sum. theol.*, I, 13, 1, Resp. [Pegis, ed., I, 113]. One could engage in theology properly so called and show that, such as Thomas Aquinas, in being faithful to the Christian tradition, conceives it, the theology of the Divine Word is a theology of language. The Divine Word is "spoken" by definition. His incarnation, when the Word is made flesh, is not without analogy with the manner in which in language the meaning incorporates itself in the word. There are, properly understood, some differences: *Verbum incarnatum habet aliquid simile cum verbo vocis . . . ratione cujus unum alteri comparatur: quod sicut vox manifestat verbum interius, ita per carnem manifestatum est Verbum aeternum. Sed quantum ad hoc est disimile: quia ipsa caro assumpta a Verbo aeterno, non dicitur Verbum, sed ipsa vox quae assumitur ad manifestationem verbi interioris, dicitur verbum; et idea verbum vocis est aliud a verbo cordis, sed Verbum incarnatum est idem quod Verbum aeternum, sicut et verbum significatum per vocem est idem quod verbum cordis.*" Thomas Aquinas, *Quaestio disputata de veritate*, qu. IV, a 1, ad 6 m.

18. Descartes, *Responses to the First Objections*. . . .

19. Locke, *Essay . . .* , II, 10; *Great Books*, vol. 35, p. 145.

20. Ibid., III, 2, 2; *Great Books*, vol. 35, p. 253. [Italics in Locke, not Gilson.]

21. Ibid., III, 3, 6; *Great Books*, vol. 35, p. 255.

[21a. Ibid., p. 251.]

22. Ibid., p. 253.

23. Naturally, Locke does not forget that there are cases in which words signify things (*Essay*, III, 2, 5, p. 254), but he firmly maintains "that it is perverting

the use of words, and brings unavoidable obscurity and confusion into their signification, whenever we make them stand for anything but those ideas we have
in our own minds." Here as elsewhere Locke uses the expression *stand for (tenir
lieu, remplacer, stare pro)* in the sense of "be a function of." In whatever manner
one may translate it, he wants to say that the idea is what the word signifies directly and immediately.

24. "*Id quod ex re intellectu concipit intellectus, dicitur verbum.*" *Summa
theol.*, I, 28, 4, ad 1 m.

25. See note 6, above. This fact constitutes (less firmly expressed because
we only approach the problem of the concept indirectly) what Mortimer J. Adler
calls "the triadic theory." The three terms in question are: "The verbal sign, the
things that we use language to talk about, and our understanding or knowledge
of these things." He specifies: "Only when the concept is treated (as in Aristotle
and Aquinas) as *that by which* we know or understand (*id quo*) [never as *that
which* we know or understand (*id quod*)], does the correct version of the triadic
theory result: the object known or understood is that which our designative words
signify; the object as understood is that which is signified. Since our concepts are
that by which we understand the objects we know, they are also that by which
our words signify these objects as known; they are themselves never the objects
signified." M. J. Adler, *The Difference of Man and the Difference It Makes*, p. 327,
n. 10 [1968 ed., amended as above]. The consequence of this is that "the concept
is an unobservable factor in behavior; it is, therefore, a psychological construct
and should be defined in dispositional terms" (p. 156). For example, one could define it as "a disposition to understand what a certain kind of object is like, whether
or not it is actually being perceived and whether or not it is perceptible" (p. 161).
The definition is as good as it can be of that which, not being a thing, is not susceptible of definition. In any case, one will note the consequence which follows
from this notion: true concepts differ from simple sensible abstraction as with
animals in that they "provide an *understanding* in addition to a *recognition* of the
perceived objects" (p. 163) [Adler's emphasis]. M. J. Adler makes a very successful
use of this essential distinction in discussing the numerous cases in which animal
reactions (to colors or even to forms) are taken as indications of a properly intellectual activity. "Perceptual" abstraction and "conceptual" abstraction ought not
be confounded.

26. Another way of approaching the problem, in a different spirit, also offers other interesting perspectives: A. de Wahlens, *Existence et signification* (Lou-
vain: E. Nauwelaerts, 1958), pp. 127–129. I see nothing to object to in the thesis
of the author, that the human word (*verbum*) exists as thought in language "alone"
(p. 127). For my part I would only say: insofar as it is thought conscious of itself.
I also admit that the word is not exactly the *sign* of thought, but its existence (p.
128). I would add perhaps only that it manifests thought by allowing it to exist
(in the modern sense of the expression). Thought only attains the concrete mode
of existence in language, although I do not feel convinced by the argument (p. 129)
against the possibility of pure thought. Alphonse de Wahlens would conceive of
it as "a power of combining significations" anterior to these significations themselves. Now, he objects, this would be an impossibility since this power of com-

bining would not be conscious either in its activity or in its effects, unless, precisely, that which it produces should be incorporated in a language which this power ought to wait upon [*attendre*] in order to become fully itself (p. 129). In this connection we repeat that the unconscious ought not be conceived of as the conscious less consciousness. "Pure thought" busies itself, not with combining significations, but in preparing them [*à en preparer*] and in creating the signs required in order to formulate them.

I also willingly subscribe to an expression attributed to Herman Kleist: "The idea does not preexist language, but it forms itself in it and through it" (Tzvetan Todorov, in *Critique*, 231/32 (1966), 750). Yes, and inversely, if thought did not preexist language, the idea could not be incorporated there; but it is true that it cannot preexist language in the same way as it is in language. This can only be its intelligible sense under another mode of existence. If, as we think, there is pure thought, it escapes observation and is only knowable to us in and by reflection on language, which is known to us. The absence of thought in animals other than man explains why it is impossible for them to speak, for, we repeat, in the present state of our knowledge, man alone is capable of speaking. "Among scientists who consider the matter, there is unanimous agreement that man and man alone uses verbal symbols and has a propositional language [*langage*] and syntactically structured speech." *The Difference of Man . . .*, p. 112. And I allow myself to repeat that if the contrary were proved, the result would simply be that, beyond man, other animals also think. It would mean that they are endowed with an immaterial power and not that thought is material or a function of matter. In order to assure oneself in what particular we are indeed here in the presence of a "constant" of the philosophy of language, see Aristotle, *Historia animalium*, IV, 9. He does not even leave out the dolphin: "For this creature has a voice (and can therefore utter vocal or vowel sounds), for it is furnished with a lung and a windpipe; but its tongue is not loose, nor has it lips, so as to give utterance to an articulate sound (or a sound of vowel and consonant in combination)" [535b 32–536a 4. Trans. D'Arcy Wentworth Thompson: *Great Books*, vol. 9, p. 62].

5. ON THE CUSTOMS OF LANGUAGE

[a. *Basic Writings of Saint Thomas Aquinas*, ed. Anton C. Pegis (New York: Random House, 1945), I, 534.]

1. Emile Benveniste, "Le langage et l'expérience humaine," in *Problèmes de langage* (Paris: Gallimard, 1966), pp. 1–13.

2. These purely linguistic observations invite the metaphysician to follow his own inclination. The present is the axial time of discourse because discourse has as its primary function to signify knowledge, that there is only knowledge of what is, and that nothing is which is not at the present. This is why the classical grammars defined the present of the verb to be as that of actual existence. Eternity can only be conceived of as a perpetual present. Following in another direction, one could scrutinize the metaphysical sense of experience in the New Novel from this point of view. This is an experience about discourse itself, abstracting from

all reference to anecdote, narration, series of events, and therefore from time. The New Novel positions itself, therefore, inevitably in the present and holds to it deliberately, whatever the grammatical tense may be that it uses: "The cinema only knows a single grammatical mode: present indicative. Film and novel agree in any case today in the construction of instants, intervals, and successions which have nothing to do with those of clocks or calendars" (A. Robbe-Grillet, "*Temps et description*," in *Pour un nouveau roman* [Paris: Gallimard, 1963], p. 164). Despite its title, "Last Year at Marienbad" is not an exception to this rule. "The universe in which the whole film unfolds is, in characteristic fashion, that of a perpetual present which makes impossible all recourse to memory" (p. 165). One cannot avoid seeing in this new development of the arts of language (for the images of the cinema are signs also) the result of a deeper conscious recognition [*prise de conscience*], neither philosophical nor linguistic but artistic and poetic, of the fact that all language defines its times with regard to the sole real axis, that of the present. That inevitably follows thus when the principle is proposed that "the work is not evidence of an exterior reality but is itself its own reality" (p. 166). With fine lucidity, A. Robbe-Grillet has perceived that from the moment when the narrative and the character (as with Balzac) cease to be the objects of discourse, time ceases to be the principal "character" of it. Everything taking place then in the mind of the author, the reader, or the viewer, the time of the work remains the only real time: that of the language, present indicative.

3. Emile Benveniste, "Le langage et l'expérience humaine," pp. 10–11.

[3a. See *The Complete Writings of Ralph Waldo Emerson* (New York: Wm. Wise, 1929), II, 1247. Here and in the other Emerson quotations I haved translated from Gilson's French unless it differs significantly from Emerson's English.]

[3b. Ibid., 1254.]

[3c. I am unable to locate the first sentence cited here; the second one is on p. 1254.]

4. Claude Bernard, *Leçons sur les phénomènes de la vie communs aux animaux et aux vegetaux* (Paris: Librarie J. -B. Ballière, 1885); reedited, with a useful preface by Georges Canguilhem (Paris: Librarie Philosophique J. Vrin, 1966), Tome I. The numbers in parenthesis in our text refer to this reedition. Concerning the formulation "Life is a creation," "Evolution is a creation" (which brings us fairly close to "creative evolution") see the "Preface" of Georges Canguilhem, p. 10. The entire scientific epistemology of Claude Bernard is an interpretation of the scientific implications of his own scientific discovery of the glycogenic function of the liver. If we are permitted to use a comparison which all the Pascalians will understand, it is his "miracle of the Holy Thorn."

[4a. For the earlier statement of this position see Claude Bernard, *An Introduction to the Study of Experimental Medicine*, trans. Henry Copley Greene (Henry Schuman, 1949), p. 93.]

5. We call attention to the analogous remarks in the *Journal* of Paul Claudel for the month of April 1911. One will only be astonished that a poet should allow himself to be seduced by possible analogies to other orders than that of the mind [*esprit*]. "There is an Archimedean principle for minds: Every strange idea introduced into the brain experiences an eliminatory thrust proportionate to the density

of the medium which it displaces. It takes an effort of which few people are capable if one would preserve for this idea the time necessary to examine it and, should the case arise, to assimilate it. Everything that is full has a tendency to reject things." The phenomenon of rejection was, with Claudel, particularly rapid and vigorous. One is not surprised that he had observed it.

The dramatic art of Paul Claudel is an experimental demonstration of the difficulty of recopying. The power of verbal creation was with him such that a first writing rarely sufficed to satisfy it. We have *Tête d'Or* in first and second versions; *La jeune fille Violaine* in two versions, followed by *L'annonce fait à Marie,* itself in two versions of which one says, "for the stage"; *La femme et son ombre* in two versions; *Le soulier de satin* in the complete edition and in a version for the stage (as if the complete edition ought not to be, in a society worthy of its poets, the proper [*veritable*] version for the stage). "*L'annonce fait à Marie,*" says its author, "is the fruit of fifty-six years of desperate patience." But is it *the same work* which lived through these fifty-six years?

6. The two movements are moreover tied by intimate connections, Dada being the elder and having played in certain respects the role of precursor. Cf. Michel Sanouillet, *Dada à Paris* (Paris: J.-J. Pauwet, 1965), pp. 420–426: "If it were necessary to condense things to the extreme, one could, it appears, be satisfied with the following formulation: *Surrealism is the French form of Dada*" (p. 420). This appears to be a more dadaist than surrealist view of the problem. But we have not taken it into serious consideration, and it moreover is doubtlessly an insoluble issue.

7. Jacques Rivière, cited by M. Sanouillet, *Dada à Paris* p. 204.

8. André Breton, *Manifestes du surréalisme* (Paris: Gallimard, 1967), p. 179 ["Du surréalisme en ses oeuvres vives," 1953].

9. Ibid., pp. 181–182.

10. Ibid., p. 117 ["Second manifeste," 1930, 1946].

11. Ibid., pp. 180–181 ["Du surréalisme . . . ," 1953].

[11a. Ibid., p. 36 ("Manifeste du surréalisme . . . ," 1924).

12. Breton, *Second manifeste,* p. 122.

13. S. Mallarmé, "Avant-dire au Traite du Verbe de René Ghil," in *Oeuvres complètes,* ed. Mondor and Aubry (Paris: La Pleiade, 1945), pp. 857–858.

14. S. Mallarmé, *Oeuvres complètes,* pp. 433–434, 442–443, 477. The meaning of the poem is to be found again above all in the very vocabulary of Mallarmé: the obsession with the translucency of the vacuum, of the clearness of ice, "clearness which encloses the substance of nothingness," ibid., p. 439. Cf. P.-P. Richard, *L'univers imaginaire de Mallarmé* (Editions du Seuil, 1961), p. 75; note on page 55, and IV, 5, "The fictive negativity: Igitur," pp. 185–195 and 237–240. Cf. V, 2: "The missed metamorphosis," pp. 251–256.

It is not impossible that a passage from Baudelaire's memorable essay on *Theophile Gautier* had held Mallarmé's attention. "There is in the word, in *speech* [*verbe*], something of the *sacred,* which we protect from becoming subject to chance. To handle a language [*langue*] knowledgeably is to practice a sort of evocative sorcery." *Speech* and *sacred* are underlined by Baudelaire. Valéry, though hardly a metaphysician and still less a theologian, will write nevertheless: "Honor of men,

Saint *LANGAGE*" (capitals by Valéry himself). Without closely examining the nature of this apparently sacred delirium, one can at least ask oneself if Gautier's phrase did not inspire Mallarmé's reflection on the evocatory sorcery of speech [*verbe*] and did not suggest to him the plan of a language from which all chance would be, if possible, eliminated.

15. Jacques Scherer, *Le "Livre" de Mallarmé*, Initial Research on Unpublished Documents. Preface by Henri Mondor . . . (Paris: Gallimard, 1957, 3rd ed), p. 2. Processes of reasoning are not absent there, adds the poet, "but we ignore them; they themselves become designedly mysterious."

16. It is interesting, and perhaps significant, that, before Valéry, Mallarmé may have thought of a science of language to furnish a "method" which would make possible a science "of the general expression of our mind." "We have not understood Descartes," he wrote at the same time, "foreigners snatched him up, but he stirred up French mathematicians. One must take up again his movement, studying our mathematicians." [Mallarmé, *Oeuvres complètes*, pp. 849, 851: Page of the *Discours sur* (sic) *la méthode* (underlined).] [Gilson's bracketing.] A study of the poetic trinity Vinci-Teste-Valéry would not be without philosophic profit, although it might be rather difficult to adopt a negative attitude with regard to metaphysicians without knowing it. It is difficult to understand well writers that one has not read in one's youth and carried about for a long time in oneself, but it appears to me that the work of Maurice Blanchot prolongs what has today become a literary tradition. See, in *Critique* 229 (1966), 580, these remarks of Roger Laporte: "Mallarmé transmuted the alchemical project of the Great Work into that of the Book. Valéry did not effectuate this Book, but all his writings are the dream of it, the dream of Monsieur Teste. It is impossible to read Blanchot: critical studies as 'narratives' [*recits*], without living under the powerful attraction of a Book which exercises a fascination more especially redoubtable as it is ever future . . ." etc. This is the very title of the book of Maurice Blanchot, *Le livre a venir* (Paris: Gallimard, 1959). See also, in the same installment of *Critique*, pp. 544–545, the remarks of Michel Foucault on *La pensée du dehors*.

17. "Everything that can be thought, can by the same token also be formulated verbally." Justus Hartnack, *Wittgenstein und die moderne Philosophie* (Stuttgart: W. Kohlhammer, 1962), p. 40. This is an univerifiable proposition, for if there is some thought not yet formulated, it escapes us. In order to maintain the contrary, one must admit either that there is no unconscious thought or, if there is such, that it is identical to conscious thought less consciousness.

18. On the problem of the translation of philosophical writings see the remarks of M. Heidegger in *Questions I* (Paris: Gallimard, 1968), "Author's Prologue," pp. 9–11. These few pages may require long reflection, for if the language in them is clear, their thought is profound. The position of the philosopher of Fribourg is that: "by the translation, the labor of one's mind [*pensée*] finds itself transposed into the spirit [*esprit*] of another tongue [*langue*], and thus undergoes an inevitable transformation. But this transformation can become fecund, for it causes the fundamental position of the question to appear in a new light" (p. 10). What he wants to say appears to me thus: first, that faithful translation from one language [*langue*] to another is not possible (without changing the meaning); sec-

ond, that translation ought, therefore, to consist in an effort to think anew *the same problem* from the lexical and syntactical givens of another language [*langue*]; third, the question being the same, translation into another language [*langue*] of the response proposed by a philosopher constitutes in itself "a breaking of new ground for the question posed in common. It conduces to mutual comprehension in a superior sense" (p. 11). There are therefore two distinct settings [*defrichements*: ground-breakings] of the same question. In order to take account of these remarks, it appears to me that I would not be wasting my time in trying to translate one of Heidegger's works from his language [*langue*] into mine. I would rather feel invited to an effort to assimilate his thought, followed by another effort to join to it the givens of my own language [*langue*]. My translation would be then less an expression in French of what M. Heidegger said in German than what Heidegger himself would say of the problem if he thought it in French. I ought to acknowledge that I do not see this operation very clearly, and since I imagine that the difficulty is the same for Heidegger himself, I have trouble not perceiving in his response, so courteous, the trace of a philosophical humor in very good taste.

[18a. For the English translation see Ludwig Wittgenstein, *Tractatus Logico-Philosophicus*, trans. D.F. Pears and B.F. McGuinness (London: Routledge & Kegan Paul, 1966), esp. pp. 6–7.]

19. André Breton was practiced in this sort of literature: "*Ce jeune apache qui de la paume de sa main colle un pain à sa môme*": we leave it to the reader to search in the text for the example that follows, which would have made Rabelais envious: Letter from Breton to Picabia, 16 October 1922, in the correspondence edited by Michel Sanouillet, *Dada à Paris* (Paris: J.-J. Pauvert, 1965), p. 524. Here is a metathesis whose noble origin encourages me to cite it: "Dites, les invasions des Perses et Mèdes, ne dites pas, les invasions des m. . . .s épaisses." He who taught it to me in 1913 is today an illustrious philologist and a member of the *Institut de France*.

20. I have culled this example of a "fine *chiasma*" from M. Jean-Marie Benoist, "Marcuse, un Aufklarer contre les lumières," in *Critique* 258 (1968), 951.

21. Germaine Decaris and Pierre Mac-Orlan, *Paul Gilson* (Paris: Pierre Seghers, 1959), p. 109.

6. THE SPOKEN WORD AND THE WRITTEN WORD

1. Ludwig Wittgenstein, *Le cahier bleu et le cahier brun*, followed by Norman Malcolm, *Ludwig Wittgenstein* (Paris: Gallimard, 1965), p. 336. [The French edition has not been available to me. For this comment see Norman Malcolm, *Ludwig Wittgenstein: A Memoir* (London: Oxford University Press, 1962), p. 24: "The thoughts that came out were 'stale', or, as he put it to another friend, the words looked like 'corpses' when he began to read them."]

2. Ibid., pp. 339–340. It is true that "what enabled him to follow in this fashion the thread of the inspiration is, he said to me, long precedent reflections and numerous notes on the questions which he dealt with during these classes" (p. 336). The classes were not any less exposed to the hazards of improvisation

for it. "Often we have heard him exclaim to himself: 'What I am about to say is idiotic!' 'What a sorry professor I make!' 'I am only capable today of uttering foolishness.' And he asked himself at times if he were able to proceed with it, but generally he gained possession of his thought again, and I have only rarely seen him abandon his exposition before the time when the course ended" (ibid., p. 33). "At the end of each exposition, Wittgenstein was exhausted. He experienced a profound disgust for himself, for all that he had said, for all that he did not know how to say. It often happened that after the end of a class he would dash headlong to a cinema" (ibid., p. 340). This last characteristic, more common than one would suppose, concretely expresses the discouragement and fatigue which the continual perception of the essential inadequacy of speech to thought engenders in him who speaks. One imagines that "the mode of existence of professors, and most particularly that of professors of philosophy, was odious to him" (p. 343). Descartes already shared this sentiment.

3. Cited by Werner Heisenberg, *La nature dans la physique contemporaine* (Paris: Gallimard, 1962), pp. 113–114.

4. I cite at random: *arie* (interjection), *echoumacher* (one of the cuttings of the vine), *Armagna!* (a Burgundian insult), *en ribouler* (escape again, recover from illness: I [sic] *n'en a pas riboule*), etc. Paul Claudel willingly made use of these words. He made them up as required: "And the tawny *brebillettes* of the hazel tree! And here are the sweet *minonnets*"; "Like the peeping [*piaule*] of a nest of *crinches* (young crows) . . ."; "this *morfondement*" [chilling to the bone] (we certainly use the words *morfondre* and *morfondu*). Naturally Claudel uses certain grandiloquent words of which few are provided by himself: *s'affourcher, taille-mer* (marine); *rouelles* (little wheels; today a butcher's term for round slices of beef); *occlure* (the antonym of to open: occlusion,); etc.

5. Concerning the cause of this fact see above chapter I, n. 9.

6. I think here of the admirable Dr. Johnson, of whom Boswell has reported to us so many amusing traits in this respect. We would see pedantry there if with him the natural language had not been, since his birth, the written language. "How is your toothache?" someone asked this little boy one day. Response: "Thank you, sir, the pain is abating."

7. A. Martinet, *Éléments de linguistique générale*, p. 7. "But the contemporary linguist, confronted with expressions like '*la lettre que j'ai écrit*', '*occasion à profiter*', '*la femme que je lui ai parlé*', objects to the virtuous indignation of the purist as well as to the exaltation of the iconoclast. Here he simply sees facts which he must note and explain in the framework of usages where they appear." If, as the same linguist justly says (p. 7), "in ordinary speech, 'language' [*langue*] properly designates the faculty which men have of understanding one another by means of vocal signs," all that which within the structure of language expresses this desire for mutual comprehension is brought into relief by linguistics. It appears to me that an iconoclast has good pretext to rejoice here: he is only wrong to be an iconoclast. As to the purist, virtue has nothing to do with his indignation, if he is so naive as to feel it. There are linguistic reasons why the correct formulas should have been preferred to the others: *écrit* is readily understood, but *écrite* is more logical (logic is an inherent component of language); on occasion *à profiter* is there

substituting for *à saisir*, because *mettre à profit* it too long, but "to profit" is understandable; "the woman of whom" is better than "the woman whom," simply because one doesn't *speak* a woman (unless one is a magician), but one speaks *of* a woman. It seems that, raillerie or indignation aside, for they are in fact irrelevant, the way the language [*langue*] is used may have introduced here a formal distinction corresponding to a distinction of meaning and that the linguist cannot remain indifferent to a linguistic fact of the first order. It is true that, as we have noted, while entirely refusing to recommend "a method which makes total abstraction from the meaning of the significative units" (ibid., p. 34), the same linguist reproaches this method above all with the enormous "consumption of time and energy" that it would require. It does not appear to him, in itself, contradictory and impossible.

8. J. Derrida, *De la grammatologie* (Paris: Editions de Minuit, 1967). I note this book for the importance of the subject, but the language [*langue*] which the author uses being often unintelligible to me, I do not feel myself authorized to relate its conclusions. I had hoped to clarify them for myself by reading the study which M. Gerard Granel devoted to him, "Jacques Derrida et la rature (sic) de l'origine," in *Critique* 246 (1967), pp. 887–895; but this study being written in the same language [*langue*] as the book, I found myself no further along. Incidentally, the "erasure" [*rature*] in question is the *Durchschreibung* of Heidegger. One fears lest this linguistic [*langagière*] epidemic propagate itself. According to a review (*The Times Literary Supplement*, July 11, 1968) of Andre Jacob's book (*Temps et langage* [Paris: Armand Colin, 1968]), "the masters of style, and also to a certain extent of philosophy," of this author "appear to be Heidegger and Hegel (in that order), which makes it difficult for the reader to follow him." This diagnosis applies without qualification to the writings of certain French grammatologists of our time. Yet, it must be added that the words "difficult to follow" are, in the case of M. J. Derrida, litotes.

9. We were tempted elsewhere to describe the attitude of Cicero on this point. His witness is of the first importance and ought not suffer from the contempt, unfortunately justified, which philosophers feel for his speculative attitudes. There, on the terrain where he was master, he was truly excellent. See "Eloquence and Wisdom according to Cicero," in *The Phoenix* (Toronto) 7 (1953), pp. 1–19.

10. The question is one of knowing if algebraic signs have a meaning. Cf. J. Derrida, *De la grammatologie*, p. 12, n. 1, and the works of E. Ortigues (*Le discours et le symbole*) and those of G.-G. Granger (*Pensées formelles et sciences de l'homme*), which are found cited there.

11. Aristotle, *Rhetoric*, I, 1, 1355b.

12. Rev. Fr. Samson, of the Oratory, read the Lenten sermons which he preached at Notre Dame in Paris. Hardpressed by the crowd, I one day found a seat in the gallery, right in front of the pulpit. I heard him execute a magnificent *crescendo allentando* culminating on the sustained and detached words: DEUS/CARITAS/EST!!! Upon which, skillfully gathering in his left hand the page that he had just read, and without taking his eyes off his audience, he adroitly passed the sheet to an associate seated behind him on the highest step of the stair; the latter whisked it away without anyone in the nave of the church being able to per-

ceive it. The contrast, fascinating for me, between the prophetic tone of the orator and the meticulous precision with which he executed this little show, has never left my memory.

13. I do not know if I mislead myself in saying that the most uncontrolled verbal acrobatics of Shakespeare, which, I imagine, no one could invent other than under the written form, always, or at least most often, remain perceived by the hearer as improvisations of great style. He writes the spoken word as one would speak it if one were Shakespeare. Who else than he could have invented, in writing, that spoken description of speech? Cf. *A Midsummer Night's Dream*, V, 1, 14–17. When the translator of Shakespeare is a professor, he transposes the spoken word of the poet (who nevertheless uses his pen: "the poet's pen") into more presentable written form. Thus, V, 1, 326, "With hands as pale as milk," becomes in French: "With your hands as white as white dairy products" [*De vois mains blanches comme un blanc laitage*] [see *A Midsummer Night's Dream*, V, i, 345, in G. B. Harrison, ed., *Shakespeare: Major Plays and Sonnets* (New York: Harcourt, Brace, 1948), p. 297]." This is, perhaps, "better written," in any case, it is "more written" than would have been: "*De vois mains pâles comme le lait.*" It is therefore less spoken, less theatrical.

14. The difference bursts forth in the case of musical language: the passage from the spoken to the sung always remains artificial. Moreover, the singers who know how to speak are exceedingly rare. The artifice of the *recitatif* alternating with the *aria* always has something false about it, even when it is a Berlioz who "puts to music" the words of a Weber. Consequently, with Wagner the appearance of "continuous melody," then with Debussy that of the word continuously chanted. The alternation of prose and verse (*chante-fable*) is analogous to that of the spoken and the sung from which it derives. When an orator practices speaking and reading, he comes up against analogous difficulties, of a sort which are never completely resolved.

15. See J. Derrida, *De la grammatologie*, p. 17, n. 1.

16. "To think? . . . To think! That's to lose the thread." P. Valéry, *Oeuvres* (Paris: La Pléiade, 1960), vol. II, p. 379.

17. Aristotle, *Rhetoric*, I, 1, 1354a; I, 2, 1356a 30.

18. The two modes of scientific knowledge are syllogistic deduction and induction. These forms of argumentation are necessary in science properly so called, probable in dialectic, simply persuasive in rhetoric; but there is no persuasion without probability in some degree. Rhetorical argumentation is a sort of dialectic without rigor. Thus, for induction, instead of proceeding by a more or less complete enumeration as in science, one contents oneself with citing several examples, at times only one. For deduction, one contents oneself with those incomplete syllogisms called enthymemes, which the *Petit Robert* defines correctly: "an abbreviated form of the syllogism, in which one implicitly understands one of the two premises or the conclusion." He gives an example: "I think, therefore I am," Descartes' celebrated enthymeme. Thus, by a highly humorous turn, an inference that Descartes considered as the first of all evidences and the foundation of all scientific knowledge passes today for an instance of syllogistic persuasion of the lowest rhetoric: that in which one leaps over one of the premises. Descartes, natu-

rally, energetically protested against this interpretation of the *Cogito*. He has not reasoned, he says, from the major premise of a syllogism of the form: Everything that thinks, exists; now, I think, etc. . . . This is doubtless true, but Aristotle would conclude on the matter that the first principle of a metaphysics which presented itself as more certain than any mathematical knowledge was an artifice of rhetoric, which conclusion could certainly be sustained.

19. Valéry appears to have held the idea of philosophy as inseparable from that of system (*Oeuvres*, II, p. 1528). It is doubtlessly in this sense that he said: "I am not by any stretch of the imagination a philosopher" (II, p. 1503), and, for my part, I am among those who willingly would praise him for it. More profound is the remark made elsewhere: "I rejected not only literature [*lettres*] but still more philosophy almost entirely, among the Vague Things and the Impure Things to which I objected with all my heart" (II, p. 12). On those vague things, among which he included the domain of philosophy, note the development, which concludes: "The result of this is that *in order that there might be philosophy, it is necessary that no verification should be possible* (Oeuvres, II, p. 1529). Assuredly, for the verifiable is science, but it is not sufficient that there should be no verification for there to be philosophy. It is further necessary that there be rational knowledge of the unverifiable. This is not contradictory if there exist one or many areas of reality whose nature should be such that neither mathematical nor physical verification apply to them. We will say that it is always possible to say nothing of them. Yes; but Valéry has precisely above all spoken of that: no mathematical or experimental verification is possible of what we call the spirit, of the meaning of the word, of the advances of "the language animal" [*l'animal langage*], of the operations which preside over the conception of the work, over its development, over its maturation. This impossibility holds for the very nature of the observer and for that of the observed. Valéry had had the feeling for it, and this it is which inspired one of his most profound thoughts, one which he expressed under many forms, notably: "The act of writing always requires a certain sacrifice of the intellect" (*Oeuvres*, II, p. 11); cf. p. 1313: "The first sacrifice to viable literature is the *sacrifizio dell' intelletto*." He calls himself a writer by temperament nonliterary; nonphilosophical also; but what about scientific? But that nature "which is nonliterary" (p. 1313) is the author of a work which is only of consequence in literature. It would be hard to cite a single proposition of his on language which might be scientifically verifiable by any method whatsoever.

20. See the "Preface" written for the second English translation of *La soirée avec M. Teste*, Pléiade, II, pp. 11–12: "This is to say that the results in general – and consequently the works – are of much less importance to me than the energy of the worker." This whole text amuses itself with parodying the first part of the *Discourse on Method*. The remembrance of Descartes presided, moreover, in the subscription to *La soirée*. Cf. p. 1381.

21. Speaking of his teaching at the Collège de France, Valéry said with unparalleled vigor: "At any rate, I could not flatter myself with fashioning poets, the only demonstration that could justify or confirm a 'Poetics,' in the usual sense of the word. But taking this in all its original simplicity, I ventured to treat at my

best . . . the matter of the *fabrication* of 'works of the mind' in general: These are the works which mind destines for its own use, which mark out and propose to it its proper growth. Perhaps I had ought to say and write *Poietics* rather than *Poetics* in order to avoid all misunderstanding, as does that physiology which speaks of hematopoietic and galactopoietic functions. But I admit not to have dared. Whatever the case may be, it is the completely primary idea of MAKING [FAIRE] or fabricating that I intended to express." *Oeuvres*, II, p. 1605 (italics and capitals are Valéry's). And all that follows, admirable for its lucidity about the idea of a *Poetic Economy*, where artists of every order, literary and other, are the producers, where there is therefore consumption, supply and demand, and so on. That which was important to him was the very *generation* of the works. "I was tempted, nevertheless, to deepen their study in the intimateness of the internal work of the producer, to refer to my own personal experience, searching at least to make precise the most general conditions of that work, to the extent that the producer himself can be aware of it" (p. 1606). It is infinitely regrettable that Valéry should not have dared to put into usage the word *poietic*, perfectly fitting, and saying well what he wants to say. Others than he, who have gone back to it for their personal usage, lack the authority necessary to impose it. It responds nevertheless to a mental necessity.—Incidentally, we will note the free usage of the word *mind* [*esprit*] to designate that which is the proper goal of literary production: *fabrications of the mind for the mind.*

22. *Oeuvres*, II, p. 1314.

7. THE *SEVENTH LETTER*

1. Plato, *Phaedrus,* 257B. The great philosophical debate over the respective merits of the spoken and the written word extends from 259 to the conclusion of the dialogue. Note particularly 274B–275A. [At 257e it is Socrates, and not Phaedrus, who makes the suggestion. See "Phaedrus," trans. R. Hackforth, in E. Hamilton and H. Cairns, eds., *Plato: The Collected Dialogues* (New York: Bollingen, 1969), p. 503. Subsequent references to the Platonic corpus in brackets will be from this edition. Here I have translated Gilson's French.]

2. Ibid.; see the myth of Thoth, 274–275. Rhetoric is at the center of the debate because it is preeminently the art of speech [*parole*] once written. A spoken rhetoric is not re-presented well. Beyond the general advice that a veteran of the speaker's platform can give to a beginner, and the criticism that he can address to him, the teaching of the rhetorician loses itself in the vague. Cicero certainly did not pronounce his discourses in the form in which he revised them for posterity, but his *Rhetoric to Herennius* could only be conceived under the form of a written work.

3. *Phaedrus,* 276AB.

4. *Confessions,* XI, 3, 5 [see *The Confessions of St. Augustine,* tr. E. B. Posey (London: J. M. Dent, 1942), p. 255. I have translated Gilson's French].

5. *Phaedrus,* 278A, *ad sensum.*

[5a. "Letters: VII," trans L.A. Post, in Hamilton and Cairns, ed. cit., 341c–e (p. 1589). In this and subsequent passages from the "Seventh Letter" I have translated Gilson's French.]

6. The "Seventh Letter" takes up again here a theme that we have come across already developed in the *Phaedrus*, 275d. M. Jacques Derrida appears to understand this passage as applying to the relation of writing to the word [*vocable*]. I may moreover be mistaken about the meaning of M. Derrida's writing itself (*De la grammatologie*, pp. 58–59). In any case, invited by him to reread this passage of the *Phaedrus*, I do not succeed in understanding it as concerning the relation of the written sign to the spoken discourse, or, in modern terms, of exposition or oral conversation to the written book and, as we say today, to the printed word. Plato's repugnance for the written word was nothing near that which the book would probably prompt him to, to say nothing of its vulgarization by the mass edition, the periodical, and the digest. But the quantity is not at issue here. That which the *Phaedrus* and the "Seventh Letter" emphasize is the state of dereliction of the written word which, left to itself, is open to the possible incomprehension of all, its father not being there anymore to defend it. In case of need a man explains himself; a book cannot explain itself.

7. Mallarmé, "Le mystere dans les lettres," *Oeuvres*, Pleiade edition, p. 373. "The mystery in language" would be a very fitting title for the present writing.

8. Sainte-Beuve, *Nouveau Lundis* (Paris, 1807), t. VII, pp. 35–37.

9. One will be astonished perhaps that I should not take into consideration the work of Marshall McLuhan, in which the talent and virtuosity of its author have merited a deserved success: *Understanding Media: The Extensions of Man* (Signet, 1966); *The Medium Is the Message* (Bantam, n.d.). In French: *La Galaxie Gutenberg* (Mame, 1968). This copious but engaging thought is of the sort where one catches oneself in a pleasant net, not without asking oneself if its mesh if real or imaginary. The most solid idea appears to be that we leave the age of print (Gutenberg's age) in order to enter, or reenter, into an age wherein the oral transmission of thought, thanks above all to the means of mass communication, takes the upper hand once more. M. McLuhan believes himself (perhaps, for he is very subtle) the prophet of a new age and of a culture in a new form, an age into which, still imagining ourselves to be in the age of printing and of the book, we enter backwards, without perceiving the fact. I see only one objection to this thesis, but it is so large that one can hardly believe that M. McLuhan may not have perceived it, and if he perceived it, one can hardly believe that he believes himself completely serious in his enterprise. The objection is that, in order to announce the end of the Gutenberg galaxy he himself should have had recourse to the book, and even to books which sell in hundreds of thousands of copies. As a continuation of these words he has at present launched a review, which is the preeminently super-Gutenbergian *medium*. This dazzling triumph of the written and the printed over the oral and the spoken is a refutation of the central thesis of the author all the more decisive in that it would have been strictly impossible for him to diffuse it to the vast public by means of those *mass media* which he announces are going to replace the book. His personal experience is, therefore, that of the absolute primacy of writing as a means of communicating ideas. He

had to make himself read in order to be understood. No verbal pirouette will extract him from his own trap.

10. Saint Augustine, *In Joannis Evangelium*, I, 1, 8, *PL*. 35, 1383.

8. TWO DIGRESSIONS

1. *Actes du XIII Congres des Societes de philosophie de langue francaise* (Neuchatel: LaBaconnière, 1966), II, "Le Langage," pp. 29–30.

2. Ibid., p. 30. Incidentally, note the precision that our linguist imposes on himself: "Our domain will be the language called ordinary, common language, to the express exclusion of poetic language which has its own laws and its own functions" (p. 30). M. Emile Benveniste certainly has the most precise reasons for introducing this distinction, which is just, since he speaks as a linguist. Since we speak as a philosopher, we can, without contradicting him, fail to introduce it. Mallarmé remains for us the same when he composes *Les mots anglais* for the use of classes and when he imagines *La catastrophe de Igitur*. The same verbal creation is at work in "ordinary" language [*langue*] and in that of the poet. Even if the poet is not often satisfied with displaying the poetry of common, ordinary language (I believe I owe to Francois Coppée the small compensation of noting his capability in this respect), the poet appears to the philosopher to demonstrate what the act of speech [*parole*] has of its own in its first issuing forth. Thus the favored title which poets give to this so freely: the word [*le verbe*].

3. "Linguists accept this idea completely, empirically; I do not know if among philosophers it has been scrutinized for itself. To speak truly, it is one of the immense problems concerning so many sciences which is not properly dealt with by any. I only see logicians who may be occupied with it, most especially in America, the School of Carnap and of Quine." Linguists give proof of wisdom in empirically accepting the object of their science. Philosophers have scrutinized it for itself, as have still more theologians, but neither of them have claimed to give "scientific" responses to this problem. With respect to the logicians, the problem not being in any way within their competence, we might expect that they would leave it alone: "to speak truly, in their preoccupation with rigor they have set aside every attempt at direct definition of meaning [*signification*]. In order not to fall into psychologism, they have replaced the analysis of meaning [*signification*] by the objective criterion of acceptability, proved by means of tests, according to whether the predicates are or are not accepted by the speaker" (E. Benveniste, *La forme et le sens* . . . , p. 31). When we grant that speakers exchange intelligible remarks, it is too late to define meaning [*signification*].

4. Not wishing to follow in detail the development, but to put the meaning of it in relief, we set aside many remarks which are perhaps for the linguist those to which he attributes the most value. Nevertheless, here is one of them for which the philosopher has a predilection. "In the sciences of nature the units are in general identical portions conventionally cut out of a specific continuum; there are thus quantitative units, identical and interchangeable, in each discipline of nature. Language is completely different. It does not rise up from the physical world

[. . .] but quite to the contrary from the dicontinuous and the dissimilar. This is why it does not allow of being divided, but of being decomposed. Its units are a limited number of basic elements, each different from the other, and these units group themselves to form new units, and these in their turn can form still others, at a level each time superior to the previous one." Ibid., p. 32.

5. Ibid., p. 34.

6. Ibid.

7. Ibid., pp. 35–36.

8. Ibid., p. 36.

9. Ibid., p. 37.

10. Ibid., p. 37. [The passage is in fact on p. 34.]

[10a. But note: as Gilson has quoted the text of Benveniste, and, not or, joins the two conditions. See fn. 10 above. Benveniste's French reads: "Pour qu'un signe existe, il faut et il suffit qu'il soit recu et qu'il se relie d'une maniere ou d'une autre à d'autres signes." (Emphasis mine.) Ibid., p. 34.]

11. I put myself quite certainly out of the game here. I am all the more certain that if my objection were pertinent, M. E. Benveniste would have foreseen it. It is too obvious to have escaped such a perspicacious observer. Further, defining semiotics, he specifies that "the sign has always and only generic and conceptual value. It does not admit therefore of particular or occasional signification. Everything that is individual is excluded. Circumstantial conditions are held not to have occurred" (p. 35). Insofar as I understand this position, it appears to me to entail the consequence that proper names of persons are not signs: Julius Caesar, Jesus Christ, Napoleon I are not signs. If one admits this, and M. Benveniste is in any case free to decide whether it is so (semiotic is a common noun, and the imposition of names is unconstrained [libre]), I recognize that my argument is null and void. This fact allows me at least to understand that M. Emile Benveniste may have tacitly eliminated it. I must then remain in that other perplexity: If, semiotically speaking, "Adolf Hitler" is not a sign (a verbal manifestation of what one thinks), what is it?

12. Let us listen once more to the words of M. Emile Benveniste himself, for we greatly fear that we misunderstand his thought: "We set forth, then, this principle: everything that belongs to semiotics has as its necessary and sufficient criterion that one can identify it in the heart and usage of language [langue]. Each sign enters into a net of relations with and oppositions to other signs which define it, delimit it, in the interior of the language [langue]. Whoever says 'semiotic' says 'intralinguistic'. Each sign has in itself that which distinguishes it from other signs. To be distinctive, to be significant, is the same thing" (ibid., p. 35). Our own difficulty is that of understanding how the sign can be "received as provided with signification in the community of those who use the same language [langue]" (p. 34) without a semantic activity being introduced at some moment whatever, be it only that of the speaker vis-à-vis himself, in the constitution of the sign "provided with signification."

13. Ibid., p. 36.

14. Ibid., p. 37.

15. Ibid., p. 39.

16. Ibid., p. 38, for very true and very "real" remarks on the reasons why we always have at our disposition a quite considerable number of different expressions "for the purpose of setting forth," as we say, *the same idea;* same page, on the "subtle mixture of liberty in the statement of the idea (semantic order), and of constraint in the form of this statement" (ibid.); why the signs "the least restricted in the interior of the semiotic repertoire of the language *to be, to do, thing, that,* have, as words, the most frequent use" (p. 39).

17. Ibid., p. 39.

18. Ibid., pp. 39–40.

[18a. Cf. Immanuel Kant, *Critique of Pure Reason,* trans. Norman Kemp Smith (New York: St. Martin's Press, 1965), pp. 65–91, esp. pp. 80 (sec. 7, A39–B56), 82 (sec. 8, A42–B60), 83 (A43–B61).]

[18b. See *The American College Dictionary* (New York: Random House, 1962), under "building": "BUILDING generally connotes a useful purpose (houses, schools, business offices, etc.)." I have translated Gilson's French in the text.]

Subject Index

Name Index